Leadership Issues
in the Information
Literate School Community

Edited by
James Henri & Marlene Asselin

LIBRARIES
UNLIMITED
A Member of the Greenwood Publishing Group

Westport, Connecticut ● London

An edition of this book is available for sale in Australia, New Zealand, and Hong Kong. James Henri and Marlene Asselin. 2005. *The Information Literate School Community 2: Issues of Leadership*. Wagga Wagga, New South Wales: Centre for Information Studies, Charles Sturt University (ISBN: 1-876938-72-2). The book is part of their Topics in Australian Teacher Librarianship series. For more information, consult their website at http://www.csu.edu.au/cis.

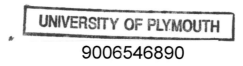
British Library Cataloguing in Publication Data is available.

ISBN: 1-59158-184-2

First published in 2005

Libraries Unlimited, 88 Post Road West, Westport, CT 06881
A Member of the Greenwood Publishing Group, Inc.
www.lu.com

Printed in the United States of America

The paper used in this book complies with the Permanent Paper Standard issued by the National Information Standards Organization (Z39.48-1984).

10 9 8 7 6 5 4 3 2 1

Leadership Issues

in the Information

Literate School Community

Contents

Acknowledgements

Conceiving and producing an edited work is a labour of love, especially when the contributors come from all parts of the globe. This volume is no exception. The editors express their appreciation to the team of contributors to this volume without their dedication to the project it would not have happened. The editors also thank Ruffina Thilakaratne of the University of Hong Kong and Anne White of the University of British Columbia for the editorial support they have contributed to the project. Without their support the project would still be a draft.

James Henri and Marlene Asselin

Introduction and Context

James Henri and Marlene Asselin

Who Should Read this Book?

This book will be of interest to the many players and stakeholders who work in and/or conceptualize about modern schools including principals, teachers, teacher librarians, information technology coordinators, educators of teachers and teacher librarians and their students, as well as educational policy makers and parents.

The Context of this Book

The first significant work on the notion of information literate school communities (*The Information Literate School Community* 1999) argued for the leadership role of the teacher librarian within an emerging vision of schools in the 1990s – that of professional communities where physical and intellectual access to, and purposeful use of, information are critical foundations of teaching and learning. Rapid globalization, hastened by developments in information and communication technologies, means that these foundations for our schools have grown more complex (*Adolescents and Literacies in a Digital World* 2002, Bruce 2002, Bigum 2002, *Learning for the Future* 2002, Lankshear & Knobel 2003). Schools are running to catch up to directions from the last decade. For example, organizational structures have certainly begun to shift from hierarchies to communities, and core curriculum, especially that of literacy, has expanded to include some of the lower-level literacies of information. However the leadership role of the teacher librarian remains unrealized. Authors in this book tackle the issues teacher librarians must face to become leaders in the new emerging vision of schools.

Contexts for Teacher Librarian Leadership in Today's and Future Schools

To establish a framework for views expressed by the authors, the editors have identified four major developments that are shaping current thinking and practices of teaching and learning:

- New learners
- New literacies and multiliteracies
- New and multiple identities and communities
- Teaching as a political activity

The issues that teacher librarians face if they are to become leaders are embedded in these contexts. Knowledge of these forces – not suspicion, condemnation or wishful thinking that they will go away if we ignore them – is essential for any opportunity for leadership. Each author in this book firmly believes that teacher librarians have a powerful potential role in the new visions of education being shaped by the four forces, but there are challenges in attaining that role, challenges related to restrictive policy, unrealized leadership behaviours, limited views and practices of literacy generally and information literacy particularly, and untapped use of technology to maximize teaching and learning in the school. However, the authors also argue that teacher librarians are well equipped to shape educational innovation in their schools because of their global view of the learners, teachers, and curriculum and their expertise in information and information and communication technologies. All the authors offer experience and powerful insight into ways that teacher librarians can construct their roles as vital to present and future learning communities.

While recognizing that the four influences on education are highly interrelated we will attempt to distinguish them by highlighting essential concepts underlying each one. Following this discussion, we will introduce the individual chapters composing this volume.

New Learners

Serious attention to the notion of student-centred learning demands dropping old assumptions about methods, places, and goals of learning. Students born since 1982 now populate our schools and represent a unique generation, known as the Millennials. A growing literature describes this generation (e.g., Gee 2000 and 2002, Howe & Strauss 2000, Negroponte 1995, O'Reilly 2000, Tapscott 1998). According to high school seniors (class of 2000), the Millennials consider themselves to be in the vanguard of a new generation and feel part of something coming after (Millennial Surveys 2000) They are growing up connected to the world and each other; they use technologies fearlessly and seamlessly to communicate with known and unknown others and to shape their lives; they are action-oriented problem solvers and see technology as their primary tool; they define their identities by shared interests and experiences, not race, class, gender or locale; they herald creative thinking, empowerment, and problem-solving as key qualities in the new global economies; and they see themselves as competent pioneers in their personal and shared futures. Those not actually born within this generation – and that includes many teachers – are inevitably and forever outsiders to the ways of being and thinking that identify the Millennials.

For the Millennials, school is only one site of learning, and not the most significant one. While Millennials are aware of the importance of school for their future, they are also aware that many of the core credentials, skills, experiences, and identities necessary for success in the world are not gained in school, but rather outside school at home, in activities, travel and on the Net (Gee 2002, p. 74). Indeed, these real life activities engage them in processes of learning that are deeper and richer than the forms of learning to which they are exposed in schools (Gee 2002, p. 78). Their regular learning processes represent known principles of effective teaching and learning, such as situated practice or authenticity, choice, integrated versus hierarchial skill practice, a high degree of interactivity, just-in-time instruction, and scaffolded learning. Is it any wonder that Millennials turn off in school when past assumptions of teaching and learning still prevail? The school library offers a learning environment unique from classrooms because it provides more opportunities to honour the learning processes preferred by Millennials. Teacher librarians need to tap the practices which embed these processes more consciously and strategically and actively strive to become instructional leaders in the school community.

New Literacies and Multiliteracies

What was counted as literacy a generation ago (let alone 500 or 1000 years ago) has changed dramatically. To function effectively in society now requires more than basic reading and writing with old technologies or print materials. Today in our workplaces, in our communities and in our private lives, we use a variety of print and electronic technologies to communicate and learn. In recent decades literacy researchers began to examine the many different ways of reading and writing in cultures and groups other than those of white Western upper-middle-class. This work forms the foundation of the concept of multiliteracies (New London Group 1996). Literacy is now conceived as both more expansive and complex than ever before.

Most often new literacies refer to the unique ways of reading and writing with the new technologies of information, communication and multimedia. New literacies refer both to new forms of texts or post-typographic (digital) forms, and to new ways of using text to shape new ways of thinking such as zines and scenario planning (Lankshear & Knobel 2003). Thus new literacies are more than new types of texts and processes in an old world but are situated in what Castells (1996) calls the era of informationalism which is oriented towards technological development, that is toward the accumulation of knowledge and towards higher levels of complexity in information processing (p. 17). In this way, new literacies are never fixed or definable, but constantly evolving.

While many adults are learning how to be comfortable with new technologies and the new literacies they spawn, today's youth have been bathed in bits since birth (Tapscott 1998) and regard technology as an inherent and integral means of creating themselves and the world. As Alvermann (*Adolescents and Literacies in a Digital World* 2002) notes, digital culture locates adolescents in new ways – ways that necessarily challenge earlier views on what counts as literacy, for whom, and when (p. ix). The problem is that numerous highly influential (and powerful) literacies exist that hold privileged places within contemporary everyday culture, but are not accounted in school learning in any significant way (Lankshear & Knobel 2003, p. 24).

The question of what aspects of new literacy needs or should be taught in schools is controversial. Clearly, Millennials live and breathe and craft their world with new literacies, and these abilities should be leveraged for learning in schools. On the other hand, some researchers have identified new literacy skills that students need help learning: searching and locating information on the Internet, comprehending hypermediated text, and critically evaluating online information (Kinzer 2003, Leu 2002, Todd 2004). Again teacher librarians are well-positioned to lead in these aspects of new literacies, but need to re-situate what they often regard as their domain – information literacy – in the currency of the larger literacy literature, i.e., within new literacies.

New literacies are not limited to technical and intellectual competencies, but include critical social abilities necessary for living in today's diverse and multicultural world. Thus critical literacy perspectives should also shape education in the new literacies (Street 2003). A sociologically-based critical perspective of information literacy goes beyond the cognitively-based application of critical thinking to information literacy that is commonly held by teacher librarians. What is needed is an understanding of critical thinking beyond the sense of detecting flaws in logic, factuality, or argumentation (Kapitzke 2003, p. 46). Students should be taught not only to learn with and through information but, most importantly, to learn about the political, economic and cultural production and use of information and knowledge (Kapitzke 2003). This dimension of information literacy is where teacher librarians lag behind, and they do so at the cost of much needed leadership in the educational community.

New and Multiple Identities and Communities

Globalization, diversity, and the rapid development and proliferation of information and communication technologies have altered how we define our personal and social lives. The Millennials are master-carvers of their identities as they continuously shape and manage their personal landscapes on the Internet. They construct their own curriculum and create their own learning tasks, processes, and tools. They see the Internet as a way to continuously connect with ever-shifting online communities established through a desire to share multiple and diverse identities. They put themselves on the line to the world through such new modes as blogs, ezines and chat rooms, and are unaware of the traditional processes of publishing their voices. Innovative educators see a major source of school reform in students' passionate focus on their multiple communities by framing schools as sites of knowledge providers and producers for students' communities (Bigum, Lankshear & Knoebel, in process). Teacher librarians need to apply more fully their training in information and communication technologies to facilitate students' intense and sophisticated use of networks to enrich teaching and learning in their schools. Teacher librarians can lead the development of schools as sites of *collaboratories* (Lunsford & Bruce 2001), which are distinguished by values and practices already held by teacher librarians: shared inquiry, intentionality, active participation and contribution, access to shared resources, technologies, and boundary crossings.

Teaching as a Political Activity

The three trends described above demand a significant shift in how we view teaching as more than covering a prescribed curriculum and using conservatively-interpreted effective instructional methods. While the concept of teaching as professionalization is now well-rooted in preservice and inservice teacher education, teaching as a political act (Apple 1996, Freire 1998, Giroux 1981 and 1988) is finally coming out of the closet as issues of social justice, globalization, ethical use of information, and empowerment take a more prominent place in the curriculum and classroom.

Teaching and curriculum has always been a socialization process and, therefore, a political activity. The difference now is that globalization, and what Castells (1996) calls the rise of the networked society, has put the politics of education in our faces. Amazingly, many people in education appear to have chosen to keep their eyes averted from or closed to this reality. At worse, some carry on ignoring new learners, new literacies, and new communities. Others attempt to placate by layering the new onto deeply-embedded educational structures and practices thus appearing to be innovative while preserving tradition (as is typical of many government educational innovations). Equipping schools with new technologies does not mean that new literacies are being taught and used to learn. In school library media programs, the adaptation of a critical (or sociological) perspective means enabling students to not only be able to access information, but to uncover agendas in information and take critically-informed positions in matters that truly count in their present and future worlds. While the real world and real learners race ahead, learning in school is becoming less and less what James Gee calls *efficacious*: what a child does now as a learner must be connected in meaningful and motivated ways with mature (insider) versions of related practices (Gee, Hull & Lankshear 1996, p. 4). Teacher librarians have an opportunity to shape education as a transformative process, not one that maintains the status quo. Helping students develop a critical dimension of information literacy as part of new literacies is begging for leadership and teacher librarians should step forward boldly.

Introduction to the Chapters

James Henri, in his chapter, attempts to deconstruct the meaning of the key defining concept for this work, that is, the information literate school community. This is achieved by relating it to other concepts that attempt to refocus and redefine the nature of school. He argues that our understanding of the information literate school community is very much linked to our understanding of information and of information literacy. He portrays information as the process of becoming informed and information literacy as mastery of the processes of becoming informed.

Cushla Kapitzke opens her chapter, *Whose community? Which knowledge? A Critical (Hyperliteracies) Take on Information School Communities,* by raising the obvious question about the many new phenomena peppering our educational landscape: New for whom? She suggests that these new notions reflect adult anxiety about what is unfamiliar and alien to them, but altogether routine to those who have not known otherwise, i.e., the Millennials. She presses us to move past debating the pros and cons of ICT-based changes in forms of text and spaces for learning and teaching and instead, accept that flux and confusion are here to stay, and be knowledgeable about these developments. Like other contributors of this book, Kapitzke argues the need for teacher librarians to rethink theory and practice, specifically in literacy. She reviews perspectives of critical literacy and hyperliteracy and explains their placement in the literacy curriculum in one educational system (Queensland, Australia).

Louise Limberg's chapter, *Informing Information Literacy Education through Empirical Research*, like Kapitzke's, presents serious concerns about how information literacy is being taught. She first establishes a view of information literacy that is multi-faceted for multiple purposes (e.g., finding facts, analyzing information, critiquing information), therefore requiring instruction aimed at development of a repertoire of strategies and understandings. She then reports findings from three of her studies, each one data-rich and representing significant samples, about what teacher librarians actually teach about information literacy. These findings are uncomfortable and disturbing. Limberg concludes with an urgent call to teacher librarians to begin the dramatic action that is necessary to break up cultural patterns of doing and teaching research and recreate instruction to fully support the complexity and depth of advanced models of information literacy.

The chapter *Curriculum Integration and Information Literacy: Developing Independent Learners* by Jedd Bartlett describes an innovative program designed to bring the principles and characteristics of the concept of the information literate school community to life. The program (named Base 6 to represent its six key features) uses student-centred teaching and learning approaches that are focused on developing autonomous, self-managing learners, student self-esteem and motivation, and the skills appropriate to lifelong learning. Bartlett concludes the chapter by identifying the strategies that were most successful in achieving in each stage of the program and the most compelling indicators of success – the teaching and learning in the school.

Elizabeth Lee also looks at literacy teaching in her chapter, *Reading and the Information Literate Community*. She reminds us, as did Sigrun Hannesdottir in her foreword to the *The Information Literate School Community* (1999) book, that "the skill to read is the foundation on which all other literacy skills rest", and that "(t)here is no information literacy possible without the basic skill of reading" (p. ii). Lee provides teacher librarians with a well-established research-based model of reading development by Jean Chall, a prominent reading researcher. Lee emphasizes that being able to read is just as critical in a technological society and that teacher librarians can play unique roles in supporting students reading development throughout their years of school.

Dianne Oberg and James Henri shift the focus from teaching to the role of the principal in their chapter, *The Leadership Role of the Principal in the Information Literate School Community*. Their focus on the principal rests on the assumption that a whole-school approach is necessary in developing an information literate community and that the critical role of the teacher librarian is particularly dependent on the support of the principal. They begin by constructing a profile of the role of the principal as determined from a review of the professional and research literature. They then explain how they extended learning about the role of the principal in developing the school library program in their international study of seven countries. They argue that an expansion rather than a reconceptualization of the role of the principal is needed to advance the place of the school library in the learning community.

Anne Clyde's chapter, *Policy, Social Justice and the Information Literate School Community,* sends a powerful message about the resource and educational role of the school library in all aspects of social justice, including gender equality, democratic government, economic opportunity, intellectual freedom, environmental protection and human rights for all people. Clyde works from the premise that in school communities that prioritize the pursuit of teacher and student mastery of processes of becoming informed, human rights and social justice will be of enormous importance. Clyde argues for the inclusion of social issues in school library policy by drawing on a range of educational and political documents as well as international and national policies in the school library field. Through concrete examples, she points out the shortcomings of current school library policy in supporting the right of youth to access information on such critical issues as HIV and sexual orientation.

In her chapter, *Scaffolding and the Information Literate School Community: Knowledge Building*, Sandra Lee uses the concept of knowledge management from the corporate world to examine if and how teachers have adapted what they know about building knowledge in the classroom to building knowledge in their teaching profession. She begins with an overview of major views and components of the literature of knowledge management, and distinguishes schools from corporate environments of professional practice. She then compares perspectives of knowledge building of the teacher (constructivism and scaffolding) and student (from knowledge as the way things are to knowledge as semi-autonomous artifacts).

In their chapter, *Teacher Librarians: Mirror Images of Teachers and Pioneering Voyagers*, Jean Brown and Bruce Sheppard establish that for schools to transform into learning communities more successfully, new models of leadership must take hold: If we are to develop learning organizations, the professional leadership of teachers must be developed. Taking the next step in their argument, they propose that teacher librarians need to be mirror images of other teacher leaders while also bringing added value as leaders in teacher librarianship. From their extensive, multi-method research program in leadership for change in schools and districts, Brown and Sheppard describe the four areas of competency required to meet this goal: (1) knowledge base; (2) technical skills; (3) personal, interpersonal and team skills and (4) a particular system of values and beliefs.

Sue Spence's chapter, *The Teacher Librarian Toolkit for an Information Literate School Community*, offers a treasure trove of first-hand methods of integrating information and communication technologies in teaching and learning. She explains the changing contexts of learning, in which technology is inherent and an inquiry-based interdisciplinary approach to teaching and learning concepts prevails. She introduces a variety of technological scaffolds for learning, featuring a structure she developed for her school community that supports resource-based learning and examines the natural role of the teacher librarian as professional development leader in these new teaching and learning contexts.

The following two chapters focus on specific international contexts of educational change and how teacher librarians can lead within these contexts. Lesley Farmer's chapter first outlines some of the major agents of change of education in North America including redefining good education, recognizing changing demographics, understanding the influence of the economy, being accountable, and integrating technology. Within each dimension of change, she offers implications for stronger roles for teacher librarians. She also describes key changes within the school library profession and how these changes represent potential pivotal roles of teacher librarians within the changing educational environment.

Linda Selby and Maureen Trebilcock describe a powerful initiative in New Zealand designed to generate change through professional development. As in many countries, professional development in New Zealand has moved to localized contexts where individual learning communities, at a variety of levels, control their own inservice in contrast to past top down externally-controlled models. Infolink, the program discussed in this chapter, is based on two major principles of effective professional development: coaching involving in class observation, and sharing of best practice. The goal of Infolink is improving teachers' educational practice through changing their attitudes and beliefs and to equip teachers with the knowledge and skills to improve their practice, thereby offering better opportunities in student learning. Infolink provides an effective model not only for teacher librarian education but also for all educational partners in moving their schools towards information literate communities.

Ken Haycock, in his chapter, *System Issues and the Information Literate School Community*, focuses on the unique role of another level of educational partner, the education authority, whether that be at the district, provincial/state or national level, or any combination thereof. He sets out the components of a policy framework that must be in place to ensure full participation of all members of the learning community: statement of the purpose of the school library program, definition of the roles of the partners, definition of terms, clarification of roles and expectations, provision of ongoing professional development, and definition of best practice.

The last chapter, *Preparing Preservice Teachers as Members of Information Literate School Communities,* by Marlene Asselin regards yet another, and sometimes overlooked, educational partner. She begins by reviewing trends in educational reform and in teacher education reform. The current professionalization view of teacher education rests on constructivist notions of teaching and learning, teaching as a collaborative activity, and teaching in constant change. Unlike past models of teacher education where learning was abstract and isolated from real children and schools, and where unequal power relations characterized teacher and student teacher interactions, effective teacher education now assumes the use of authentic tasks, authentic environments and mentoring. Based on these concepts of current teacher education, Asselin presents three Canadian models of educating preservice teachers about school libraries and the literacies of information and concludes with recommendations for developing initiatives that prepare preservice teachers as members of information literate school communities.

Understanding the Information Literate School Community

James Henri

Introduction

Not very long ago few people were using the terms "information skills", "information literacy" and "learning to learn", whereas today they are appearing with gay abandon in the most surprising places. The issue is no longer a concern about the currency of these ideas but rather it is about the proliferation of meanings that are attributed to them. The idea of the information literate school community is a fairly recent idea (Henri 1995). Yet quick and dirty Internet searches, using Google and AltaVista, found 171,000 and 78,289 records respectively: An indication, at least, that people are beginning to use this concept. As more and more people use the concept its meaning will change and adapt to meet particular purposes. It is likely that the concept will be misused because it is misunderstood. The purpose of this chapter is, therefore, to tease out the meaning that can be attributed to the information literate school community within this volume.

The challenge with this undertaking is that the idea of the information literate school community is both a concept and a working model. From a theoretical perspective the task is to draw a picture of an information literate school community that is defined by boundaries, even if those boundaries are somewhat fuzzy. From a practical perspective the concept has to be versatile enough for it to be applied. If we can make sense of "information" and "information literacy" then we should also concern ourselves about what we mean by "the information literate school community". Philosophers have argued for centuries about the meaning of concepts such as "good", "miracle" and "truth", and, although there may not be agreement about their meaning and although nothing in our world may match any particular definition, the ideas of "good", "miracle" and "truth" are nevertheless useful, and even of practical significance. Borrowing from Cooper and Boyd (1995) the information literate school community can be viewed as "a philosophy as well as a place; it is a way of being as well as a working model. It is a mindset as well as a map"

Henri (2000b) declared that: "A school community that places a high priority (policy, benchmarking, funding, and evaluation) on the pursuit of teacher and student mastery of the processes of becoming informed can be regarded as an information literate school community". This is the definition that underpins the argument in this book.

The idea of the "community" suggests more than an organization that is student focused. Community is something that transforms thinking within the school and does so in such a way that the transforming pulls the world of school and the world outside school closer together. Collaboration and collegiality are key measures of community well-being and are partial indicators of the existence of an information literate school community. But as Cooper and Boyd (1995) noted:

> Collaboration, rather than isolation, unfortunately, is a foreign practice to many educators. For most teachers, the adult in the next classroom is not someone they confide in about matters of teaching practice because it is too threatening. There is no time for teachers to collaborate even if they want to. In most schools, teachers do not see each other teach; they do not know each other's disciplines.

The idea of "high priority" suggests that the school is interested in implementation of innovations rather than in mere lip service to ideas. Issues pertaining to the information-literate school community will be featured in staff meetings and will be drivers of administrative rules and norms of behaviour. Professional development and induction programs will feature agendas that underpin critical elements of the information literate school community. Fostering, stimulating and evaluating elements of the information-literate school community will not be seen as highly problematic or as low priorities but rather will provide measures against which school success is evaluated.

"Mastery of the processes of becoming informed" suggests that the purpose of schooling is to bring to maturity young peoples abilities to think and reason interdependently. The emphasis is on construction (Groundwater-Smith 2001) and not on instruction (Henri 2004). Research reports will highlight elements of information literacy and point to the students' progress as learners. Success in subject learning will provide evidence of mastery of elements of learning.

In essence, the information literate school community describes a school community that places a significant priority on transforming information into knowledge and in turning knowledge into information. The members of this community search for meaning and application of knowledge and must, therefore, be equipped to deal with information as raw material, as a partial construction, and as an end product. The search for meaning is important at both the corporate and individual level. At the corporate level, policy and culture must work together to ensure that the focus of the school is on learning and that information literacy is appropriately supported as the key enabler of learning. At the individual level both students and teachers must be encouraged to monitor the attainment of information literacy.

The Learning Community

The idea of the information literate school community belongs to a broad family of concepts such as the "learning school" (Lincoln 1987) or the "learning organization" (Senge 1990, Watkins & Marsick 1993) or the "community of learners" (Brown 1997, Schön 1983 and 1990) or "collaborative learning communities" (Cooper & Boyd 1995). It also has an affinity with the ideas that underpin knowledge management particularly as promoted by the "Japanese School" (Nonaka 1994, Nonaka, Toyama & Konno, 2001) where knowledge management is seen to address the need to create knowledge spaces (Nonaka & Konno 1998) and reward personal understanding.

The information literate school community draws from and meshes with emerging learning theory and provides a sound reason for reconceptualizing and, ultimately, reengineering the places we call schools. Abbott and Ryan (1999, p. 66) claim that:

> As scientists study the processes of learning they are realizing that a constructivist model of learning reflects their best understanding of the brain's natural way of making sense of the world. Constructivism holds that learning is essentially active. A person learning something new brings to that experience all of their previous knowledge and present mental patterns. Each new fact or experience is assimilated into a living web of understanding that already exists in that person's mind. As a result, learning is neither passive nor simply objective.

Abbott and Ryan suggest that for the brain's predisposition toward constructivist learning to thrive, consideration must be given to all aspects of a child's learning environment. Therefore, building an information literate school requires and demands a departure from the stereotypical thinking that places teachers into classrooms to teach subjects. The culture, the architecture, and the relationships that dominate school must be holistic and flexible rather than myopic building blocks called classrooms. Schools must be places and spaces where people learn to learn and this must be transparently obvious and demonstrable.

Social constructivism attempts to explain learning as a community endeavour rather than as a merely personal pursuit. This community emphasis can be seen in Brown's (1997) community of learners and the parallel idea of communities of practice (Wenger & Snyder 2000). Within these communities, the focus is on shared responsibilities and mentoring relationships where loosely-coupled groups of people come together through shared expertise and passion for learning (Weick 1976). This argument was passionately put by Senge (1990) who noted that, while all people have the capacity to learn, the structures in which they have to function are often not conducive to reflection and engagement.

Senge claimed that learning organizations are:

> Organizations where people continually expand their capacity to create the results they truly desire, where new and expansive patterns of thinking are nurtured, where collective aspiration is set free, and where people are continually learning to see the whole together (Senge 1990, p. 3).

Nevis, DiBella, and Gould (1995) suggest that organizational learning is the "capacity or process within an organization to maintain or improve performance based on experience".

The dimension that distinguishes learning organizations from more traditional organizations is the mastery of certain basic disciplines. They are:

- Systems thinking: the ability to comprehend and address the whole, and to examine the interrelationship among the parts. Systems thinking provokes the incentive and the means to integrate the disciplines and is generally oriented toward long-term vision.
- Personal mastery: the discipline of "continually clarifying and deepening personal vision, of focusing energies, of developing patience, and of seeing reality objectively" (Senge 1990, p. 7). People with a high level of personal mastery are lifelong learners.
- Mental models: "deeply ingrained assumptions, generalizations, or even pictures and images that influence how we understand the world and how we take action" (Senge 1990, p. 8).
- Building shared vision: The practice of shared vision involves the skills of unearthing shared "pictures of the future" that foster genuine commitment and enrolment rather than compliance.
- Team learning: viewed as "the process of aligning and developing the capacities of a team to create the results its members truly desire" (Senge 1990, p. 236).

Building the Learning Community

Taking their cue from Senge, Watkins and Marsick (1993) talk of six action imperatives that underpin a learning community. The principal and teachers in a learning community:

- Create continuous learning opportunities
- Promote inquiry and dialogue
- Encourage collaboration and team learning
- Establish systems to capture and share learning
- Empower people towards a collective vision
- Connect the organization to its environment.

These imperatives provide a framework for, and some understanding about, the actions that are needed to sculpt the learning community. These actions look very much like knowledge-building (See Chapter 9).

Senge (1996) has more recently placed emphasis on the forces, or energies, that work to mould the five disciplines of the learning organization. In this way he has focused attention on leadership as the overarching force (or glue) that enables coherence within the organization and that creates the impetus for continuous innovation. He argues that leadership cannot force meaningful change but it can create the ingredients for a dynamic learning culture. He argues that leaders must develop personal learning strategies, and understand the context in which they work. Leaders must model what matters. They must create an environment in which people are open to new ideas, responsive to change, and eager to develop new skills and capabilities.

More recently, Lee (1998) suggested that a key feature of school as a learning community is that it is networked. He claims that "contrary to the simplistic views expressed by many who have not ventured into the online world, the technology provides the opportunity for enhanced social interaction, both on and off the Net". This idea, at least in part, provides a reminder of the idea that "the medium is the message" (McLuhan & Quentin 1967).

A networked community is, however, not necessarily a learning community. Lee suggests that empowerment does not flow from the connection of schools to the Internet but rather from the way that schools use an educational rationale to drive that connectivity. In other words, access to more and more information is of little value unless a school places high value on equipping its community in the processes of becoming informed. Clearly the quality of learning is in large part determined by the learner's access to relevant and pertinent information, and by the desire and determination of the school community to foster information literacy. First things must come first. "Fingertip access to the contents of the world's libraries may not benefit a child who has difficulty reading one book" (Beswick 1986, p. 8). The reward structures and support structures established by school leaders will be drivers of teacher behaviour. Schools that do not provide support for teacher learning can expect that teachers will be less motivated to learn than teachers in schools with a supportive environment. Principals who allow (even encourage) teachers to make mistakes as they learn are more likely to witness long term improvement than are principals who are wedded to a focus on student learning (Henri, Hay & Oberg 2002)

The learning organization concept has received wide support but as Garvin (2000) notes this support is predominantly conceptual rather than research-orientated. In practice achieving learning organization status may be much more difficult than creating the theoretical model. It is certainly true that some schools practice the six action imperatives proposed by Watkins and Marsick (1993) but the force still appears to remain with traditional-style schooling. Hawamdeh (2003) suggests that knowledge-sharing is the key force behind the learning organization and it is the potential weak point. He portrays individual learning within the organization as "selfish learning". Selfish learning occurs when individual goals and vision do not match corporate goals and vision. Examples of selfish learning in schools are:

- Multiple teachers preparing the same lessons
- New teachers having to develop lesson plans without recourse to a database from which they can retrieve previously used materials
- Teachers attending professional development courses without reporting their learning, and its potential application, to the wider school community

Tichy and Cardwell (2002) identify similar concerns about the learning organization model. They suggest that learning without teaching is a root cause of the knowledge-sharing challenge. They state:

> [A] Teaching Organization adds a critical expectation that everyone will be a teacher as well as a learner… Teaching Organizations work because they set in motion and sustain what I call a "Virtuous Teaching Cycle"… This continuous learning and teaching chain is fundamental if an organization is to make the best use of available knowledge and generate new knowledge
> (p. 54).

Fullan (2001) also argues that school systems and corporations suffer from the knowledge-sharing problem. He notes that:

> Corporations and school systems have much more in common than we thought. They are not identical, but they both would be better off (and hence so would society) if they strengthened their capacity to access and leverage hidden knowledge (p. 105).

Fullan's articulation of the knowledge-sharing problem as "hidden knowledge" is very much in the tradition of leading Japanese writers in the knowledge management field (Nonaka 1994, Nonaka & Konno 1998, Nonaka & Takeuchi 1995) who have placed great emphasis on knowledge-building as the primary concern of knowledge management.

School Culture

The picture of a typical school is of an architecture that makes accessing and leveraging knowledge for learning extremely complex. This is why leading-edge schools are experimenting with forms of working (that do not resemble traditional classroom structures) and the organization of teaching that demands a fundamental reassessment of the role of, and an understanding of learning spaces and information in schools. Some schools are fundamentally open spaces where teachers are connected, both physically and electronically; some schools are fundamentally closed spaces where teachers rarely see each other. Some schools are drowned in information; some schools use information as the oxygen of learning. If schools are serious about being informed, if they want to forge a school community where both teachers and students are comfortably and competently using a wide range of information services and products, they will place a priority on the effective use of teaching and learning methods that equip learners with knowledge construction skills.

Schools that recognize that becoming informed is a struggle of making sense from inconsistencies and incompleteness are likely to hold the view that learning is nothing less than self-understanding – reformulating information for oneself. Compare, for example, the science teacher who tells students what to expect from an experiment with the science teacher who creates an environment in which students discover what the great scientists discovered before *but* allows for the possibility that all is not yet set in stone and perhaps the students can discover something new.

Knowledge-sharing is strong when community and collegiality are valued, but, as Thomas, Kellogg, and Erickson (2001) suggest, it is essential that these shared values about relationships become embedded in practice and become an essential part of school culture. Schein (1985, p. 9) refers to culture as "a pattern of basic assumptions – invented, discovered, or developed by a given group as it learns to cope with problems…that has worked well enough to be considered valid and, therefore, to be taught to new members as the correct way to perceive, think, and feel in relation to those problems". Eventually cultural behaviour is taken for granted and this can be a strength or a challenge.

Deal and Peterson (1999) argue that school cultures are complex webs of traditions and rituals that have been built up over time and which are shaped by principals, teachers, and key people who reinforce, nurture, or transform underlying norms, values, beliefs, and assumptions. School culture affects a staff's receptiveness to professional development as a vehicle for change. Cohesion of purpose comes out of a strong culture. If the culture is both successful and strong it will be the prime element to the successful improvement of teaching and learning (Fullan 1998, Rossman, Corbett, & Firestone 1988). If the culture is both unsuccessful and strong it will be a major roadblock to school improvement and understanding the school's culture will be the prerequisite for any internal or external change agent (Stoll 2003).

Kuhlthau (1993a) has developed a set of primary inhibitors and basic enablers that may help in understanding the information literate school community. She found three primary inhibitors in programs that seemed to have stalled, that is, to have been unable to develop effective collegial teaching and learning: lack of time; confusion of roles; and poorly designed assignments. Stalled programs show evidence of lack of time both for instructional planning and for students to engage in information literacy activities. The lack of instructional planning prevents the development of new or enhanced instructional roles: the teachers give the assignments; the librarians find the resources; and the principal is not involved at all. The student assignments are not integrated into the classroom curriculum; they are often regarded as add-ons, as optional enrichment activities, rather than an essential part of curriculum-based learning.

Kuhlthau (1993a) found that four basic enablers were present in successful programs: a team approach to teaching; a shared understanding of learning as a constructivist process; a shared commitment to lifelong learning; and competence in developing learning activities and strategies. Successful programs show evidence of the teachers, the librarian, and the principal working together to facilitate, develop, and implement instructional programs. Each person on the instructional team has essential roles to play – finding time for the instructional team to work together, ensuring that the assignments fit within the school's philosophy and goals, designing the assignments on an information process model, ensuring that the appropriate information resources are available, teaching the required information skills, and monitoring and assessing student work. The instructional team understands that students bring different understandings to their learning and that their new learning builds on what they already know; the team engages students in problem-based inquiry as one way for students to learn how to learn. The instructional team is focused on helping students to take responsibility for their own learning and to develop the skills for learning that are essential within and beyond the school. The instructional team develops assignments through innovation and experimentation; they are trying new approaches in order to enhance student learning.

While Kuhlthau was primarily concerned with library programs and teacher and teacher librarian interaction, her findings demonstrated that basic enablers are not simply opposites of primary inhibitors. That means that creating information literate school communities involves addressing both kinds of indicators, developing the basic enablers while eliminating or ameliorating the primary inhibitors. This is consistent with the findings of research in educational change.

Understanding Information

A major challenge for a school that seeks to become an information literate school community is to understand the nature of information and to unlock the complex relationships among data, information and knowledge and to promote and sustain a culture and an architecture that will allow opportunity for knowledge-building. This process of understanding occurs within a culture that is more comfortable for students than it is for teachers because the processes of informing that dominate today did not even exist when most of today's teachers were born. Today's dominant forms of communicating are the playgrounds of the young, and adults have always been wary of spending time in the playground. As we witness the pace of change ever accelerating, imagine the difficulties faced by the teachers of tomorrow. Previous ideas of teacher comfort, which impeded student learning, are no longer acceptable. The new teacher comfort must be about constant adaptation to change. The information literate school community is a community in which change is accepted as the norm and teachers are supported through allocation of resources – time, mentors, access to professional development – to enable them to be prepared for change.

Information has two properties; it is both a medium of exchange and a store of wealth. In addition, information can have both a public and a private value. Public information is that information that is readily available for wealth creation. Private information is that information that has been used for personal wealth creation (personal knowledge, you might say).

Information has both passive and active attributes. When information is used actively it facilitates exchange. Inactive information is information that is waiting to be used. Such information is held inside filing cabinets, inside textbooks, inside networks, and in school libraries: It is held inside containers. But when information is active it entails a process of informing. Informing happens inside brains. It changes opinions, attitudes, strategies and so on, by offering evidence.

If a school considers information as a store of wealth, it will collect information and measure it. Such schools are interested in the size of a library collection, the number of books each student borrows, the qualifications held by teachers, and the amount of information stored inside student heads as preparation for tests. A classroom in these schools will be characterized by transmission of information from teacher and textbook to student notebooks. Students will download huge quantities of material from the Internet, they will grind the photocopier to a standstill, in the hope that some form of osmosis between the copied material and their minds will occur. Knowledge, *not* understanding, is the hallmark of such schools. McGregor and Streitenberger (1998) aptly describe students in these schools as scribes.

A parrot can talk, but doesn't know what it says. A machine can copy, but it has no idea of the value of what it is copying. Electronic text can be copied and pasted into new places, but without the application of the mind it has no new meaning. By definition, copied material lacks originality and therefore it lacks meaning. Scribes and sign-writers copy for a living and the quality of their work is measured against the accuracy of the imitation. For the most part learning is about making something personally understandable from a range of information sources.

Quality teaching is about supporting students in their quest for exploration. Through the processes of becoming informed, they mature as researchers who grapple with the adequacy of their information sources and skills. Such researchers do not investigate information as if it were a needle in a haystack (the answer is there somewhere, the trick is to locate it); rather, their information pool is a rich laboratory providing evidence for personal examination. As teachers and students work together to construct knowledge in this way they share an understanding that the process of becoming informed and constructing knowledge involve all of the dynamic processes of thinking, feeling, and acting.

Information requires knowledge to be both created and understood. Evidence of knowledge is provided via information. Knowledge of information in action is needed to produce knowledge. Learning is what happens when knowledge and information collide in a dynamic way. The transformation of information into knowledge occurs within the mind of individuals, and knowledge becomes information once it is articulated. This means that one person's information can be another person's knowledge. The creation of knowledge is a product of the interplay of previous knowledge with new information. All information needs knowledge to be decoded and some of that necessary knowledge may remain tacit.

Stenmark (2002, p. 2) argues:

> In a corporate setting, not only information creation but also information seeking and information interpretation are actions that describe the interaction between knowledge and information. By monitoring these actions, the organization can learn where certain kinds of knowledge reside and thereby leverage the tacit knowledge of its members. Individuals benefit both by being able to find knowledgeable colleagues and by being themselves identified as knowledgeable.

Stenmark draws inspiration from Schön (1983 and 1990), who claimed that new understanding comes from reflection; and that requires the practitioner to mentally "step back" while observing his/her own actions. Such reflection, however, can only take place when the practitioner is not fully preoccupied by the action itself. The traditional classroom setting is unlikely to provide an arena that allows a multitude of formats and interactions and impedes the possibility for dialogue which provides the opportunity for reflective practice.

Environments for Teacher Mastery

Schön's idea of the reflective practitioner has been highly influential, but his claim that such reflection necessitates an arena had largely gone unnoticed until Nonaka and Konno (1998) promoted the idea of "*ba*" or knowledge space. *Ba* refers to the space of emerging relationships among people. It is a place where information is interpreted and possibly transformed into knowledge. *Ba* is a combination of physical, ideational, virtual and organizational space or contexts for human interaction within a team or organization (Talisayon 2004). Four types of *ba* are:

1. Originating *ba*: it is the place where persons share experiences, feelings, emotions, and mental models. Such context can fully empathize and/or sympathize one's emotions and physical senses in order to facilitate the transfer of tacit knowledge. Love, care, trust, and commitment emerge in this *ba*, and it forms the basis for socialization process among individuals.
2. Dialoguing *ba*: this perhaps is the *ba* following the originating *ba* where mental models and skills are shared, converted into common terms and articulated as concepts through dialogues. It supports externalization process. Dialoguing *ba* can also be facilitated with a selected mixed of participants with specific knowledge and capabilities interacting with each other.
3. Systemizing *ba*: this may be articulated as "cyber *ba*", where explicit knowledge is combined and disseminated and could be easily assessed by the public. ICT technology such as groupware, intranet and databanks are some examples of systemizing *ba* that allow people to interact effectively and efficiently.
4. Exercising *ba*: it is a more individual-based context where knowledge from virtual media is internalized. Exercising ba "synthesizes the transcendence and reflection that come in action, while dialoguing *ba* achieves this via thought." (Nonaka, Toyama & Konno 2001)

The information literate school community suggests a space where human minds are equipped to master informing processes and where those human minds are provided the opportunity to coalesce: that is, there is a need for both ability and opportunity. But are the adults who are drawn into teaching compatible with the pursuit of these? Or are they typically adults who choose less collegiality, rather than more? Are our teachers equipped and provided with the ongoing support that they need to enable them to lead the forging of such communities? There is, in fact, significant evidence that teachers are not necessarily efficient learners within today's dominant information paradigms and more specifically, there is evidence to suggest that teachers are not necessarily information literate (Henri 1999a, O'Connell & Henri 1997). Indeed, Moore (2001) noted that:

> We have evidence from several studies, however, that many teachers are themselves uncertain where to begin with information literacy and need assistance in translating a good idea into good classroom practice. This problem is compounded for those who interpret information literacy in terms of technological skills that they personally lack! (See also Bruce 1997, Henri 2001, Moore 1998 and 2000)

The idea of an information literate school community challenges the suggestion that teachers don't have to be information literate. It suggests that the quality of a school's teachers is its most important asset and, therefore, developing a culture that ensures space for ongoing collegial teacher renewal is essential. Renewal and growth are dependent upon reflective and collegial practices that are embedded in school culture. Schools that focus upon maintaining high-quality teachers (that is, teachers who constantly practice and model the processes of becoming informed) will, as a by-product, achieve high-quality learning outcomes.

Teachers who master the processes of becoming informed have the ability to:

- recognize the need for information and understand that stress and uncertainty are essential components of the process of becoming informed
- pose essential questions (McKenzie 1997), develop ideas and solve problems
- use a variety of data-gathering strategies
- locate appropriate, relevant and pertinent data
- assess data for quality, authority, accuracy, and authenticity
- adopt and use the practical and conceptual tools of information and communication technologies to create meaning (shared understanding)
- understand form, formats, location, and access methods
- format and publish in textual and multimedia formats

By placing emphasis on teacher mastery, the information literate school community provides an environment in which students are most likely to be able to understand why they need to be information literate and teachers are able to be role models of good practice.

Stuck schools (Rosenholtz 1989) provide reasons why change won't happen. Teachers don't understand, teachers are too busy, parents will object, and so on. Moving schools look for solutions through collegial focus and the desire for constant improvement. Schools that are focused in a direction of information literacy see constant change as the norm and set policies and practices within this context. Schools that want to be information literate communities create conditions that enable that to happen. Characteristics of stuck schools include: fixed-length inflexible timetables, lack of pertinent professional development, emphasis on out-of-class work rather than the quality of the learning environment, lack of meaningful engagement with the local community (Bigum 2004), and assessment by subject. Characteristics of information literate schools include: emphasis on policy development, authentic process-driven assessment, integrated and flexible curriculum, and a strong role for specialists such as the curriculum coordinator and the teacher librarian.

Almost by definition, teachers who focus on process have a complex and holistic perspective within schools and it is these particular teachers who are positioned to drive cultural norms away from the fixation on classrooms and subjects towards a much more organic view of schooling as community.

Learning and knowledge are both complex concepts and raise complex issues, but both are inextricably linked with information. How a school thinks about information will ultimately shape attitudes and approaches to learning and knowledge-building. Traditionally, when a student said "I need information", s/he meant "I need an information source from which I can copy". In the information literate school community "needing information" is more likely to mean "I need to know how to be informed on this topic".

Mapping the Information Literate School Community

Henri (1995) articulated a tentative set of benchmarks that could be used to assess a school's progress towards information literacy culturing. The list, given below, appears to be equally applicable today. The list has been classified by focus.

Whole school focus

- The school has a set of information policies in place
- The school has adopted an information technology plan
- The school has an Internet portal. Learning is the dominant consideration in its design and maintenance
- The school has benchmarked information competencies that are expected of students at key points in their school career
- Information skills are taught/learned across the curriculum and in the context of authentic content learning
- The process of learning from information – of constructing knowledge – is always the focus of teaching and learning.

Principal focus

- The principal demonstrates information leadership
- The principal fosters knowledge management, requires timely information for corporate decision-making, and provides the resources to make this possible

- Information leaders (ICT coordinator, teacher librarian) are members of the key curriculum committee

Teacher focus

- The school supports the professional development of staff with respect to information literacy
- Teachers demonstrate that they are excellent learners
- Teachers talk, dream, plan and teach as a team rather than as a group of individuals
- Teachers seek evidence that students are constructing their own meaning

Teacher librarian focus

- A significant percentage of school funds are budgeted for the provision of information services
- The school understands and defends the role of the teacher librarian, as articulated in policy documents
- The school requires that the teacher in charge of information services be a qualified teacher librarian

Student focus

- The school requires students to build electronic portfolios of evidence of their level of information literacy
- The school monitors the information work demands that are placed on each student. Careful scrutiny is applied before students are requested to locate information outside school
- Reporting on student achievement focuses on how the student is maturing as a learner
- Teachers encourage student collaboration in many aspects of their learning
- Learning contexts are varied and involve students in the meaningful use of a wide range of information resources
- When students are required to undertake homework that involves a step(s) in the information process, teachers consider issues of social justice, equity, and the domestic demands placed on students
- Students are encouraged to provide constructive feedback to teachers with respect to information based learning tasks
- Students maintain logs or other records of their learning – the successes and challenges – and are involved in self-assessment

The shift in focus from teaching to learning; the shift in focus from stand-alone subjects to integrated learning; the shift in focus from one teacher to 30 students to flexible teaching teams and student groupings; the shift from assessing knowledge to assessing learning; the shift from classrooms (and teachers who are in charge of classrooms) to learning spaces; and the shift from individual foci to a whole-school focus – together these represent a revolution in thinking about schooling.

Schools that are serious about substantive change and adopting a "learning to learn" paradigm are encouraged to construct and mould information literate communities where teachers are themselves information literate. This shift in thinking brings with it many shifts in practice and has special implications for the role of the teacher librarian and the purpose of information services in schools (Henri, Boyd & Eyre 2002).

How might the teacher librarian act as a catalyst for change? Consider the following:

Policy development

- Encourage discussion about the effect an information policy might have on teaching and learning
- Encourage the involvement of all staff in the formulation of an information policy, considering how such a policy might affect them and their teaching programs
- Argue that the library is a duty area and that all staff should be scheduled there throughout the year
- Be involved in the development/revision of homework policy/practice. Argue that typically students should not be involved in information seeking tasks out of school but could use home time to manipulate information
- Participate in lobby groups in support of such matters as the development of union policies on working conditions, responsibilities, rights, etc.

Information services

- Map the information resources in the school so that these can be matched against curriculum requirements. Identify unmet information needs
- Use program budgeting to ensure adequate funding is allocated to support resource based learning and the provision of information services
- Identify skills-based learning goals from curriculum documents and develop levels of performance indicators for the identification of information literacy
- Ensure that the school is up-to-date about current information services/sources and the ways that these can be used to support/resource the curriculum
- Encourage teachers to call upon teacher librarian expertise
- Seek funding from outside school sources to support school-based information literacy initiatives

- Ensure maximum patronage of the library through extended opening and eventually through electronic access
- Disseminate professional reading to colleagues

Learning and assessment

- Provide a significant contribution to the development of whole-school information literacy programs
- Encourage the use of assessment techniques that demonstrate the acquisition of information-based competencies
- Model lifelong learning by testing and trialing information skills/strategies
- Collaborate with teachers to integrate information skills/strategies into teaching programs
- Fight vigorously for an unscheduled library timetable and maintain an open-door policy for information seekers
- Reinforce the desirability of student self-assessment and the use of metacognitive tools (thinking/learning logs etc.)

Integration of ICT

- Ensure that the school is aware of the educational potential of available information technologies and that information technology needs are prioritized with the allocation of appropriate funding
- Argue for the integration of information technology into all teaching programs

Continuing professional development

- Ensure that teachers are efficient library users
- Provide teachers with strategies to implement/integrate information skills/strategies into their teaching programs
- Educate teachers/students about such issues as copyright, privacy, intellectual property rights and freedom of information
- Arrange for the demonstration of information technology sources, services and products
- Participate in the professional development of other teacher librarians
- Read widely in such areas as information technology, educational administration, librarianship, and education

Conclusion

Clearly the relationships among, knowledge, information and learning are extremely complex, but this complexity ought to be something that schools explore rather than ignore. Traditional transmission pedagogies are suited to a bygone era because they ignore complexities and because they accept the bankrupt proposition that knowledge can be transferred in the same way that information is transferred.

When the information literacy focus shifts from students to teachers then the role of the teacher librarian and of the principal as information leaders must shift too. Teacher librarians must shift their services and their allocation of time towards teachers. Principals must make that happen by driving school policy and rewarding school practices that reflect these changes. Indeed a school community that places a high priority, in terms of policy, benchmarking, funding, and evaluation, on the pursuit of teacher and student mastery of the processes of becoming informed can be regarded as an information literate school community (Heppell 2003).

3

Whose Community? Which Knowledge? A Critical (Hyperliteracies) Take on Information Literate School Communities

Cushla Kapitzke

Changing Times: Changing Libraries and Literacies

The jargon of *new*speak has emerged recently within educational circles in response to the avalanche of change that is currently transforming society, schools, and schooling. For example, along with a host of "posts" (post-industrialism, postmodernism, post-structuralism, post-colonialism), the term "new times" is often used to differentiate the present from the immediate, but passé, past (Dizard 2000, Hall 1996, Luke 1998). Professional literatures, scholarly research, government reports, and policy documents alike are peppered with the "new languages", "new literacies", "new media", "new workplaces", and "new poor" that educators need to account for in this "new information age" (Castells, et al. 1999, Dertouzos 1997, Dovey 1996, Fairclough 2000, Gee 2000).

Yet, use of this loose qualifier invites the question, "New for whom?" Is the change "new" to the young people who are making it happen as they are objects of adult theorizing about it? Or does the conflation of "new" with "novel" and "modern" say more about the educationalists who use the term so profusely, yet so uncritically? Is it possible that, rather than denoting an historical disjuncture, the term "new" reflects adult anxiety about what is unfamiliar and alien to them, but altogether routine to those who haven't known otherwise? With this in mind, I intentionally use the term "changing" to contextualize the following discussion about libraries and their literacies in what are fluid and unpredictable social and educational environments.

What, then, are the changes that have destabilized the pedagogical logics of libraries? First is the proliferation of new textual forms. Examples of these are the ezines, Internet chat, animé, text and video messaging, email, and computer gaming through which many young people today communicate and learn. Second is the shift to digital and online spaces and portals for teaching and learning. Of most interest here are the pressures placed on school library media centres from globalization and the increasing commodification of information. Irrespective of whether one is positive and proactive, or pessimistic and reactive in the face of these changes, the point is that the postmodern condition with all its flux and confusion is here to stay. Because there are benefits and drawbacks to all change, the challenge for teacher librarians is to be knowledgeable and upbeat about these developments.

Working as they do at the frontline of curricular renewal, technological innovation, and professional development, teacher librarians and cybrarians are well positioned to be leaders of school reform. Indeed, within the existing parameters of their education, certification, and professional practice, teacher librarians have a reputation for initiative and excellence. Yet an inability to meet the high expectations to which they aspire, combined with narratives of crisis around print-oriented libraries, has created a healthy sense of uncertainty and reflection on the parameters and outcomes of school library media centre work (Crawford & Gorman 1995, Wisner 2000).

With this in mind, the present chapter argues that, if school cybrarians are to capitalize on current opportunities for educational reform and social change, there is a need for them to rethink theory and practice. My aim here is to show that effective leadership in school library media centre and cybrary contexts requires a paradigmatic shift in terms of literacy pedagogy. I begin with an overview of critical literacy and hyperliteracies approaches as a starting point for reassessment of the cultural ideologies and pedagogical practices of library practitioners. Such approaches assume that, irrespective of the issue at hand – whether policy, benchmarking, or funding as addressed in this volume – these developments and debates manifest within, and need to be considered part of, historical, social, political, and economic contexts. In sum, I believe that more of a sociological perspective on these issues is required. To defend this claim, I begin by describing an Australian educational initiative around critical literacy education, and illustrate its classroom practice with a discursive analysis of a familiar library information resource. Because critical literacy approaches require problematizing one's own assumptions and practices, a reappraisal of the concept "information literate school community" follows the textual analysis. The purpose of this deconstruction is to assist teacher librarians to achieve their potential for visionary leadership in these "changing times".

Critical Literacies and Hyperliteracies

For two decades now, school library media centre practitioners have used the information literacy framework as their primary literacy pedagogy. Bruce and Candy's (2000) volume shows the extent to which this model for library research and resource-based learning has been adopted worldwide. But recent theoretical work by Kapitzke (2003a and 2003b, Luke & Kapitzke 1999) has shown that the framework as it is currently understood and enacted is conceptually limited. The latter corpus argues that it is not educationally sound to think of information literacy as a single, neutral pedagogical approach or "framework", the application of which will produce predetermined, universal learning outcomes. Instead, Kapitzke views information literacy as a social construction, a discourse that both enables and constrains library work and learning outcomes. Most importantly, because it is "done" differently with different texts in different literacy events, using different pedagogical practices embodying different power relations, the information literacy framework has differential educational consequences for different groups of students.

Kapitzke's work draws heavily from critical literacy studies, which in turn, are informed by critical social theory. Because these theories form the philosophical bedrock of the hyperliteracies framework proposed by her, a brief review of both concepts follows. Note that the term "critical" used here has a different meaning from that of the critical *thinking* paradigm. Critical *social* theory emerged during the 1920s with theorists of the German Frankfurt School, who sought to explain the continued power of capitalism and the failure of Marx's socialist revolution. Several waves of critical theory have occurred since then, but the common threads of this work are the concepts ideology, dominance, and discourse. These ideas are used principally to explore the reproduction of social inequity through processes of language, knowledge, and power. Hence, the first principle of critical educators is a commitment to progressive social change through critical understanding and praxis, or action.

Whilst its meaning is highly contested, critical literacy is generally understood as a repertoire of practices that problematize and interrogate, deconstruct and reconstruct text. Critical literacy entails "talking back" to text by asking questions of it to elicit its social power. This is necessary because most meaning in text is implicit. That is, it resides below the surface level of vocabulary, grammar, and punctuation. Working at the surface level of text, or within the text itself, enables only reading and/or viewing that is complicit to its meaning and power. Alternatively, critical questioning of the external dimensions of text elicits its "politics", which comprises the site and source of its action and effect on the world. A *socially* critical reading of text disclosing these implicit meanings requires analysis of the contexts of its production and consumption.

Lohrey (1998), for example, describes seven such contexts, any or all of which teacher librarians could explore with students as part of the process of selecting and evaluating learning resources. These are the contexts of:

- situation (the institutional, school library media centre setting of text selection and use);
- form (the text type);
- author (questions of authorial (in)visibility and authority);
- voice (modes of address embodying formality or informality);
- genre (links between cultures, events, and text types);
- rhetorical strategies (the micro grammatical constructions and macro structures); and
- worldview (the text's epistemology, or approach to truth and knowledge as constructed in and by the text).

This simple framework enables readers and viewers to mine the dimensions of a text's power and, thereby, to reflect on their own discursive assumptions. This literate practice is different altogether from an information process model that approaches text to "find" and "extract" information for a library report or assignment. A key assumption of critical literacy approaches is that text is not an object with a specific meaning residing in it. Rather, it is a *co-creation*, a shared process arising from the blending of textual conventions and the text user's discursive history.

No single "silver-bullet" model for the teaching of critical literacy has emerged, and nor should one. Indeed, the above is just one form of many critical discourse analysis and systemic functional linguistic approaches that are used in classrooms today with oral, print and multimodal texts (Fairclough 1995, Gee, Michaels & O'Connor 1992, Lemke 1996). Critical literacy approaches are also variously deployed in media studies and cultural studies programs (see, for example, Semali & Pailliotet 1999).

The wide range of methods available to literacy educators, including teacher librarians prompted Kapitzke (2003a) to devise the notion of "hyperliteracy". The term encapsulates the notion of being literate about literacy, and refers to critique of the information process itself, as students are provided opportunity to consider their positioning as information users and producers. This is not the place to provide a more detailed exposition of that term, and I refer the reader to the aforementioned body of work. The present paper nevertheless is based on the premise that, given opportunity and scaffolding, even small children are able to contextualize and problematize text. To counteract would-be naysayers to the notion of six-year-olds identifying and contesting the values and ideologies of "The Three Bears" (patriarchy) or The Wiggles (consumerism), the following section provides an overview of one Department of Education's state-mandated critical literacy policy initiative.

Mainstreaming Critical Literacy: An Australian Initiative

In this Australian initiative, school literacy debates and agendas have centred expressly on social critique (Education Queensland 2000a). While acknowledging that curricular and pedagogical innovations alter in the process of their implementation at the classroom level, Education Queensland has made a concerted effort to conceive the teaching of literacy as critical engagement with the social texts and discourses of a changing world (Education Queensland 2000b and 2001). Their Four Resources approach to literacy instruction specifies four repertoires of practice that critical readers deploy (see Luke & Freebody 1997). They are:

- *Coding Practices:* The resources that students draw from to crack the conventions of a text's symbolic system. This entails asking how the marks, sounds, and movements of a text combine to "mean".

- *Text-meaning Practices:* The semantic resources that students as members of cultural and subcultural groups utilize. This entails understanding how the text and the student draw from and reproduce meaning through their union.

- *Pragmatic Practices:* To enable students to develop practical understanding of the social uses of text, students consider how text is used and how it can be used differently.

- *Critical Practices*: The resources students draw from to analyze text. How is the text selective? What are the interests and agendas of the person who wrote the text? Which voices and values are present and which are absent?

These dimensions are neither discrete nor hierarchical but are used at any year level and in any literacy event such as a shared reading or writing session using video footage, magazines, advertisements, textbooks, storybooks, or web sites. In simple forms, children are taught aspects of mode, modality, and pronominalization through which they analyze how particular textual genres construct ideological versions of the world (cf. Fairclough 1989).

Putting Theory into Practice

Let me illustrate this approach with an example of an analysis like those undertaken in Queensland classrooms. The selected text is the *National Geographic Online* magazine web site (National Geographic Society 2003). I chose this information resource because of its relevance to library work and the possibilities it offered in terms of critical textual analysis. Dating back to 1888, the *National Geographic* magazine is published by the National Geographic Society and recognized as a prominent educational institution in the United States and abroad. Yet, despite its status as a traditional learning resource and the National Geographic Society's claim to being the "world's largest *nonprofit* scientific and *educational* organization [emphasis added]", values inscribed in the content of this web site are overtly commercial. The purpose of this exercise is to show how, in recent years, corporate capitalism has eroded the time-honoured distinctions between news, education, and entertainment. Furthermore, it illustrates how web sites like this provide rich texts for student study of the genres, *infotainment* and *edutainment* (Scanlon & Buckingham 2002).

This analysis deals specifically with the 2 June 2003 edition, the homepage of which featured the new *National Geographic Kids* magazine. [1] Brilliant colours, dazzling images, captivating animation, and Flash-enabled icon movements leave no doubt about the blending here of factual information and market-oriented values that target children through pleasure. Before going any further, let me preface my case with the assertion that leisure and (re)creation are integral to children's well-being. Children deserve and need pleasure, but they also deserve honesty from adults. My concern here is with profit-making motives that are cloaked by discourses of "educational" purpose and content. For example, the web site's "About Us" information states that the "mission" of *National Geographic Kids* is to *"entertain*

---

[1] Consistent with the post-structuralist principle that 'truth' is socially constructed through the legitimation of knowledge, this is my interpretation, my take, on the text. It is informed by my personal values, understandings, and agendas, which I am able to express, having been asked to contribute to the current volume. This does not impute to these views more credence than other readings and (re)constructions of the text.

children while educating and *exciting* them about their world [emphasis added]". There are two doses of pleasure here, namely, "entertain[ment]" first and "excite[ment]" last. Education is present (for parents?), but downplayed by its middle position in the list. The text's author describes the magazine as "an interactive, multitopic magazine" covering "animals, entertainment, science, technology, current events, and cultures from around the world". We all know how entertaining animals are to children, so the order of these categories – animals first, followed by "entertainment" and other "cultures" last – reconfirms that *National Geographic Kids* is "the magazine that makes it *fun to learn* about the world" [emphasis added].

Using the Four Resources model, clearly, there is much to entice children to comprehend the text at the level of graphophonic (language) and semiotic (image) coding (see Figure 1). Plenty of animals (e.g., guerillas advertising Nintendo Gameboy computer games; a kitten on the cover advertising the *National Geographic Kids* magazine; and wolves used to advertise the "Amazing Animals Fun Fact" segment of the web site) woo the viewer to explore the *Stories, Games, Sound Off! Try This!* and *Surprise* features offered within the site's precincts. Working at the cultural level, students could share their rich stores of knowledge on advertising, narrative, sports, and media culture that enable them to understand the meanings and activities of the site. They could consider how children of poorer nations and majority cultures would or would not understand these texts and their values, and the reasons for this. As text users, students could explore the genre of magazines (leisure and/or educational, print and/or online) and create their own.

The following mini-analysis comes from the site's *NG Explorer*, which describes itself as a "Classroom Magazine". A heading, *Guides*, on the left of the page, contains a list of hyperlinks to features such as *Adventure and Exploration, Animals and Nature, History and Culture, Maps and Geography*, and *News*. These topics are redolent of print-based, nonfictional categories, which traditionally claimed to provide impartial, factual information for teaching and learning. But this informational text could make no such claim because the contexts of situation (a for-profit magazine), form (web site), voice (marketer), and worldview (instrumental/commercial knowledge) function to create the desires and dispositions of consumers rather than the rational qualities of the "informed" citizen of liberal democratic educational discourse.

Numerous features of the site illustrate this point, but this analysis focuses on the *This Month's Game* item. Comprising an "Ice Cream Challenge", the feature's opening page invites viewers to play the game by tempting them with images of mouthwatering, jumbo ice cream serves atop cones decorated with cherries, sprinkles, and chocolate drizzle. The sassy interrogative, "Think you've got the scoop?" accompanying the images proffers a challenge that cocky "tweenagers" and adolescents would find hard to resist. Use of the direct second person ("you") and copious scatterings of wry puns throughout the activity (e.g., "You know these ice cream facts cold!" "Like Nero, you rule") appeal to the viewer's self-image and confirm him/her as perceptive negotiators of consumer culture who understand and enjoy the hip and playful language of advertising.

A "Play the Game" hyperlink hails the reader by asking, "Want to know more about this sweet subject [sic] before trying the game? Get the scoop [sic] from our Ice Cream article". The accompanying *article* provides social and historical information on ice cream but, notably, closes with references to two of the largest ice cream manufacturers in the United States. This strategy of product placement through covert mention of these "ice cream empire(s)" promotes brand awareness and loyalty in the targeted consumer group, namely, school children.

The activity itself comprises ten multiple-choice questions, most of which deal with historical information about the manufacturing of ice cream and consumer behaviour. Examples of the questions are: "About how much do Americans *spend* on frozen desserts each year?" "When did the first ice cream factories open?" and "What is the *best-selling* flavor of ice cream? [emphasis added]". A complicit reading of factual information (e.g., Americans spend $20 billion annually on frozen desserts) could encourage the spending of pocket money on the sweet rather than on alternative foods or consumer items. A single image of either a person or a rich icy sweet accompanies each of the questions. The choice of close-ups in the camera shots of the adults and children establishes a close personal or social relation between the participants represented in the images and the viewer. Most are looking directly at the viewer, the purpose of which is to "demand" closeness to and collusion with the text's message. The image of children with ice cream on their faces and holding cones containing enough of the sweet to feed an entire family could legitimate excess, self-indulgence, and gluttony.

The Four Resource approach requires students to think about gaps and silences in text. For example, no mention is made of the social or health care implications of consuming such large quantities of bad food. What would the American Medical Association or the National Heart Foundation have to say about the $20 billion statistic? Why were these organizations not given opportunity to engage in debate about the statistic, which is presented here as a source of national identity and pride? A more balanced – and socially responsible – approach might have provided nutritional information on, for instance, the preservatives in ice cream that have been linked to allergies such as the asthma epidemic in western societies.

Another omission is the children of minority communities. The inference can be drawn from this that the site was constructed to target mainly white, middle-class children with money to spend on this expensive food item. Power is present in all representations of self and other, and dominant social groups construct their identities through definition and positioning of the Other (Hall 1997). In this case, white children are positioned as consumers, but poorer, non-mainstream groups are excluded, and thereby represented as irrelevant to corporate America. Could these be the "discarded" classes who are of "no value in the black holes of informational capitalism" (Castells 1998, p. 165). Indeed, the context of voice for the whole *National Geographic* web site represents most poorer, majority people groups through custom, costume, and culinary delight: as the "exotic other". Their crucial role as producers, markets, trading partners, and sources of labour in the interdependent global economy is overlooked.

Content in both the *National Geographic Kids* and the *NG Explorer* magazines works at the level of isolated and sensationalized fact. Who cares, for example, that a giant squid's eye is as big as a human's head? Or that a two-headed tortoise was found in South Africa? This trivia was part of a front-page feature entitled, "Today's News". The other "news" items included two stories on the animation movie *Finding Nemo*, a report that a "witches" market in Bolivia was experiencing "brisk sales in spells", and an announcement that a U.S. team had produced the first "mule clone". I am of the view that this kind of macabre superficiality is an affront to the intelligent curiosities and mature sensibilities of young people. Despite the claim that the *NG Explorer* is an "educational" site and a "classroom magazine", the lack of substantive ideas and perspectives precludes productive engagement with disciplinary content and process, or with important social issues of interest and some urgency to young people.

Commercial interests, on the other hand, are strongly represented. Of the thirteen articles in the archive of the "Stories" section, six were nature stories, five drew from popular culture (movies), and two were overt advertisements. The nature stories were about jungle frogs, polar bears, and "lion ghosts" of Africa that had eaten 135 men. It is reasonable to presume that this content on exotic animals would have little relevance to the lives of the socially-advantaged students who would be accessing the site. Furthermore, one of the two advertisements promoted the "top" three water park rides in the United States. This level of attention to entertainment and fun parks within the genre of a learning resource represents a different kind of political economy of information production and distribution from the past. Whilst profit-making has always been integral to publishing, marketized "learning" spaces like these form a new kind of educational and social relation with learners. Traditional children's books constructed insulated and safe alternative worlds into which the reader imagined him or herself. By contrast, these texts direct reader/viewers to the here and now via the goods and services through which they frame their identities as members of a consumer society.

A hyperliteracies "take" is not a framework but a standpoint, a way of being that treats texts – like the *National Geographic* web site – as an object of critical analysis as well as a source of pleasure and learning. This perspective would present multiple and contrasting viewpoints on what is considered geographical and social knowledge by problematizing knowledge and examining who decides which knowledges are visible and valid. Through critique that respects these hybrid knowledges by recognizing the popular appeal and importance of the texts in the lives of children today, hyperliteracy practices would encourage learners to ask, How are high-status knowledges either legitimated or devalued by publishers, schools, and their cybraries? And in what ways are language and image integral to processes of inclusion and exclusion through curricular work undertaken in school library media centres and cybraries? This consideration of social diversity and inclusivity within curricula brings the notion of "community" into analytic focus.

Rethinking the Information Literate School

As public educational spaces, school library media centres have historically forged ties to local communities by means such as links with public libraries. Indeed, recent national policy documents on educational innovation advocate the creation of working partnerships with local communities (cf. Benton Foundation 1996). Communities of practice, learning communities, and professional communities are other variations on the theme of mutual benefit deriving from consensus and collaboration between key educational stakeholders.

Yet, acknowledging the constructedness of literacy necessitates problematizing the notion of "*the* information literate school community". Within school library media centre professional literatures, the notion of community has escaped scrutiny to date. But my critical bells start to ring with the definite article, "the". "The" is usually taken to mean, "the only one". This begs the question, To which community does "the" refer? Can there be a single information literate "community"? What are the texts, values, and literacy practices of this community? Is it the book-oriented – or "wired" and now "wireless" – middle-class community that library cultures embody and perpetuate? What meanings are attributed to community, and how can teacher librarians create learning communities for *all* students, not just for those whose textual cultures are compatible with school ways?

For more than a century, the term "community" has been associated with positive things like extended families and close neighbourhoods. Community conjures the familiar and comforting, and evokes feelings of security and sentimentality. Many ideas about community in education come from the work of John Dewey (1916) and his small "l" liberal approach to education. Dewey's focus was on the individual and the shared life of human beings, on common interest and endeavour. Indeed, Bauman (2001) shows how, more than ever, we look nostalgically to notions of community as an antidote to the pressures and sterility of life today.

> For us in particular – who happen to live in ruthless times, times of competition and one-upmanship, when people around seem to keep their cards close to their chests and few people seem to be in any hurry to help us, when in reply to our cries for help we hear admonitions to help ourselves… the word 'community' sounds sweet. What that word evokes is everything we miss and what we lack to be secure, confident and trusting. (Bauman 2001, p. 2-3)

Community values stand for the kind of world that no longer exists – if it ever did – and for which most people long. Yet, this sense of belonging that communities endow derives from the acquisition of social capital and cultural markers that also establish communal boundaries. Too frequently, we forget that markers of identity exclude individuals and groups as much as they include them. Too often, we fail to notice that the flipside of consensus and conformity is difference and dissonance.

What is it then that coheres an information literate community? Hoggett (1997) defines three variables upon which a sense of community rests: Place (e.g., territorial or geographical location); Interest (e.g., religious affiliation, sexual orientation, or ethnic origin); or Communion (e.g., an intangible spirit of community). Which of these form the basis of the information literate school community? Is it place (the library), interest (love of reading), or the communion that the latter two endow on those who connect through them?

Place is not a basis for community here because libraries are no longer physical, place-bound entities, but increasingly are virtual spaces. Indeed, Selwyn (2003) shows how mobile technologies (phones) are reconfiguring the temporal and spatial frames of young people's lives by freeing them from the constraints of embodied presence and communication. E-technologies are eroding the fixedness of schools and their print-based cultures, and diminishing old forms of symbolic power that were maintained through information access and use.

Is the status of being "informed" a sufficient basis for community? In reality, there is little empirical evidence to suggest that such an entity as an "information literate community" exists. Who identifies as belonging to the community apart from the teacher librarian? Only one chapter of twenty in the first edition of *The information literate school community: Best practice* (1999) provided grounded research on the issue. That author conceded, nevertheless, that "none" of the primary schools involved in the research "could be said to be information literate school communities" (Moore 1999, p. 118). Finally, interest too is an insufficient basis for information community considering that school library media centres are used for many reasons other than formal learning. Given all of this, is the notion of being informed about information a sufficient basis for such disparate groups as teachers, learners, parents, school administrators, and community members to develop affinities worthy of being called a "community"? This is a dubious claim considering that as much difference occurs within these groups as between them. Tremendous differences in age, language, culture, gender, religion, level of interest in learning, and access and affinity for library usage requires teacher librarians to denaturalize and rethink the notion of "being informed" within a homogenous information "community".

Which Way Forward?

So what does this mean for cybrarians, teacher librarians, media specialists, and directors of information services who have responsibility for providing effective and equitable information services? The argument presented here highlights the reality that much of the disciplinary expertise of the traditional teacher librarian derives from outmoded concepts that are print-based, place-bound, atheoretical, and apolitical.

An explanation for this dilemma facing contemporary librarians can be found in Wiegand's (1996) critical biography of Melvil Dewey (1851-1931), founder of the library profession. Wiegand lays bare Dewey's prejudices of race, gender, and class that were "stitched" into the fabric of the Dewey Decimal Classification System, public library collections, and library education programs (p. 371). Dewey based his conception of librarianship as feminized work on assumptions of consensus and service because, ultimately, its purpose was to serve capitalism's need for a literate but passive workforce. To that end, he recruited mostly women because they provided a cheap and compliant source of labour that would pose no threat to the disciplinary canons of the literary and scientific (male) experts of the time. Dewey's legacy, therefore, was a loss of opportunity for serious intellectual engagement and critique of dominant masculinist discourses, and, eventually, the deprofessionalization and marginalization of librarianship in the hierarchy of professions.

To improve their status and authority, and to obtain political power and pragmatic influence as leaders, teacher librarians need understanding of the ways in which language and discourse function in the service of power, or its lack thereof. The want of critical sociological discernment in library studies and educational programs continues to hamper reform agendas. At this bold assertion, I hear you asking "What does sociology have to do with libraries?" A sociological outlook requires what C. Wright Mills called *the sociological imagination* (Mills 1959), which links single entities (e.g., school library media centres) to broader social issues and processes. Questions raised by a sociological approach might include, How do school library media centres and cybraries reflect and affect historical continuities and transformations, technological developments, and changes in economic and social relations? What sorts of reading and writing subjects do school library media centres frame? Which learning identities do the processes and practices of school library media centre work enable and constrain? More sociologically-informed approaches would provide teacher librarians with a socially-critical take on their disciplinary direction and literacy pedagogy.

By contrast, the information literacy "framework" focuses on printed text and works at the level of code-breaker and meaning-maker. That students today understand and enjoy the temptations of technotainment and Disney discourse provides an opportunity for curricular renewal and change. In cooperation with classroom teachers, teacher librarians can engage students in hyperliteracy practices that would make discourses of information, entertainment, and consumerism the focus of higher-order thinking and substantive conversations about economy, media, society, and culture. As Gallego and Hollingsworth (2000) show, recent developments around social literacies are challenging conventional school ideas about what counts as reading and writing at the same time as governments are retreating to high-stakes, skills-based testing and enforcement of school funding tied to outcomes.

Considering what is at stake for them and their young charges, teacher librarians need to be part of these important debates. Transformative leadership entails genuine reflective practice, engagement with contentious issues, and tough dialogue. Existing confusion over roles and identities that bridge the spaces and logics of print and electronic textualities provides evidence that some in the profession are tackling these challenges and debates. But there aren't enough of these brave souls; furthermore, they are hampered by an obsolete theoretical paradigm. Because there is no space outside of language, meaning, discourse, and politics, teacher librarians and cybrarians need to be upfront about their positionality and ideologies. Instead of retreating behind a façade of an unattainable neutrality of resources and services, they can and must be overtly normative about their visions and agendas for change. Being committed professionals is necessary, but not sufficient. That commitment needs a professionalism that is both contextualized and politicized.

Informing Information Literacy Education through Empirical Research

Louise Limberg

The chapter builds on findings from three research projects on the interaction between information seeking and use and learning. The studies have adopted different perspectives on information seeking and learning, either a learning (student's) perspective or a teaching (teachers' and librarians') perspective. Complementary theoretical frameworks have been used in the studies. A sociocultural perspective, as well as a phenomenographic view of learning and knowledge, is adopted in this research. The aim of the chapter is to draw upon conclusions from these studies and discuss implications about changes needed as regards information literacy education. A wider purpose is to illustrate how empirical research may inform professional practice in information literate school communities.

Points of Departure

The first point of departure for this chapter is that, as I see it, research-based knowledge about how students experience information seeking and use is an essential requirement for setting up and maintaining purposeful information literate school communities. There is an abundant body of literature expressing librarians' notions and convictions about information seeking and use (Limberg, Hultgren & Jarneving 2002, Loertscher 2001). However, for these notions to be useful for teaching, they must *meet* students' understandings in order to challenge them in learning processes. A second point is that, in schools, a lot of things keep going on, "but which have escaped remark only because they are always before our eyes" (Wittgenstein 1997, p. 415). That is why I think it necessary to closely observe and analyze not only students' learning processes and outcomes in libraries and classrooms, but also the activities of librarians and teachers involved in information literacy education. A deeper, empirically grounded, understanding of both learning and teaching information literacy is required to enhance learning outcomes.

Three Studies

This section of the chapter will present the design and main findings from three research projects. Projects 1 and 2 take the learning perspective, i.e., the perspective of the students. Project 3 focuses on the teaching perspective of information seeking and use, i.e., that of teachers and librarians.

1. Experiencing information seeking and use and learning

The aim of the first study was to explore the interaction between variation in students' experiences of information seeking and use and qualitative differences between their learning outcomes (Limberg 1999a and 1999b). The study was undertaken in 1993/94 and set in a naturalistic learning situation, where senior high school students (18 to 19 years) were engaged in a learning assignment requiring independent information seeking and the use of a wide range of sources. The topic of the assignment was "What will be the positive or negative consequences of a possible Swedish European Union membership?"[1]

The objective to study variation led to the choice of a phenomenographic research approach, developed since the 1970s, in order to study variation in students' learning (Marton 1994, Marton & Booth 1997). The twenty-five students worked cooperatively in five groups, each group choosing one of five subtopics, developed through brainstorming in the class. Each student was interviewed three times during the process: (i) in the early phase of the assignment; (ii) during the phase of intense information seeking; (iii) after conclusion of the assignment. The interviews were semi-structured and focused specifically both on experiences of information seeking and use, and on students' development of the knowledge content of the assignment.

Analyses of interviews focused on five aspects of information seeking as expressed by the students: their *relevance criteria*; their experiences of *information overload*; their criteria for judging when they had *enough information*; their criteria for assessing the *cognitive authority* (cf. Wilson 1983) of information sources; and their experiences of *bias*. These aspects emerged from the manifest content of the interviews and led to the identification of three major ways of experiencing information seeking and use, described in three categories. The most important difference between the categories is related to the students' various *approaches* or *intentions*. The intention of the A-category was to lay hands on a *ready-made answer*. The B-category focused on *choosing the right side* based on the relative quantity and availability of information from opposing sides, and the C-category aimed at *creating an answer* based on thorough scrutiny and analysis of a variety of information sources, and the relationship between these sources. Approaches to and understandings/experiences of information seeking reflect each other. The categories are described in somewhat more detail as follows:

---

[1] In November 1994 a referendum on Swedish European Union membership took place. The issue was Yes or No to membership, as from 1 January 1995.

A. Information seeking as fact-finding

meaning that students were looking for discrete bits of facts or the right answer to a specific question. Ease of access, physical as well as intellectual, was an important criterion of relevance. Information overload was solved through avoiding vast amounts of information. Biased material was considered not useful due to a lack of facts.

B. Information seeking as balancing information in order to choose the right side

implying that the meaning was to find enough information for forming a personal standpoint on the controversial issue of Swedish EU membership. The most important relevance criterion was that information should allow students to cover their subtopic, and to retrieve information from both sides, i.e., in favour of and opposing a Swedish EU membership. The approach to bias implied efforts to strike a balance between sources from opposing sides and then to let one weigh down.

C. Information seeking as scrutinizing and analyzing

meaning that information seeking was experienced as seeking and using information for understanding a topic. In this case, when the topic happened to be a controversial issue the students thought of information seeking as critically evaluating and discovering relations between various information sources. The most important relevance criterion was that information should provide different perspectives on the topic. Biased material was used to discover values and motives underlying various sources and to structure ways of argumentation for different standpoints in the sources.

A second main theme for analysis of the interviews was focused on students' understandings of the content of the assignment. Qualitative differences between students' learning outcomes were identified and described in three categories, which were grounded in students' understandings of the subject matter of the task as expressed in the last interview. A check between these categories of learning outcomes and the teacher's assessment of the students' written reports indicated strong consistency. A comparison between the three ways of experiencing information seeking and use and the three ways of understanding subject content shows great coherence. Those students who experienced information seeking as fact-finding according to category A also achieved a learning outcome as described in the A category, and the same is valid for categories B and C. The coherent pattern of students' experiences is presented in Table 4.1.

Table 4.1. *Conceptions of information seeking and use and of subject content*

Category	Information seeking & use	Learning outcome
A	Fact-finding: finding the right answer, concrete evidence.	Consequences of EU membership could not be assessed due to a lack of facts. Only fragmentary knowledge was gained about the European Union.
B	Balancing information in order to choose the right side: finding enough information to form a personal standpoint on the issue.	Possible consequences of membership were related to the subtopic. The EU was understood as mainly economic cooperation.
C	Scrutinizing and analyzing: critically analyzing information sources; finding different perspectives; trying to reveal values in information.	EU membership was considered as a matter of ethical or political decision or commitment. The EU was seen as a power block.

These findings indicate a close relationship between students' ways of experiencing information seeking and use and their ways of understanding the subject content. It is evident that an understanding of information seeking as fact-finding was not purposeful for the complex learning issue. However, there is no simple cause-effect relationship but it is more of an interactive relationship. The findings show that students' different ways of understanding the subject matter of the task did influence the ways in which they seek and use information. Likewise, differences between students' understandings of information seeking and use influenced their learning of subject content. Differences between students' various approaches to information seeking influenced both their information seeking and use and their learning outcomes. There is an obvious relationship between students' varying *approaches* to information seeking and use and their learning outcomes. This finding correlates with some of the earlier core findings of phenomenographic research, which show that there is a close relationship between students' approaches to an assignment and their learning outcomes (Marton & Booth 1997). My findings point to variation in *approaches to information seeking* as a decisive aspect of the task with implications for learning outcomes.

In view of these research findings, a question of overriding interest in an information-literate school community is how librarians and teachers can help students develop information literacy, since the notion of fact-finding is too restrictive when related to a complex issue. However, it is important to remember that all information seeking does not take place in complex learning environments and that fact-finding may be an appropriate approach when related to other types of tasks. This implies that the goal of teaching information literacy should be for students to develop a *repertoire* of various understandings of information seeking and use, and to be able to apply various approaches appropriately to various tasks, contents and situations (cf. Bruce 1997, Limberg 2000). I shall come back later in the chapter to discuss this issue and propose some steps in that direction.

2. Learning through the school library media centre

The second project, *Learning through the school library (LearnLib),* concentrates on how students use the library, as well as other information paths and sources, in order to seek and use information for their assignments. This three-year project is to be concluded at the end of 2003 and findings have been presented internationally in (Alexandersson & Limberg 2003, Limberg & Alexandersson 2003). Our research interest is thus directed to the library as a means of acquiring information for learning tasks. The main research question for the LearnLib project is: How is the school library media centre used as a cultural tool and how is its content constituted, that is, how may students learn subject matter in their interaction with the school library media centre? Two theoretical perspectives have been combined to form the framework of the study. With a sociocultural perspective on learning, we consider students' contact with artefacts and people in and through the school library media centre as participation in a socialisation exercise where the school library media centre can be understood as a cultural tool with a communicative function. With a phenomenographic research approach we study variations in students' ways of comprehending phenomena.

The empirical material covers data from 260 students in eleven classes (from 8-year-olds to 19-year-olds) and eighteen members of staff (teachers, principals and library personnel) in seven schools. The schools participated in a two-year development project to strengthen the pedagogical role of their school library media centre. Data were collected mainly through so-called field notes, that is, from observations, interviews and talking to students, teachers, principals and library staff. All empirical data were generated from concrete learning processes related to students' assignments, from introduction to presentation and conclusion. We also collected documents, scrutinized artefacts and administered a questionnaire to all 260 students from whom we received 245 responses.

Major findings from the LearnLib project concern how students interact with artefacts in the library and what they learn through this interaction. Results indicate that information seeking in the eleven observed classes is characterized by procedure rather than content. Information seeking is commonly understood as fact-finding. Students' primary ambition appeared to be to get factual information, and then to assemble it in a final product, a report, a booklet or a web page. This fact-finding approach was prevalent, regardless of the type of source used by the student; books, the Web, multimedia resources, film, etc. There are surprisingly small differences as regards approaches to information between various age levels. However, we have examples of students actively engaged in their assignments and seriously using available tools in the library to explore a topic. These examples are characterized by individual students' genuine curiosity to investigate a problem generated from a personal interest, e.g., "Why am I so tall?" (Boy, 15 years). Teachers or librarians rarely challenge the view of information seeking as fact-finding. Our data indicate that notions and experiences that the students develop through their assignments mean that "research" is to choose a topic, to find one or several sources, to read, to write and to present. To formulate questions seemed not to be part of students' conceptions of "research".

A striking result of the LearnLib project is what we have chosen to call the "transport and transformation of text". There are frequent examples in our material of how students interact with texts in a book or on a web page, transforming text through rewriting it somewhat, changing a few words, reducing the amount of the original text, and then transporting it into their final report.

The following citation captures how this is done:

> I borrowed a book on dolphins, picked out words from the book. I jotted these down
> in a little notebook as rough notes, then I wrote out my real version and then I painted
> a front page and then I put the whole thing into a booklet and the job was done.
> (David, 11 years)

On the whole, the students were positive towards the work method and considered it both fun and enriching. But we may wonder what students learned about the subject matter of their topics through their research. We may also be certain that what students actually learn does not necessarily correspond with the teacher's intention. One conclusion of the LearnLib study is that the question regarding to what extent and in what ways teachers and librarians can develop educational support structures can be decisive for what and how students learn from their own research. Such support should be directed both to the way of doing research (the process) and the learning object (the content). The observed focus on the final product of an assignment needs to be questioned and challenged.

Major conclusions from the LearnLib project are that students' interaction with artefacts in the library, and their communication with fellow students or adults, are determined by the school context, where students define their task according to the school's discursive practice, that is, that the school is a non-research environment, not based on genuine research questions but on the understanding that there are right answers to find, compile and re-present. This forms the basis for information seeking as fact-finding and, research, as transport and transformation of text. To support more genuine research-based learning, the school's discursive practice needs to be dramatically challenged through conscious and systematic intervention from pedagogues, such as teachers and librarians.

3. Experiencing teaching information seeking and use

The aim of the third, still ongoing study *Information seeking, didactics and learning (IDOL)*, is to explore librarians and teachers' various *experiences of teaching* information seeking and use related to students' learning assignments. The project is designed to observe possible changes in ways of teaching over three years and runs from 2001 to 2004. One major question in this study is: What do teachers and librarians teach about? (i.e., what is the knowledge content of information literacy education according to the participants in the study?) Other questions concern what difficulties the participants discern in students' information seeking and use for particular learning assignments and what participants say that they can do about such difficulties.

A phenomenographic approach was also chosen for this study, entailing that the empirical data are collected through interviews, which are tape-recorded and later transcribed. The protocols are analyzed through repeated readings to identify similarities and differences in order to develop categories of description of teachers' and librarians' various ways of experiencing information literacy education. Sixteen pedagogues, (eleven teachers and five librarians) in three schools, grades 5 to 12 (students' ages 11 to 19), take part in the project. Individual interviews have been conducted with the participants three times on various aspects of information literacy education, and always related to concrete learning assignments which were carried out in classrooms and libraries.

Preliminary findings of this study indicate some interesting contradictions about what difficulties teachers and librarians observe in students' information seeking and use, and what they tell us about their teaching to help students develop information literacy. A summary of difficulties related to information seeking and use identified and described by project participants concern (i) reading ability, (ii) ability to formulate various types of questions, (iii) ability to analyze and synthesize material from various information sources, and (iv) effective use of time. Students' reading difficulties concern many aspects, according to our informants; reading strategies for various types of texts, e.g., web pages or nonfiction, too limited vocabulary, a lack of ability to interpret or understand the message in a text. Several teachers claim that the students who have insufficient reading ability tend to focus more on fact-finding than those who have better reading skills. Difficulties concerning the formulation of questions are to be found along various dimensions of students' learning processes, e.g., research questions for assignments, search queries, as well as analytical questions when using information sources.

Students' use of time during information seeking is claimed to be inefficient, according to the participants. The remedy seems to be that teachers and librarians advise students about specific sources, URLs or search engines to use. In our material we have several examples of both teachers and librarians aiming at more effective time use through actively directing students away from the Internet and towards printed sources to be found in the library. The idea of teaching students about a specific order to follow between types of sources during their information seeking also emerges as a common strategy. Thus, while project participants emphasize the importance for students to learn to reflect on their own knowledge and actions, to formulate relevant questions, to use time effectively, to critically evaluate their sources, to analyze and synthesize information from a variety of sources, these issues do not seem to be included in the content of teaching. Teaching and scaffolding seems to focus on advice about types of sources, specific texts or sources, rarely on how to formulate questions or evaluate information sources critically.

A comparison between the main contents of teaching emerging in our material and the main issues which students ought to learn or improve according to our informants is presented in Table 4.2.

Table 4.2. *Contents of teaching and items identified as important to learn*

Teaching on information seeking	*Difficulties for students related to information seeking*
<ul><li>to direct students to the right source, channel or site</li><li>to recommend a certain order to follow between types of sources</li><li>to teach about the process of information seeking</li></ul>	<ul><li>reading ability and reading strategies</li><li>to reflect on knowledge and actions</li><li>to formulate questions</li><li>search queries and search strategies</li><li>critical evaluation of sources</li><li>use of information (interpreting, analyzing and synthesizing)</li><li>effective time use</li></ul>

Table 4.2 indicates a striking gap between what teachers and librarians identify as important for students to learn about information seeking and use, i.e., the desired knowledge content, and what they actually say that they teach about. The descriptions of desired knowledge content touch upon various dimensions in students' tasks which together constitute the entire learning process, from topic to questions, through information seeking and use to substance and meaning in presentations. Our findings confirm the view of information seeking and use as integrated in the learning process, and as needing to stand out much more clearly as knowledge content in teaching and learning. These findings confirm and strengthen Bruce's conclusions of the need for evaluation of information literacy curricula and the usability of research results for such evaluation and further development as regards information literacy education (Bruce 1997, p. 172-173).

The three items listed under teaching are similar to those described by Kuhlthau (1993b, p. 11) as a source approach, a pathfinder approach and a process approach. However, "to teach about the process of information seeking" may not actually be consistent with Kuhlthau's "process approach". In our material the process of information seeking constitutes the actual content of teaching and may be interpreted as teaching on a metacognitive level, in order to encourage students to reflect on their own process of information seeking and to prepare them for what they may expect about information seeking as part of their learning task. This is not the same as actually supporting students along the process and adapting information services to the different phases of the process, as described by Kuhlthau. Certainly, the metacognitive level of teaching about the information search process and adapting interventions to support students during the process may be combined. The information search process as teaching content seems to aim towards the goal of students *understanding* the process, while a focus on the right source or the right order to follow is aimed at teaching students to *do right*. "To do right" indicates that information seeking is characterized by the bibliographic paradigm based on structure and order, as well as right or wrong. On the other hand, teaching for understanding the process is more related to users' uncertainty (cf. Kuhlthau 1993b) and may encourage students to reflect more actively on their own information seeking and learning.

Summarizing Conclusions

The three research projects, undertaken over the last ten years, have led to conclusions that are consistent as regards some major issues of information literacy education in school contexts. The findings concern three essential features for strengthening the development of students' information literacy: (i) the need for *experiences of variation* in learning; (ii) the *identification of the knowledge contents* of information literacy education; and (iii) the need for *breaking the school's discursive practice* as a means of bringing in more genuine research-based learning. All these issues constitute great challenges for leadership on various levels in school communities and will require that teachers, librarians and administrators act both cooperatively and individually in their various professional capacities and in their specific different environments. It will also involve action both in pedagogical practice, in professional development, and as regards policy measures. The discussion in the second part of this chapter is intended to illustrate how research findings may be useful for information literate school communities.

Implications for Strengthening Information Literate School Communities

Variation in Teaching and Learning

Conclusions of the research presented above have emphasized a need for information literacy curricula to formulate goals in terms of students developing a *repertoire* of understandings of information seeking and use, since the notion of fact-finding did not serve a qualified outcome of a complex learning task. The idea of developing a repertoire of various understandings is different from the prevalent attitude in library and information science literature, which often adheres to one model or list of skills to be taught. A repertoire of understandings implies that a learning outcome would be that students can adopt one of several approaches to information seeking, adapted to a specific task and situation.

A repertoire of understandings will require that students can tell the differences between one approach and another. To achieve this, students need to experience variation. In the case of information literacy education, variation can be introduced through a range of measures. Practising teachers and librarians might use categories of description resulting from research to explain information seeking to their students (cf. Limberg 2000). Teachers can also invite students to apply various approaches for specific topics or tasks. For instance, teaching information seeking could use the notions of *fact-finding*, to *choose the right side* or to *create an answer*, and apply them to different situations. Patterns of variation may also be introduced in teaching through sometimes inviting students to seek information on a topic without instructing them where to search and how to formulate queries. The task should be for students to document their search paths, decisions taken at crossroads, criteria of relevance and evaluation of documents, and then to let students compare and analyze their experiences. The objective of such comparisons should be to focus on the critical features of the differences between various approaches as regards essential aspects of information seeking such as search strategies (selection of channels or types of sources), relevance judgments and evaluation of sources. These features should persistently be related to the character and the content of the task at hand. These suggestions agree with a substantial body of research claiming that for meaningful learning to occur, students must experience patterns of variation. Encountering variation when learning at school prepares students for participating in the social practices of future communities of learning (see Marton & Trigwell 2000).

Assessment of students' work should provide meaningful feedback to learners about the quality of their achievements. As I see it, listings of a large number of skills included in information literacy standards risk to reduce information literacy assessment to the observation of correct or incorrect behaviour. Such standards are basically founded on a behavioural view of learning which is not compatible with the constructivist views of learning that the advocates of information literacy tend to support. Categories of description resulting from phenomenographic research are usable for assessment because they are rich in content and structure and they build on differences between the critical features of information seeking and use (Limberg 1999a). The categories are hierarchically related to each other in an outcome space, which make them well suited for assessment.

Identifying the Knowledge Contents

The question of identifying the knowledge contents of information literacy education is an important didactic task. Our research findings tell us that there is a need to reconsider common practice, which seems to be highly focused on instructing students on the right procedures and technicalities related to online or web-based information seeking, underpinned by assumptions about "right" and "wrong" procedures.

According to the findings of the referred research projects, critical features of information seeking and use are a capacity to formulate various types of questions, to develop an awareness about relevance criteria or judgments about when you have enough information in situations of overload. The research findings indicate that teachers and librarians often do not direct their efforts to students learning such contents, but instead try to help students *avoid* to have to make judgments and choices of their own through advising them about precise sources or sites. The discovery of a gap between the actual teaching contents and the desired learning contents can be used for analyzing possible ways of developing information literacy curricula. Again, the description of various approaches to information seeking and use related to a complex learning task should be useful for identifying an appropriate content for information literacy education.

Learning to formulate questions for research, for search queries or for the analysis of information sources, also needs to be part of the content of teaching. This will require that teachers devote time and effort in discussing with students various types of questions and the types of answers that they may lead to. Instead of repeatedly letting students pursue their "research" guided by simple factual questions – for instance on wolves' diet preferences, habitat, and number of offspring – teachers should encourage more complex and dynamic questions. For example, there are a great number of books and other types of information on wolves for children. Through them Swedish children may learn that wolves have a well-developed social life in families, that they are an endangered species and that they are seldom dangerous for human beings. Through the media children learn that some people want to kill wolves. Children may conclude that these people are evil. In order to understand a controversial issue like this, students might work with a question like, Why do people in the forest area of Värmland want to shoot wolves, whereas people in Stockholm want wolves to live and to be protected? Working with such a question would introduce students to different points of view and controversies based on different interests as a contrast to conclusions about "good" and "evil" people as the basis of opposing views.

As I see it, the essence of the change needed concerns a shift from a focus on procedure and order towards a focus on more abstract and the more exciting contents of information literacy as regards what is at stake and what is crucial for becoming an information literate person. Such contents of information literacy can only be taught in relation to the content of information, implying that they have to be discernible, but integral, parts of learning assignments on a range of subject matters.

Challenging the School's Discursive Practice

It was pointed out above that the fact-finding approach to information seeking seems to be related to a school's discursive practice, based on the school as a non-research environment. This is contrary to the overall goals of education in Sweden and in many other countries, where independent and critical use of information and capabilities of analysis and synthesis from various sources are highly valued. It is also acknowledged that information and communication technology creates new demands on schools and citizens in our democratic societies. The research results show that the students need both support and guidance in order to become participants in the learning environments that constitute the school, including the library.

Now the question is, How can the school library media centre contribute to changing the school's discursive practice? Research findings indicate that school library media centres may embrace a special potential for contributing to such change. In his study on literacy in the library, Dressman (1997) concluded that classrooms are seen as "spaces devoted to literacy as work", and libraries as "spaces devoted to literacy as the pursuit of personal desire". As I see it, this implies that an awareness of the library as a space allowing more freedom and independence than classrooms should be more consistently utilized by teachers and librarians for introducing a school discourse of intellectual knowledge formation, questioning ready-made answers and the widespread tradition of "fact-finding". Cultural traditions are strong. Challenging or breaking up cultural patterns may require quite dramatic action. It will need teachers, librarians and administrators who are knowledgeable, creative and courageous, and at the same time persistent and flexible. It will also demand that students tolerate uncertainty and doubt in their pursuit of meaningful learning, through questioning, critical thinking and creativity. For this to be possible teachers, librarians and students must look upon each other as fellow creators of knowledge.

Conclusion

In this article I have stressed the usability of research findings for developing information literacy education. One aspect of the mastery of becoming informed would be for professionals in information literate school communities to focus on becoming informed about relevant research and to use research results in creative ways for enhancing students' learning of information literacy.

Acknowledgement

The LearnLib and the IDOL research projects are being funded by The Swedish National Agency for School Improvement (previously The Swedish National Agency for Education).

Curriculum Integration and Information Literacy: Developing Independent Learners

Jedd Bartlett

Introduction

In 2001 we began a new way of learning and teaching at Kuranui College with the introduction of Base 6, an inquiry-based, curriculum integration program. A key element in this program is the student-centred inquiry process, supported by a comprehensive set of information literacy skills. The program was developed through a desire to implement student-centred teaching and learning approaches that were focused on developing autonomous, self-managing learners, student self-esteem and motivation, and the skills appropriate for lifelong learning. During the planning and design process Base 6 has evolved into a two-year program for year 9 and 10 students that incorporates many of the characteristics of the information literate school community (Henri 1999), including

- school-wide information policies and information and communication technology (ICT) plan
- benchmarked information literacy skills
- portfolios developed and maintained by students
- information literacy skills across all curriculum, learned and practised in context
- learning contexts varied with a wide range of resources
- resource-based learning rather than resource-based teaching
- an unscheduled library timetable
- a collaborative teaching team
- student drafts included in assessment
- information tasks negotiated between teachers and learners
- regular feedback built into the assessment and evaluation of student work

- student goal-setting and self-assessment as key elements in student learning
- teachers as learners

This chapter describes the journey undertaken by the Base 6 teachers at Kuranui College. Over a period of two years we designed and implemented a program which we call Base 6. It is at present in its third year, with around half of the College's students at the year 9 and year 10 levels enrolled in the program. Base 6 is a primarily a curriculum integration program combining achievement objectives from the English, Social Studies, Science, and Health curriculum areas. Students carry out extended individual or collaborative inquiry-based projects, driven largely by their own questions and interests. The program takes place during ten to twelve block-scheduled hours each week, with the remaining periods used for the other junior college options and programs.

The Base 6 Program

Our aim was to implement a program that

- was able to respond to the diverse needs of learners
- focused on outcomes rather than subjects
- built on students' desire to inquire
- included students in decision-making
- encouraged collaborative learning
- made connections with real life situations and problems
- utilized the power of information and communication technologies
- fostered relationships with students
- was designed with an holistic perspective

We were seeking to overcome the barriers inherent in a typical secondary school, including

- one hour blocks of "teaching time"
- students moving from room to room
- curriculum separated into distinct blocks of content
- lack of student motivation towards prescribed curriculum

Base 6 is named after the six key features of the program – active learning through inquiry, independent student-centred learning, authentic contexts, collaborative learning, ICT enhanced learning, and building connections to family and community. There is a strong emphasis on students becoming increasingly information literate as they practise and develop the competencies required for independent inquiry, using a six-stage information literacy framework.

Students are able to use ICT in their classrooms throughout the program. The teachers in Base 6 work as a team to provide a flexible and integrated approach to teaching and learning, using a systematic process of planning and review to improve student learning.

There is a strong emphasis on individual goal-setting, and an emphasis on quality reporting of student progress and achievement, with extended parent-student-teacher interviews at the end of every term when students report on their learning, share their successes, and prepare goals for the next term.

The design and implementation process involved five distinct stages:

1. Developing the vision
2. Curriculum development
3. Professional development
4. Program implementation
5. Evaluation and review.

1. Developing the vision

Kuranui College is a small, rural New Zealand secondary school in the South Wairarapa. The College is located in Greytown and students are drawn from a wide area, with over eighty percent traveling to and from school daily by bus. Kuranui's roll has fluctuated for some years between 490 and 520. The majority of the students live in the small towns of the South Wairarapa, with the remainder drawn from the diverse rural community.

The Base 6 project grew out of a process of school review and self-improvement at the College. The Principal, the Board of Trustees and the management team made a decision to focus on raising student achievement and learning expectations, and making Kuranui College an educational centre for the 21st century. Together they developed a vision statement and a set of strategic objectives for the College, aiming to regain the confidence and cooperation of the local community by assuring quality care and teaching programs were restored and maintained at Kuranui.

The Board of Trustees contracted education consultant, David Hood, as project facilitator and mentor in 1999. Hood has always had a particular interest in ensuring quality learning in New Zealand secondary schools (Hood 1998). His primary task at Kuranui was to work with the Board of Trustees, school management and staff to establish an environment in which people worked together on common issues, were receptive to the idea that change was required, and that positive change was possible and achievable.

Hood initially spent several weeks talking with staff individually and in groups to identify their issues, their concerns and their hopes for the College. This process was an important step. Asking teachers to talk about their beliefs for education and learning at Kuranui not only provided them with an opportunity to clarify their own beliefs, but also gave Hood a picture of teacher strengths and possible outcomes of the process of staff consultation. Hood worked with the staff in a process designed to turn the strategic goals into a number of projects or educational programs. The interviews with staff members had provided valuable information that was brought to these goal-setting sessions to ensure that the issues, concerns and hopes identified by staff were addressed. As a result of these sessions, a set of clear, prioritized objectives for the College were developed.

The process adopted provided opportunities for staff to respond collectively to the strategic goals set by the Board, to define objectives and to prioritize them, to make suggestions, individually or collectively, as to how the objectives could be actioned, and to participate in projects as they were defined. The process was a democratic one and the result was a very strong sense of ownership on the part of those staff involved.

Change management

A change management group was formed, consisting of senior staff members and teachers who had an interest in shaping the future direction of the school. These were people who had a passion for a particular project that would meet some of the strategic goals. Their key task was to lead and oversee the change process.

College staff were then asked to contribute their ideas on specific projects which would help the College meet strategic goals and objectives, with a clear focus on improving the quality of learning experiences for students. Eleven project briefs were developed and submitted, including proposals for support teachers for students with learning styles, a second-chance centre for young adults, a catering "academy", and a plan for classroom upgrades. The change management group considered that many of the proposals could be subsumed under two major new initiatives, one focused on the junior school, the other on the senior school. The junior school project, which eventually became Base 6, would be developed around thematic approaches to learning in a home-room setting.

The staff members who had proposed these projects were then required to develop a full project outline, which were included in a comprehensive application for school improvement funding submitted to the Ministry of Education. The bulk of the funding sought was targeted for teacher-release days for planning and workshops, and for the provision of professional development.

The first step for the junior school project team was to develop a vision and mission statement that would guide the planning of the new learning environment. The team had to combine the school's strategic objectives with current research about how people learn best, and the needs and characteristics of the junior college students at Kuranui. Out of these discussions was developed a comprehensive statement that outlined the goals and shared beliefs for the project, including:

- We will work in partnership with the family and community to educate responsible, lifelong learners who possess the skills, knowledge, creativity, sense of self-worth, and ethical values necessary to survive and be successful in a rapidly changing, culturally diverse, global society
- It is our goal to provide a learning environment that fosters the development of information literacy skills and student-centred learning.

2. Curriculum development

Using the mission statement as a guide, the junior project team then embarked on the next stage of their journey – the development of the Base 6 program, in particular developing common understandings about the pedagogy on which the learning and teaching would be based. For the teachers on the team this became a learning journey, where they developed new understandings and accumulated new knowledge about the various elements that were to form the basis of the Base 6 project. These perspectives guided curriculum development:

> In the 21st century the prime purpose of secondary schooling should be to develop independent, self-managing learners with the basic knowledge and skills which adequately prepare them for the challenges they will face, and their futures (Hood 2002).

> The integrated curriculum rests on the premise that mastering thinking skills, not mere information, is the object of a high school curriculum (Cushman 1993).

> Much of the best educational research and practice today is pointing to a concept of curriculum and learning in which pupils increasingly take responsibility for setting their own learning objectives, based on authentic, real world challenges within their own environments. To achieve these objectives, learners' activities require a multidisciplinary approach and skills, and should be pursued in collaboration with classmates (Hartwell & Vargas-Baron 1998).

Curriculum integration

In the process of project development, the Kuranui College's Change Management Group had decided that the junior school project would be developed around thematic approaches to learning in a home-room setting. Exploration of thematic learning approaches led the project team to curriculum integration. Curriculum integration is a term used to describe a variety of different approaches to the delivery of the curriculum, so the project team's first step was to decide what curriculum integration would mean for them.

In discussions with teachers in integrated studies programs at other secondary schools and from the selection of readings used during the professional development, several key theorists and practitioners had emerged, in particular James Beane. Professor James Beane of the National College of Education at National-Louis University, Milwaukee, Wisconsin, is an important figure in the field of curriculum integration, who has written many articles and books on the subject. His book *Curriculum integration* (Beane 1997) provides a history and theory of curriculum integration and was extremely useful during the Base 6 planning year.

Beane (1998) describes the thematic or multidisciplinary approach as being based on correlating two or more subjects in relation to an organizing concept, theme, or issue. This approach has long been used in New Zealand primary schools and can overcome the problems for teachers and students associated with fragmented programs based completely on separate curriculum areas, such as the crowded curriculum and limitations on time.

Curriculum integration, as Beane defines it, is a departure from other approaches. It is an approach to curriculum design that "promotes personal and social integration through the organization of curriculum around significant problems and issues, collaboratively identified by educators and young people, without regard for subject area lines" (Beane 1998). While knowledge is drawn from the traditional disciplines, students move from activity to activity, rather than from subject to subject during the school day. Curriculum integration, with an emphasis on real-life themes, authentic contexts, and constructivist learning, appeared to provide teachers with a way of organizing the curriculum in line with our project goals.

Curriculum integration models are characterized by

- independent student-centred learning
- active construction of knowledge
- student ownership of learning
- an emphasis on skills, attitudes and knowledge rather than content
- teacher as facilitator rather than expert or lecturer
- negotiation of curriculum coverage between students and teachers

Constructivism

Constructivism, a theory of cognitive growth and learning, is based on the premise that students actively construct their knowledge, rather than simply absorb ideas delivered by teachers, or somehow internalizing them through repeated exposure or practice. As students actively create, interpret and reorganize knowledge, teachers plan learning experiences to stimulate a connection between students' prior knowledge and new information or knowledge. Because constructivism emphasizes hands-on problem-solving it does not suit a traditional secondary school curriculum delivered with traditional teaching approaches.

In a constructivist learning environment (as promoted in, for example, Henson 2004),

- learning starts with students' existing knowledge
- learning focuses on issues important to students
- the learning process focuses on primary concepts not isolated facts.

- teachers focus on making connections between existing and new knowledge
- students are encouraged to analyze, interpret, and predict information
- teachers also use open-ended questions
- teachers promote extensive dialogue among students.

As for assessment, constructivism leads to less emphasis on standardized testing and the allocation of norm-referenced grades. Because constructivism is especially suited to multidisciplinary studies, the most appropriate way to measure learning is to make assessment part of the learning process, by including opportunities for students to undertake self and peer assessment.

Inquiry-based learning

From the very beginning of the planning year it was apparent to the project team that there was a clear inter-relationship between several of the elements that were to make up the program. When it became time to consider the learning approach that would enable students to achieve the program goals and outcomes, we knew that it would involve active construction of knowledge by the learner, using information gathered in an area of personal inquiry focused by the students' own questions, supported by a set of information literacy skills, and this led us to consider inquiry-based learning.

Inquiry-based learning is a student-centred, active learning paradigm that emphasizes research, critical thinking and multidisciplinary study to achieve learning outcomes. Because inquiry begins with a student's own question, problem or issue, the process engages students as they use questions to motivate their inquiry process.

Information literacy

An information literate school community fosters the development of information literacy through the teaching and learning of information skills. The Base 6 teachers looked for a framework for the inquiry process that was based on a set of information literacy skills that could be taught to all students, and supported by all teachers. Using one clear inquiry learning model or framework would mean there was a common learning environment and would allow for consistency in teaching strategies. The inquiry learning model used in Base 6 is based on Gwen Gawith's six-stage Action Learning approach (Gawith 1988). This provides a framework that students learn and practice as they become increasingly independent, self-directed learners, and develop the skills of information literacy.

The Base 6 teachers completed the Infolink course delivered by the Auckland College of Education, in which teachers work through the stages and strategies of the Action Learning model with students as they plan, implement, monitor, and evaluate their learning. The process has a focus on cognitive strategies modeled by teachers and encourages students to think about their learning and to assess the process of learning.

This inquiry process and an associated set of information literacy competencies is now actively taught to all Base 6 students throughout the year and is used as a basis for student inquiry in each project.

Information and communication technology

ICT can create many options and opportunities for learners, encouraging student-centred learning, active, exploratory, inquiry-based learning, collaborative work, the transfer of skills and knowledge, creativity, critical thinking and informed decision-making (New Zealand Ministry of Education 2002). In the planning of the Base 6 program, the project team could see that a comprehensive information literacy program would greatly assist students in the effective use of the ICT available to them.

Computers in each of the classrooms would provide access to online resources, and would be used by students to locate their own information, test ideas, receive feedback, and work collaboratively with other students or experts.

3. Professional development

During the planning year Base 6 teachers were involved in a range of professional development activities. These were:

- encouraging the development of a staff library
- discussion of readings with peers
- discussion of program elements with experts
- visits to other schools
- workshops covering specific learning theory and practice
- Infolink, an Auckland College of Education information literacy course

Once the Base 6 program was underway the emphasis of the professional development was on mentoring teachers, teacher self-reflection and self-review and strategies for student learning through ICT.

4. Program implementation

It is 10.30 on a Friday morning. As a visitor to Kuranui College, you enter the Base 6 area. In one of the classrooms you find eleven students, five of them sitting around the pod of three computers. The classroom contains an array of tables in a range of configurations, and there are several discussions taking place as the students work on a variety of tasks. Two boys at one computer are composing an email message to a Wellington furniture supplier, asking about ergonomic designs for school chairs. Three students at a large table covered in art materials share their design plans for a publicity brochure and a large flipchart to be used for a presentation about smoking to the other year 10 students. A student tells you that the teacher is in the College library with a group of eight students, while two students are out of school videoing evidence of vandalism in the town centre and three other students are interviewing a health inspector at the local Council.

These students have spent eighteen hours over the past two weeks carrying out investigations into various features of the school and local environment that affect people's well-being, and are building up their knowledge about the issues they have identified so that they can take action to address them. They are at the end of the third week of Project 5; Healthy Environments. The underlying concept for the project, decided by the students and teacher, is that it is important to take part in creating a healthy school community and environment by taking responsible and critical action for the long-term benefit of all members of the community.

The project incorporates achievement objectives from the Health, English and Social Science curricula, and the process that the students follow will see them taking action on a school environmental issue (Health and Physical Education), undertaking social decision-making and inquiry (Social Studies Processes), and combining verbal, visual, and dramatic features to communicate information to an identified audience (English; Visual Language).

The learning environment

The Base 6 program at Kuranui College takes place in a specially designed learning centre, with students spending up to three hours in the centre each day of the week, for a total of ten hours. During that time, in a typical week, students spend seven hours on an inquiry project and three hours on specialist lessons that are designed to support the project. These specialist lessons might be related to curriculum areas, focus on skills required for the use of computer applications, or they might be activities designed to support students in the skills and strategies of inquiry learning.

There are three staff members working with the fifty students at all times. The students undertake two four-week inquiry projects in each ten-week term, with a buffer period between, when lessons are offered to cover material not covered in the projects. Examples of these are sexuality workshops and science laboratory experiments.

In the design of the Base 6 classroom area, flexibility was the primary design criterion. The tables, benches and workstations can be moved so that working spaces can be redesigned to suit the needs of the students and program. In order to achieve an environment where ICT-related tasks were easily blended into the daily routines, the computers are placed where they do the most good, not necessarily in a corner or in a row against a back wall. The teachers tend to spread their workstations about so that they serve as a variety of work centres. There is not a "front" to the classroom because the focus is on learning instead of teaching, meaning that the classrooms can include "zones" for different kinds of activities. There are three or four computer workstations allocated to each of the four classrooms, and it is possible to have six or eight workstations in one room connected to the College network at any time if required. Students use the workstations to access the Internet, to access their work on the school server. Students' completed work can also be placed on the school intranet.

The timetable

For a school contemplating a program based on learner-centred inquiry, a timetable of twenty-five or more discreet periods of teaching and learning time is a formidable barrier. Student-directed learning is, by its very nature, slower than any form of teacher-directed learning, and simply cannot exist in the sixty-minute room-change environment. Rearranging a school timetable is a huge task. The degree to which school management is prepared to alter the timetable structure of an entire school to include block-scheduling depends on the level of the school's commitment to the establishment of a learner-centred environment.

The timetable requirements for Base 6 are quite specific. There has to be block-scheduling, with continuous periods running together for two or three hours each day. In addition, the four Base 6 classes have to be timetabled in the centre at the same time, so that team teaching is be able to take place. Each year this is a problematic undertaking, as the entire school timetable tends to be built around the Base 6 requirements and senior subject selection in a small school can be affected. Regular communication with the teachers responsible for timetabling is essential.

The Base 6 program

Curriculum coverage focuses on core concepts and allows for in-depth inquiry rather than a superficial coverage of large amounts of factual information. Because of the nature of curriculum integration and student-centred inquiry learning, it is unlikely that all of the curriculum content previously "covered" during years 9 and 10 is covered by Base 6 students.

Each Project is based on two curriculum areas as a major focus, with one as a minor focus. At the beginning of the project students are provided with the curriculum-based learning objectives and the skills that will be developed and assessed during the project. During the first few days of a new project teachers facilitate discussions, organize speakers and visits, share video, text- and web-based resources, and share completed project presentations from previous years. Students know that they will be expected to conduct an in-depth exploration of some aspect of the material under discussion during these days, so the process of student-teacher negotiation begins at once.

The students then decide on an area of inquiry. With teacher help, they establish prior knowledge through individual or group brainstorming and then develop the set of questions that will drive their investigation. During the writing of questions, the teacher helps the students to define their information needs in relation to the curriculum objectives.

The role of the teacher is absolutely critical throughout the project as they help students to establish ownership of the learning process through regular discussion, negotiation and checkpoints. These discussions ensure the students have set clear goals, have a clear purpose and audience in mind, and have prepared a timetable for their inquiry. While students select, analyze, and process information, the teacher acts as expert, coach and facilitator of learning opportunities and resources. There are special sessions timetabled to introduce new skills or strategies when required, such as effective search strategies or the use of online databases. Students are also expected to take part in regular discussions when the teacher encourages them to reflect on their learning and the effectiveness of the various strategies or resources that they are using. Students use the library whenever they need to, rather than in timetabled class visits, and consequently make heavy use of library resources.

Students present their findings or conclusions in a number of ways according to the topic and the audience. Teachers support them as they prepare their own criteria for communicating their new knowledge. It is essential that a climate of trust develops between teachers and students. Students are expected to work more independently, investigating individually or in small groups, and working beyond the walls of the classroom. This means that teachers must feel comfortable that groups of students can achieve the expected outcomes and must help by providing the support needed to help students succeed.

Assessment

If new approaches to learning and teaching are to succeed, then a new model of assessment is also needed. A major barrier to the move to student-centred inquiry and curriculum integration is the current assessment methodology. Assessment of memorized knowledge is easy to administer and a move to the alternative assessment, based on students demonstrating they can use information, is difficult to establish. While such assessment is already happening in some subject areas at some levels, it is a major paradigm shift for subject specialists, parents, and for the students themselves.

In the curriculum integration model, teachers can develop guidelines for assessment direction, but the most helpful assessment is developed through teacher and student collaborations. Through these collaborations, school benchmarks can become individualized and learning goals developed that are recognized and pursued by the student. Teachers then evaluate and reward students for achievements based upon collaborative learning interactions, cognitive skills and demonstrated competence. Teachers in Base 6 employ assessment approaches that evaluate the ongoing nature of the inquiry process, the learning outcomes based on the curriculum achievement objectives and the planned product.

In the Base 6 program there is a mix of teacher observation, student self- and peer-appraisal and formal marking of presented work. Our aim is that assessment will be largely formative, ongoing, in the hands of the learner (an underpinning concept for ICT-enhanced learning), collaborative and will involve peers, teachers and parents.

5. Evaluation and review

An essential element in the development of the program has been our regular evaluation and review sessions, especially those carried out during the year in which the program was first implemented. In 2001 this meant that twice a term all Base 6 teaching staff met with the program facilitator for one day, and evaluation of the previous five weeks was carried out prior to the planning of the next project. This program evaluation and review was structured around the six key elements of the Base 6 program and the learning outcomes for project just completed.

Conclusion

The developing information and communication technologies and the traditional school organization of time, space, and teachers and students clash rather than coincide. The traditional "factory" system of the last century recognized that the technologies of the time demanded a new kind of organization in order to harness their power. A case can clearly be made now for a new form of school organization that enables schools to harness the power of the 21st century technologies. These new forms will involve rearranging the relationships for learning within the school and between the school, the community and the home. Students will be able to be free of the constraints of space and timetables and will be able to spend substantial time away from classrooms, studying and learning from other environments and other cultures.

To be successful self-managing learners in such an environment they will require comprehensive information literacy skills and the successful development of these skills has been apparent in the evaluation of the Base 6 program. Program successes include

- Students have very good understanding of how to learn and of the inquiry/research processes
- Students have a high level of information literacy skills
- Students are familiar with the New Zealand essential skills and with their own level of competency
- Students are largely independent learners
- Students demonstrate a high level of self-motivation and self-confidence
- Students are choosing to remain in the program each year and numbers remain consistent
- Teachers are less dominant and less visible in the classroom
- Attendance and attitude of at-risk students is generally improved in comparison with other classes
- ICT is integrated naturally into their learning when appropriate
- Students use their local community as a resource and an audience
- There has been more classroom time available for supporting less able students

- Teachers have been enthused by their new pedagogical knowledge and teaching experiences
- Students have continued to develop collaborative work skills throughout years 9 and 10

There are clear links between these observations and the characteristics of an information literate school community as described in the introduction to this chapter.

Reading and the Information Literate School Community

Elizabeth Lee

"To learn to read is to light a fire . . . every syllable that is spelled out is a spark"
— Victor Hugo

Introduction

How is that spark lit? We all respond favourably to Hugo's statement, because, as readers, we know reading illuminates and warms our lives. Learning to read is a monumental intellectual feat mastered through instruction, support and effort. This chapter will review the stages involved in acquiring literacy, describe materials that are best suited for each stage, and suggest how a teacher librarian can support the classroom teacher and students in fostering literacy.

Learning to read is a lifelong process. The specific skills mastered at each stage differ, but there is continual growth throughout the lifetime of a reader. The extent to which adults continue to develop as readers depends upon the amount and frequency of their reading and the type of material they read. Adler's classic text *How to read a book* (Adler 1967) sets out a self-teaching technique that a motivated adult may apply to reading deeply and critically.

In becoming literate an individual has to learn how to turn a set of squiggles – the text – into meaning. Written language unlike oral language is a relatively recent development in humankind's history. Humans have a biological predisposition for the acquisition of oral language skills. They are acquired naturally in all societies through exposure to the language (Pinker 1994). Not all societies have developed a writing system to encode their language in texts. Reading is a relatively recent development and, unlike oral language, is not universally distributed. Reading is not acquired through simple exposure to a print environment; it has to be taught.

The history of writing shows us how societies have adapted and re-adapted a code, alphabetic, syllabic or logographic, to fit their language. (For a history of writing, see Olson 1994.) The alphabet used for encoding English has its roots in Phoenician, a Semitic language. It has undergone successive adaptations in the process of representing Greek, Latin, Anglo-Saxon, and Norman French. Consequently, the script does not transparently represent the sounds of modern spoken English. English spelling reflects etymology and morphological structure preserving meaning across diverse pronunciations.

Learning to read requires the individual to master a set of arbitrary correspondences. It is an accident of history as to which symbol (letter) is associated with a particular sound (phoneme) in a language. Languages differ in the degree to which the correspondences between the sounds and the letters representing them are straightforward. English is considered opaque, as there is not a direct one-to-one correspondence between letters and sounds. English uses twenty-six letters to represent approximately forty-four phonemes (Fromkin et al. 1997).

The essence of reading is the transformation by the reader of text into meaning. In the process of becoming literate, what is considered successful reading changes as the reader's skills develop. Every stage of learning to read involves the reader responding to text; the form and degree of sophistication that is brought to the text will vary with age and experience. Reading achievement is significantly related to overall academic achievement (Donahue et al. 1999).

In an information literate school community, reading will be an essential prerequisite of participation in the curricular and social activities of that community. In chapter 2 of this book, Henri discusses an approach to mapping the information literate school community, including, in relation to the whole school, "The process of learning from information – of constructing knowledge – is always the focus of teaching and learning". In order to learn from information effectively, students will need to have well-developed reading strategies and these can be supported by the teacher and the teacher librarian. The provision and availability of a range of print and electronic materials to support reading development will be an integral part of an information literate school community and the teacher librarian has specialist knowledge in this area. In this community, collaboration between school managers, teachers and teacher librarians will be a key feature of reading development in the school, so that students who become information literate have a sound basis of reading skills which will enable them to participate fully in the wider school community.

Reading Materials and Instruction

At each stage of reading instruction, the materials will vary in relationship to the level and type of reading (Gambrell, Wilson & Gantt 1981).

1. Independent-level reading is carried out for pleasure or practice by the reader without assistance. Materials should be those in which the reader can decode and comprehend ninety-five percent of the words on his or her own.

2. Instructional-level reading is carried out with assistance from a teacher through discussing vocabulary, asking questions, activating background knowledge, thus lessening the demand on the reader and using material that is more difficult than that for independent reading.

3. Frustration-level reading occurs when there is a mismatch between the reader's skills and the requirements of the text. The text may contain too many unfamiliar words and assume nonexistent prior knowledge. These three categories are used in selecting books for instructional purposes or in guiding a child's book selection.

Book Selection for Independent Reading

Teachers and teacher librarians, when guiding a child's selection for independent reading, need to take to text difficulty into account, but it is only one factor, once past the initial stage of reading acquisition. Choice is an intrinsic motivator in helping a child persist with a book.

Gender differences are another consideration in guiding book selection. There is growing concern over boys performing more poorly than girls in literacy measures. In the thirty-five countries that participated in the 2001 PIRLS study of grade 4 students, girls significantly outperformed boys (International Association for the Evaluation of Educational Achievement 2001). United States girls in grades 4, 8 and 12 outperformed boys in reading in the national testing (National Center for Educational Statistics 2002). Most troubling is the difference in performance increases from elementary to secondary schooling. A variety of reasons for boys' poor reading performance have been suggested (Hunsader 2002, Jackson 1998, Young & Brozo 2001). Significant for teacher librarians are the different preferences expressed by boys and girls (Wicks 1995). Boys prefer informational texts (Herz & Gallo 1996), male protagonists (Langerman 1990, Ollmann 1993), magazines and alternative forms of text, and enjoy materials that are slightly outrageous (hence the wild popularity of *Captain Underpants* since 1997). We need to encourage boys to become avid readers by providing, and allowing them to select, material that appeals to them.

Information Literacy

As information specialist, the teacher librarian plays a key role in enhancing the quality of instruction that children receive. At times providing it directly, as in story time or a unit on informational literacy skills, but equally as valuable is their expertise in working with teachers to support classroom instruction. Consultation with a teacher librarian broadens the resources that a teacher draws upon in planning instruction and provides an opportunity to ensure information literacy is an integral part of the planned instruction. Information literacy is still an unfamiliar concept to many classroom teachers, and the teacher librarian can support the fuller inclusion of it into instruction.

Stages of Reading Development

The matrix below outlines the developmental progression that an individual passes through in becoming literate. There are core understandings and skills that a child needs to acquire at each stage. The matrix developed by Stahl (personal communication, July 1999) is based upon Chall's stages of learning to read (Chall 1983). It serves as a framework for thinking about the relationship between developmental stages, instructional practices and resources used to support learning. Each stage will be discussed by responding to the following four questions: What is the child learning in this stage? What is the classroom teacher doing to promote literacy? How can the librarian assist the child in this stage? What materials are important at this stage? As stage 5 deals with the later stages of postsecondary education it will not be discussed.

At all stages the child needs to be exposed to a wide variety of books for different purposes: quality literature, to build an awareness of rich language usage, classic literature to ensure that the child has access to literary and cultural knowledge from the past, popular books for entertainment and informational books to learn about the world.

Stage	What child is learning	Typical activities	Teaching materials
Stage 0 – Emergent Literacy Birth to Gr. 1	Functions of written language, Alphabet, Phonemic awareness	Story reading, "Pseudoreading", Alphabet activities, Rhyming, Nursery rhymes, Invented spelling	Books (including predictable stories), Letters, Writing materials, *Sesame Street*
Stage 1 – Decoding/Early Reading Beginning Gr. 1	Letter-sound correspondences (Phonics)	Teacher-directed reading instruction, Phonics instruction	Preprimers and primers, Phonics materials, Writing materials, Trade books
Stage 2 – Fluency End Gr. 1 to End Gr. 3	Automatic word recognition, Use of context	Reading narratives, generally about known topics	Basal readers, Trade books, Workbooks
Stage 3 – Reading to Learn (Single Viewpoint) Gr. 4 to 8	How to learn from text, Vocabulary, Strategies	Reading & studying content area materials, Strategy instruction, Use of encyclopedias	Basal readers, Novels, Encyclopedias, Textbooks in content areas
Stage 4 – Abstract Reading (Multiple viewpoint) High School and Early College	Reconciling different views	Critical reading, Discourse synthesis, Report writing	Texts containing multiple views, Reference material, Magazines and journals, Nonfiction books, etc.
Stage 5 – A World View Late college, Graduate school	Developing a well-rounded view of the world	Learning what not to read as well as what to read	Professional materials

Stage 0 – Emergent Literacy

What is the child learning in this stage?

Much of this stage occurs before children enter school. In all social classes children growing up in a literate society are exposed to a wide range of print and adults who use literacy in their daily lives (Duke & Purcell-Gates 2003, Purcell-Gates 1997). This exposure develops children's print literacy and early writing. Many children also learn the alphabet and are able to recognize and name some letters before starting school (West, Denton, & Germino-Hausken 2000). Data from thirty-five countries in the PIRLS study (International Association for the Evaluation of Educational Achievement 2001) suggests that children who had early literacy experiences in the home before starting school were better readers in grade 4.

Reading is built upon the child's oral language development. A rich language environment builds the child's vocabulary and conceptual knowledge (Wells 1986). The form and amount of language that children are exposed to differs widely among families (Hart & Risley 1995, Wells 1986). Consequently the oral vocabulary and knowledge that children have available to them when they begin to read will differ, thereby affecting comprehension.

The feature of language that has the strongest relationship to learning to read is the development of phonological awareness (Ehri et al 2001, Torgesen, Wagner & Rashotte 1994). Phonological awareness is the consciousness of sounds in words. It includes being able to detect rhyme and separate sounds in words. It is a broad concept within which the concept of phonemic awareness refers to the conscious awareness of individual sounds in words. A phoneme is the smallest unit of sound in a language that makes one word different from another. The concept of phonemic awareness develops over the course of this stage and can be fostered.

For reading acquisition, in addition to phonological awareness, children need to develop an understanding of the alphabetic principle. That is, letters represent sounds; a reader can turn print into an oral word by saying the sounds associated with letters and the reciprocal understanding that oral speech can be spelled by writing the letters that correspond to the sounds in the word (Adams 1990).

What is the classroom teacher doing to promote literacy?

In the home, day-care and kindergarten class children are helped to develop aspects of phonological awareness such as rhyme, through the use of nursery rhymes, poems and finger plays that engage children in word play. Dramatic play centres should include literacy material (e.g., menus, phone books etc.) to encourage children to incorporate literacy activities into play (Christie 1990). The teacher will devote a considerable amount of time to reading aloud. Reading and discussing a wide range of books with children develops their vocabulary and conceptual knowledge, which will underpin their later reading growth (Strickland & Taylor 1989). Oral comprehension is in advance of reading comprehension until the upper elementary grades (Sticht & James 1984), so the major source of knowledge growth is listening to and discussing texts. Open-ended discussions that follow being read aloud to enhance children's learning (Beck & McKeown 2001). Finally, the child is taught letter names and teachers encourage children to write using the knowledge they have of sounds and letters, that is, invented spelling. This is a window into the child's developing understanding of how letters represent sounds; it becomes more accurate as the child masters more of the code.

How can the librarian assist the child in this stage?

A teacher librarian supports instruction by helping a teacher select books that foster conceptual and language development and by encouraging the teacher to reread high calibre books to children, as deeper conceptual understanding arises from hearing books more than once (Leung & Pikulski 1990). Reading aloud followed by discussion in small groups helps lower-income children acquire language skills and story comprehension (Dickinson & Smith 1994). The teacher librarian should continue oral storytelling with children to enrich their imagination and enhance vocabulary growth. In the current electronically-rich world that children inhabit, children benefit from having to conjure up their own inner imagery (Gambrell & Javitz 1993).

A teacher librarian can work with the kindergarten teacher to ensure children are exposed to, and learn, some traditional nursery rhymes. Nursery rhymes are a powerful tool for language appreciation and growth. The phrases "One misty moisty morning" or "The north wind doth blow" use words in an evocative manner different from that of everyday life. They contain the distilled language patterns of English. Many children are no longer exposed to these as part of family interaction. In fact, many young teachers may not be familiar with them either. Nursery rhymes can be a vehicle for developing phonological awareness (Yopp & Yopp 1992). Children who knew nursery rhymes performed better in early reading activities (Maclean, Bryant & Bradley 1987). Barton and Booth (1995) discuss ways of incorporating nursery rhymes into the curriculum from kindergarten to high school, especially addressing the learning needs of English second-language learners. Aside from the inherent pleasure that children derive from them, traditional folk- and fairy tales also contribute to building a cultural knowledge base. This familiarity with tropes and characters underpins intertextuality. Picture books, such as *The Jolly Postman*, draw upon this knowledge as an integral part of the story. A reader at any stage misses much if they lack the background knowledge that is assumed by the author, so building a child's knowledge base is a major goal.

In summary, at this stage the goal is building a love of books, be it for learning about the world, making it more comprehensible to the child, or entering realms of fantasy and imagination.

What materials are important at this stage?

Picture books, classic and otherwise, that can be shared by a parent and child or by a teacher and children – books that build an emotional bond through text. An example is *Good Night, Moon*, which creates a world of security and warmth for the young child. My inner-city kindergarten classes were soothed by having this book read at the end of the day. Books that feature rhyme, traditional and otherwise, such as nursery rhymes, traditional folk- and fairy tales, all serve to furnish the child's mind. Providing puppets and simple props for reenactment of stories or the creation of their own stories will support the child's oral language development.

Alphabet books – although care is needed in their selection, as the words used are often selected to fit a theme or because they will make dramatic illustrations. These can cause confusion if used to teach the correspondences between letter and sound. For example, the words tiger and thumb may both start with the letter T, but they do not start with the same phoneme (tiger /t; thumb /th).

Informational picture books need to be as prevalent in the library and classroom as narrative picture books.

Stage 1 – Decoding/Early Reading

What is the child learning in this stage?

This stage sees the child making the transition from oral language learning and alphabetic knowledge to learning how to decode print. To do this a child needs to integrate letter recognition, phonemic awareness and the alphabetic principle. Instruction in phonics makes these relationships explicit for the child (Ehri 1998). Children apply their phonetic knowledge more fully in writing using invented spelling. At this stage children are "glued to print" (Chall 1996). Their oral reading may be halting and slow as they work out the correspondences.

What is the classroom teacher doing to promote literacy?

In a successful literacy program a teacher provides instruction systematically and explicitly. Children receive lessons in phonics (Adams 1990, Fielding-Bransley 1997, Foorman et al. 1998), continue to work on phonemic awareness and are encouraged to write using their developing phonetic skills (Stahl & Murray 1998). Guided reading lessons focus on comprehension strategies such as retelling (Koskinen et al. 1988). Daily independent reading also is a component of the literacy program.

The teacher will continue to read aloud and discuss both narrative and informational texts to develop vocabulary and conceptual knowledge (Robbins & Ehri 1994). Books read aloud by an adult should be available to the children to pseudo-read as well. However, these books do not make suitable instructional texts or books for independent reading.

How can the librarian assist the child in this stage?

The teacher librarian has a role to play in educating the classroom teacher in the use of more informational books in the classroom. Currently, insufficient informational texts are used in primary classrooms (Duke 2000a, Duke, Bennett-Armistead & Roberts 2003). Yopp and Yopp (2000) state that primary teachers reported that only fourteen percent of the books they read aloud to their classes were informational.

In their role as purchaser, teacher librarians can ensure that the library has books that are at the independent reading level for children in this stage, in particular informational books. To support continued language development, the teacher librarian could include a poem in every library session, for example reading Sandburg's "Fog" aloud on a foggy day. Little poetry is read aloud in schools these days, a reflection of poetry's vanishing presence in modern life. If poetry is used in the classroom at all, it is usually limited to the amusing. Librarians can help reclaim poetry for children. A whole poem does not need to be read, a few lines will bring language alive.

What materials are important at this stage?

Children will need help in selecting books for different purposes. For independent reading children need predictable, controlled-vocabulary and decodable books. These three types of books serve different purposes in early reading (Hiebert 1999). All three allow children to apply their developing understanding of how language and print works. Predictable or pattern books provide the child with quick success. Once the child knows the frame sentence she can "read" the rest of the book by using the pattern and illustration. This anticipation of the outcome aids fluent reading (Clay 1991). Controlled-vocabulary books provide success by limiting the words used to a small number that the child has mastered as sight words. Decodable books allow the child to apply his understanding of phonics to read new words (Juel & Roper-Schneider 1985). The inclusion of decodable books in early reading instruction is important, as there can be a mismatch between children and materials that limits children's success (Mesmir 1999). Many of the little books for early reading now incorporate all three factors. All three types of books are helpful in providing the successful practice needed to develop the automatic word recognition that underpins skilled reading.

Choice is intrinsically motivational (Guthrie, Alao & Rinehart 1997) and children also should have the opportunity to select books that may be above their independent reading level. These books, informational or narrative, support a child's interests, providing a rich conceptual world. The quality of the illustrations is a large part of reading or pseudo-reading these books. Teaching children how to examine illustrations (Arizpe & Styles 2003) will enhance children's enjoyment and learning.

In addition, children need to hear quality literature read aloud, rich in emotion and complexity. Sendak's *Where the Wild Things Are* contains words such as "gnashed" and "rumpus" which are too difficult to read independently, but which are within six-year-olds listening vocabulary, or can become so from the context and discussion. Short discussion of evocative words, either in appreciation or for definition, adds to the experience but the emphasis should be on sheer pleasure.

Informational books for this level should have a table of contents and index to make accessing information easy, but not all books produced for this level include these features. The teacher librarian can begin to introduce children to these information literacy skills. The classroom teacher will have begun to introduce writing informational genre and children need good models. It is better to purchase one well-designed book than three that lack these features.

Stage 2 – Confirmation and Fluency

What is the child learning in this stage?

Fluent reading is essential for comprehending texts and is a key factor in reading pleasure (Dowhower 1994, Samuels 2002, Worthy & Broaddus 2002). Fluency is a reader's ability to read with speed, accuracy, and comprehension (Samuels 2002). The rapid and automatic decoding of fluent reading frees up working memory for comprehension, that in Stage One had been focused on decoding. Word recognition is the result of having mastered phonics and spelling patterns (Adams 1990, Ehri 1998, Wolf, Katzir-Cohen 2001). Children who are unsure of the connections between individual phonemes and letters face a barrier in becoming fluent. They remain working letter by letter, unlike a child who has mastered phonics and has now shifted her attention to larger units.

What is the classroom teacher doing to promote literacy?

This stage of reading instruction is essential for a child's reading success. Difficulty with reading leads to frustration, producing less interest in voluntary reading. The gap between fluent readers and non-fluent readers steadily increases because of the difference in time spent reading; good readers' skills are continually improving. Even in grade 1, good readers read ten times as many words as poor readers in the same grade. The long-term consequence of less reading is a slower rate of knowledge and vocabulary acquisition. Instruction, if it is to move the reader from word by word reading to fluency, should focus on quantity. The simplest technique is repeated reading (Dowhower 1994). Repeated reading increases a reader's speed, word accuracy, expression, and comprehension. Both normally-achieving and learning-disabled children benefit from repeated reading instruction (Dowhower 1994, Samuels 2002).

How can the librarian assist the child in this stage?

A key goal for the teacher librarian is to hook the children into exercising their newly-acquired skill. It is important to introduce children to material that will appeal to them through book talks or reading aloud material that may not be considered quality literature. At this stage the goal is to have children clamouring to borrow books. Any material or activity that increases the amount of reading is an aid to fluency, as fluency rests on voluminous reading. The research on rereading as a technique for improving fluency suggests that children should be encouraged to reread books. Teachers and parents need to be informed of the benefit of rereading.

The librarian has a role helping the classroom teacher to develop topics of substance to build the children's knowledge base, selecting material that is not superficial and trite. The majority of classroom time in elementary school is spent studying topics already familiar to children, such as family, pets, friends etc. (Hirsch 2003, Walsh 2003). Low-income children are at particular risk from this curricular orientation, as it is only in school that they are likely to encounter the vocabulary and concepts that are needed for future learning. Without involvement in meaningful units of study in the primary grades they are at greater risk of having difficulty with reading comprehension in the later stages of elementary schooling.

What materials are important at this stage?

Books that feature the use of high frequency vocabulary in interesting ways, such as Dr Seuss's *The Cat in the Hat*, provide the repetition needed for automaticity. Simple chapter books appeal to children, as they resemble "grown-up" books. Because of the decrease in the number of illustrations, the child has to focus on words to obtain meaning.

Series books serve an important function. The commonality of vocabulary across books provides that overlap which enhances automaticity of word recognition. Familiar characters, similar structure and situations ease the cognitive load for the child, while variations in the plot maintain interest. These books are frequently written to a formula, which, although potentially deadening to a more sophisticated reader, can be reassuring for a neophyte reader.

Stage 3 – Reading to Learn (Single Viewpoint)

What is the child learning in this stage?

If children are on track, decoding has been mastered and sufficient fluency has been achieved, so instructional attention now turns toward reading as a tool for learning content.

Reading comprehension has been characterized as the "essence of reading" (Durkin 1993). The past twenty-five years have seen extensive research into the basic processes of comprehension (Kintsch 1998, Anderson 1994, Rumelhart 1980). Competent readers are actively solving problems while reading, and comprehension is resulting from the interaction between the reader's prior knowledge and the message contained in a specific text (Harris & Hodges 1995). Thus the level of knowledge about a topic already held by the reader influences the ease with which they can comprehend a new text; more knowledge allows the reader to make multiple connections between the text and the world (Ericsson & Charness 1994).

What is the classroom teacher doing to promote literacy?

While reading comprehension has been a part of reading instruction since the initial stages, it should now become the major focus of instruction. Strategy instruction enhances children's reading comprehension (Pressley 2000, Pressley 2002, Pressley et al. 1989, Rosenshine & Meister 1994) and fosters active engagement in learning (Mier 1984). The teacher will be introducing and teaching comprehension strategies, often through guided reading groups in which she may model strategies and monitor children's reading comprehension.

The National Reading Panel report (2000), a meta-analysis of thirty years of research, identifies eight effective strategies for improving reading comprehension. These are: Self-monitoring; Cooperative learning; Graphic Organizers; Question Answering; Question Generation; Story Structure; Summarization; Multiple Strategy Instruction, involving a combination of the above strategies. Children should receive systematic instruction in these strategies throughout elementary and secondary school.

Vocabulary knowledge influences reading comprehension (Chall, Jacobs & Baldwin 1990). The vocabulary load in texts increases in this stage, with more abstract and technical vocabulary appearing in place of the language of everyday interaction that dominated primary level texts. Vocabulary study should be an integral part of reading instruction at this level (Graves & Watts-Taffe 2002, Beck, McKeown & Kucan 2002). Improving children's comprehension of text is the most direct way of increasing their mastery of content knowledge, the major learning goal in the upper elementary grades.

How can the librarian assist the child in this stage?

Along with sponsoring the traditional book club for local or national young readers' choice awards, a teacher librarian might sponsor a reading club that appeals to the disengaged weaker reader, focusing on student interests, e.g., a sports book club using multimedia and high-interest materials.

Smith (2001) in an analysis of school library media centres identified two features at the middle-school level that lead to higher achievement on a reading tests – the teacher librarians' selection of material for instructional units, and the teaching of information literacy skills to students.

Information literacy skills come to the forefront in this stage and children benefit from an increased instructional emphasis on those skills needed to use electronic and multimedia resources. This is most effectively achieved when the teacher librarian and classroom teacher work together to plan for the coordination of instruction. For example, the teacher librarian may provide support for content instruction by designing appropriate WebQuests.

What materials are important at this stage?

Access to a wide variety of informational resources, print and electronic, especially those that are on curricular topics. At this stage students are likely to be engaged in extensive research projects within subject areas, such as social studies and science. In order to carry out resource-based research projects, children need access to informational resources that are written at different levels of readability. Many children in the upper elementary grades are still reading at the primary level. These primary level resources are also useful with more capable children. Informational texts for younger children frequently utilize outstanding illustrations and diagrams due to the limitations of simple text. These features can serve as an additional avenue for conceptual understanding in more capable readers.

Stage 4 – Abstract Reading

What is the individual learning in this stage?

Abstract reading involves being able to examine multiple viewpoints, assess logical alternatives, and analyze texts critically. Texts are viewed as abstract objects that can be considered systematically. Each discipline has its own textual structure and specific tools for analysis of texts. Textual interpretation depends upon understanding a genre and authorial intentions (Olson 1994). The feedback loop that exists between knowledge within a discipline and the ease with which one can read and comprehend texts becomes crucial (Murphy & Alexander 2002).

By this stage there is wide variation in the skills that students bring to text. A proportion of adolescents lack the reading skills needed to learn from content area texts, much less engage in structural and stylistic analyses of text. Unfortunately for weaker readers, there is little emphasis upon directly teaching reading skills at this level.

Online literacy

Digital texts and new technologies are creating new modes of texts and practices (Bolter & Grusin 2000). The advent of multimedia information sources has changed the nature of reading (Adolescents and Literacies in a Digital World 2002, Silicon literacies 2002). A text may now be considered to be three-dimensional, with the integration of graphics, audio and video into the structure of a text.

Students need instruction in how to read interactive sources if the purpose of reading is to gain new information. Hypertext's structure allows the reader to construct her/his passage though the text. This non-linear structure requires greater knowledge of the topic by the reader, as s/he must provide the relational structure between ideas, which in print was provided by the prepositional organization of the text. As yet there has been little research on instructional practices that improve students' reading in multimedia contexts (Leu 2002).

Mastery of online literacy is mostly acquired outside of school and varies considerably among adolescents (Lenhart, Simon & Graziano 2001). Much of this mastery is not focused on using these resources as a tool for learning information but on facility with the technology for entertainment and social purposes.

What is the classroom teacher doing to promote literacy?

Teachers at this level see their instructional role as one of conveying the content of the discipline. As part of this role, teachers may utilize instructional strategies that improve reading skills, but this is ad hoc.

Performance on large-scale international studies has lead to an increased attention to adolescent literacy. Reciprocal Teaching (Palinscar & Brown 1984), a form of cooperative learning around text to improve students' reading, acknowledges the importance of social interaction for adolescents and capitalizes upon it. However instruction in improving the reading skills of below average, average or advanced students is rarely incorporated into high-school classes. Consequently many students struggle with the literacy demands of the content areas and are not able to engage with text successfully at an abstract level.

Access to the Internet, and the extent to which it is integrated into a teacher's instruction, varies widely. Overall, little attention is given to teaching information literacy skills. Whelan (2003) surveyed media specialists at the middle- and high-school level, sixty-eight percent of whom reported barriers to teaching information literacy; there was little support by teachers and little knowledge of information literacy on the part of teachers.

How can the librarian assist the learner in this stage?

Given the low knowledge of information literacy on the part of teachers reported by Whelan, teacher librarians need to take a leadership role in ensuring that information literacy skills are taught to all students. As the information specialist, the teacher librarian has an essential role in helping teachers and students acquire the informational and technical skills needed for deeper learning.

The performance of high-school students on reading tests was highest in schools in which teacher librarians planned instructional units with teachers (Smith 2001). This is echoed by Kapitzke (2001), who found on examining four library systems that the two factors that affected student academic achievement were teacher librarians providing in-service instruction to teachers, and directly working with students.

Since the range of reading abilities in a classroom widens as the grade level increases, the librarian needs to be aware of this in selecting resources – print and electronic. In particular, weaker readers may need help in effectively using hypertext for learning. The need to engage students in reading as a leisure activity remains, so classroom visits to do book talks and book groups are essential, for many students high school is their last contact with a library and a librarian.

What materials are important at this stage?

Informational resources of all types, written for a wide range of reading abilities are essential. Students need texts containing multiple views, reference materials, magazines, and journals, and literature – young adult and adult – that appeals to a variety of tastes and skills. Providing students with continuing instruction in the use of resources is the key to ensuring their use of the materials and will enhance their enjoyment and learning.

Conclusion

In a technological society reading is the preeminent tool. One can live a life without being able to read, but it is one most often spent on the margins of society. Reading underpins all aspects of education and thus indirectly determines individuals' educational achievement and employment opportunities. Literacy attainment is the strongest determinant of economic security, and adults with marginal literacy skills are much less likely to participate in job training or education (Shalla & Schellenberg 1998). As technology advances, the definition of what it is to be literate continually changes. In an information literate school community, reading will be given a high profile, as it may be the key to participation in that community for many students.

Reading is a complex cognitive process that is best learnt through systematic instruction throughout schooling from skilled and caring adults in an environment that provides access to a wide range of materials. Reading not only opens doors in society; it also opens the interior world of imagination and emotion. We are transformed by what we read. Learning to read never ends – it is the spark that sets off a lifetime of learning.

7

The Leadership Role of the Principal in the Information Literate School Community

Dianne Oberg and James Henri

The Information Literate School Community: Evolving Concept

In the English-speaking world, school library media centres have long been a part of schools, indeed as far back as the 8th century (Clyde 1999). Even though school library media centres have existed for a long time, the implementation of the school library media centre's instructional role often has been quite limited. However, where school library media centre programs have been implemented successfully, researchers have often cited the partnership between the principal and the teacher librarian as a reason for that success. There is a large body of research and professional literature in English relating to school library media centre program development and implementation. That literature points to the key role of the principal. This finding is consistent with a broad range of educational research identifying the principal as the key agent of school improvement and of program implementation in other areas such as reading education and technology integration.

School library media centre programs involve a range of innovations which can be very difficult to implement because they require changes, not only in the way that teaching and learning occurs within the library, but also in the way that teaching and learning occurs within the classrooms and, indeed, throughout the school. School library media centre programs that support student learning and facilitate good teaching practice require many changes outside the specific domain of the school library media centre. For example, teachers need to work with other teachers, they need to use multiple resources, and they need to involve their students in designing and evaluating learning projects. A whole-school approach is needed to implement a successful school library media centre program. The teacher librarian has a critical role to play, but he or she can only do this with whole-school support, and in particular, with the support of the principal.

The active role of the principal is particularly important for the development of an information literate school community (Henri 1995). The concept of the information literate school community (ILSC) draws attention to the distinctions between the school as a place of learning and the school as a learning community, placing an emphasis on the process of informing within a learning community. Information literate school communities are ones where teacher librarians are involved in teaching, where the importance of information literacy is recognized, and where everyone in the community is engaged collaboratively in resource-based, problem-solving learning. All educators in ILSCs (principals, teachers, teacher librarians, and other educational specialists in the school) understand that information literacy begins with them and that they must be information literate themselves if they are going to act as information literacy models and mentors for their students.

In this chapter previous research investigating the role of the principal in school library media centre development is reviewed, and the results of an international study of the role principal in the development of the ILSC are examined. Finally, the themes emerging from the study of the role of the principal in developing school library media centre programs and/or information literate school communities are analyzed in terms of the themes of the Kouzes and Posner leadership model presented in *The Leadership Challenge* (Kouzes & Posner 2002). This analysis presents the role of the principal in the leadership language and concepts that will be familiar to many school principals. This analysis should further our understanding of the role of the principal in bringing about change in school library media centre programs and/or developing information literate school communities. It should also have implications for teacher librarians in relation to the leadership role that they play in the ILSC.

Previous Research

The role of the principal in supporting the school library media centre program is often referred to in both the professional and research literatures as "principal support". A deeper analysis of the complex relationships among principals and teacher librarians has demonstrated that principal support involves at least four different kinds of principal practices or roles (Oberg 1995). These four practices or roles comprising principal support are used as a framework to present in Table 7.1 a summary of the professional and research literature related to the role of the principal in supporting the school library media centre program – a key factor in the development of an ILSC.

The discussion below is based primarily on the North American professional and research literature, but it appears that similar patterns may be found in school library media centre literature from other areas of the world. Because the professional literature is more readily accessible (and therefore better known), only research findings are discussed here and included in the bibliography. Readers interested in examining the professional literature should consult *IFLA Professional Report* no. 78 (Henri, Hay & Oberg 2002) or earlier articles on the concept of principal support (for example Oberg 1995).

A number of studies (for example Baldwin 1996, Charter 1982, Gehlken 1995) have found that principal support is critical to the development of school library media centre programs. Dekker (1989) found that school district administrators were also important in enabling principals to support library programs in their schools. Corr (1979) and Turner (1980) found that principal attitude was positively correlated to program implementation. Hellene (1974) and Yetter (1994) found that principal support for the school library media centre program involved such things as encouraging its use by teachers and students, integrating the program into the curricular work of the school, and providing flexible scheduling.

Table 7.1. *Role of the principal: Professional and research literature*

Developing the school library media centre program	Professional literature	Research literature
As a supervisor working directly with teachers: • outlines expectations for library use • provides professional development for teachers	Austrom et al. 1989; Baker 1980; Carson 1989; Davies 1979; Fox 1982; Haycock 1999; Kearney 2000; Loertscher 2000; Lundin 1983; Podemski 1990; Salmon et al. 1996; Yesner & Jay 1987	Charter 1982; Hay & Henri 1995; Hellene 1974; LaRocque & Oberg 1990
As a model demonstrating personal commitment: • explicit valuing of program • using program in own teaching • being visible in library	Carson 1989; Davies 1979; Fox 1982; Grant 1988; Haycock 1999; Kuehn 1975; Kearney 2000; Loertscher 1988; Lundin 1983; Morris, Gillespie & Spirt 1992; Salmon et al. 1996; Yesner & Jay 1987	Corr 1979; Farwell 1999; Hay & Henri 1995; LaRocque & Oberg 1990; Turner 1980
As a manager enabling the program: • materials/clerical staff budget • flexible scheduling • includes program as an integral part of school's curriculum work (including planning and evaluating)	Austrom et al. 1989; Baker 1980; Barron 1994; Browne & Burton 1989; Carson 1989; Davies 1979; Fox 1982; Hamilton 1983; Haycock 1999; Kearney 2000; Kuehn 1975; Loertscher 2000; Lundin 1983; Morris, Gillespie & Spirt 1992; Podemski 1990; Salmon et al. 1996; Woolls 1999; Yesner & Jay 1987	Charter 1982; Dekker 1989; Farwell 1999; Gehlken 1995; Hay & Henri 1995; Hellene 1974; LaRocque & Oberg 1990; Turner 1980; Wilson, Blake & Lyders 1993; Yetter 1994
As a mentor providing visibility/ importance: • makes time for meetings with the teacher librarian • trusts the teacher librarian's knowledge/expertise • encourages the teacher librarian's personal and professional development	Baker 1980; Carson 1989; Davies 1979; Hamilton 1983; Kearney 2000; Kuehn 1975; Morris, Gillespie & Spirt 1992; Woolls 1999; Yesner & Jay 1987	Hay & Henri 1995; LaRocque & Oberg 1990

Farwell (1999) found that, in schools with successful school library media centre programs, the principal served as an advocate for collaborative planning and information literacy instruction; the principal in such schools also provided financial support for the library program, including that needed to hire clerical staff, and arranged for teacher librarians and classroom teachers to have time during the school day to plan together.

LaRocque and Oberg (1990) in Canada and Hay and Henri (1995) in Australia found that principals working within information literate school communities provided support through: understanding and believing in a collaborative school library media centre program; recognizing the importance of the teacher librarian; ensuring collaborative planning time and other program resources; providing appropriate staff development for teachers and teacher librarians; and monitoring implementation of the collaborative school library media centre program.

Campbell (1995) found that for all high school students in a school to become information literate, principals had to move information literacy instruction into the mainstream of the school program. In order to do this, principals assumed roles of direction setters, facilitators, and communicators. Campbell also found that the themes associated with successful implementation of educational change were present where information literacy programs were being implemented on a school-wide basis – vision building, evolutionary planning, empowerment, resource mobilization, and problem-coping/monitoring. Other studies indicate the virtual rarity of principal support for, and understanding of, the school library media centre program. Studies by Hauck and Schieman (1985), Dorrell and Lawson (1995) and Kolencik (2001) found that principals rarely recognized the instructional role of the teacher librarian, while Wilson, Blake and Lyders (1993) found that many principals were hampered in their support for school library media centres by lack of knowledge about the management and function of school library media centres.

An International Study on the Role of the Principal

An international study of the role of the principals in ILSCs was conducted in 1997-1998 in seven countries: Australia, Canada, Scotland, Finland, France, Japan, and South Korea. Questionnaires, based on the framework presented in Table 7.1, were used to survey both principals and teacher librarians about the nature of principal support. The research was guided by an International Research Reference Group (IRRG) representing the seven countries involved in this international study (see Table 7.2). The members of the IRRG provided input and advice regarding the adaptation and translation of the quantitative and qualitative instruments for each country involved in the research, and planned and administered the procedures for data collection, analysis, and reporting of findings for each country.

Table 7.2. *International research reference group*

Australia	James Henri	Senior Lecturer
	Lyn Hay	Lecturer, School of Information Studies, Charles Sturt University, Wagga Wagga
Canada	Dianne Oberg	Associate Professor, School of Library and Information Studies, University of Alberta, Edmonton
Finland	Liisa Niinikangas	Information Specialist and Partner, Lighthouse Consulting, Tampere
France	Colette Charrier	President of FADBEN and Teacher librarian, Lycee Guez de Balzac, Angouleme
Japan	Setsuko Koga	Professor, Department of Education, Aoyama Gakuin University, Shibuyaku
Scotland	James Herring	Head of Department (Acting), Department of Communication and Information Studies, Queen Margaret College, Aberdeen
South Korea	Yoon Ok Han	Professor, Department of Library and Information Science, Kyonggi do University, Suwon-City

Note. Titles and affiliations as current in 1998.

Research Methodology for the International Study

Questionnaires were developed and piloted in Australia. Two questionnaire sets – one for principals and one for teacher librarians – were developed. The three instruments in each of the questionnaire sets included both closed-choice and open-ended questions.

Instrument 1 was designed to identify demographic variables including the personal and professional characteristics of the principals and teacher librarians and the characteristics of the schools in which they worked. Instrument 2 was designed to identify the level of principal support for the school library media centre program and for the teacher librarian.

Instrument 2 was divided into two parts: Part A, Perception Factors, and Part B, Belief Factors. In Part A, principals and teacher librarians first rated the level of attention they perceived the principal to give each item or task at the present using the rating scale, A Lot – Some – Little – None or Cannot Comment. Then they rated (using the same scale) the level of attention they would like to see the principal give each item or task in the future. In Part B, principals and teacher librarians were asked to indicate the strength of their views on each of the items or beliefs using the scale, Strongly Agree – Agree – Disagree – Strongly Disagree – Cannot Comment. The belief statements were designed to indicate the strength of principal and teacher librarian beliefs and the alignment between principal and teacher librarian beliefs about the role of the principal in developing and supporting an ILSC. Instrument 3 was composed of open-ended questions related to the strengths and challenges of the school library media centre, the contributions of teacher librarians to teaching and learning, the nature of information literacy, barriers to integration of information skills, the promotion of the school library media centre, and the respondents' roles in developing and supporting an ILSC. Teacher librarians were asked two extra questions related to ways they used to maintain their credibility as teacher librarians and ways that their principals could provide them with additional support.

Each IRRG member was responsible for the collection of data in their country and for the entry of those data via the World WideWeb into a database at the School of Information Studies, Charles Sturt University. The SPSS software program was used by Hay and Henri to analyze the quantitative data. Frequency analysis was used to get an overall picture of the data, and t-tests were used to check for significant differences between the responses of principals and teacher librarians. The qualitative data from the open-ended questions was analyzed using a framework and content analysis procedures developed by Oberg at the University of Alberta. The NUDIST*QSR software program, designed for use with textual qualitative data, was used to gather together all the responses to each open-ended question from the principals in each country and the teacher librarians in each country. Readers should also be aware that, because only a small part of the data from the France study has been made available in English at this time, the discussion of cross-country findings could not include the data from France.

The Role of the Principal

The questions developed for the international study explored in some depth the four aspects of the role of the principal in developing an ILSC, through supporting the school library media centre program and the teacher librarian: as supervisor, as model, as manager, and as mentor (see Table 7.3).

Table 7.3. *The role of the principal (Oberg 1995)*

Developing the School Library Media Centre Program/the ILSC	Perception Question No./Item
As a supervisor working directly with teachers	3. Facilitate professional development (PD) of staff 5. Support collaboration between TL & staff 9. Encourage staff involvement in development of SL 10. Encourage staff to invest time to CPT with TL 11. Facilitate staff PD in understanding & use of IT 12. Inform new staff re importance of collaboration with TL 24. Encourage staff to use wide range of resources in their teaching 31. Seeks staff feedback re quality of SL services
As a model demonstrating personal commitment	4. Advocate TL role in school curriculum 14. Encourage staff debate re information policy 18. Visit SL to observe work of TL 22. Seek advice from TL re whole-school information management
As a manager enabling the school library media centre program/the ILSC	1. Facilitate development of ILSC 2. Ensure information literacy in school plan 6. Ensure SLRC reflects school goals 7. Ensure appropriate allocation of support staff 8. Allocate adequate, flexible time for TL 13. Support currency/relevancy of SLRC collection 15. Ensure significant funding allocated to SL budget 16. Seek outside funding to supplement SL budget 28. Encourage information skill integration and assessment by staff 30. If TL not on key committee, PR ensures SLRC needs addressed
As a mentor providing visibility / importance	17. Engage in regular/timely communication with TL 19. Encourage TL to debate/justify current practice 20. Ask questions of TL re teaching & learning 21. Rely on TL to keep PR abreast of developments re TL role 23. Encourage TL to take risks 25. Encourage TL leadership in development of information skills continuum 26. Work with TL to develop his/her personal PD plan 27. Advocate TL as member of key school-wide committees 29. Provide time release & funding for TL's ongoing PD

Abbreviations: CPT: cooperative planning and teaching; ILSC: information literate school community; IT: information technology; PD: professional development; PR: principal; TL: teacher librarian.

The findings of the international study have been disseminated through local and national presentations and publications in all seven countries and through the conferences of two international library associations. An *IFLA Professional Report* (Henri, Hay & Oberg 2002) has been published which includes examples of the research instruments as well as extensive discussions of the findings of the study and of the methodological and other issues involved in conducting an international study.

Understanding the Role of Leaders

The work of the co-investigators in conducting a large scale international study and several small scale studies in Canada and Australia helped to develop a deeper understanding of the complex phenomena involved in implementing successful school library media centre programs. Facilitating change in school programs and transforming school culture are complex endeavours that are frequently unsuccessful. Studying schools that had been successful in these endeavours enabled the co-investigators to explain more clearly, for example, the strategies of successful collaborative educational leaders.

Kouzes and Poser (2002) define leaders as "ordinary people who get extraordinary things done". For two decades, Kouzes and Posner have studied leadership through the collection and analysis of case studies of personal-best leadership experiences. Based on over 4500 in-depth case studies, over 7500 shorter case studies, and over 500 personal interviews from both the private and public sectors from around the world, they have identified five practices and ten commitments of leadership that make up The Leadership Challenge (Table 7.4). Analyzing these practices and commitments in light of the role of the principal in developing ILSCs provide insights for principals and for the teacher librarians with whom they work.

Table 7.4. *The five practices and ten commitments of leadership (Kouzes & Posner 2002, p. 22)*

Practice	Commitment
MODEL THE WAY	Find your voice by clarifying your values. Set the example by aligning actions with shared values.
INSPIRE A SHARED VISION	Envision the future by imagining exciting and ennobling possibilities. Enlist others in a common vision by appealing to shared aspirations.
CHALLENGE THE PROCESS	Search for opportunities by seeking innovative ways to change, grow, and improve. Experiment and take risks by constantly generating small wins and learning from mistakes

ENABLE OTHERS TO ACT	Foster collaboration by promoting cooperative goals and building trust. Strengthen others by sharing power and discretion.
ENCOURAGE THE HEART	Recognize contributions by showing appreciation for individual excellence. Celebrate the values and victories by creating a spirit of community.

The Leadership Role of the Principal

The connections between Kouzes and Posner's Five Leadership Practices and the roles that principals play in developing an ILSC are quite strong, as is shown in the discussion below.

Model the Way

This leadership practice involves the leader clearly defining and expressing beliefs and setting an example by acting out those beliefs in practice. This practice is very similar to the role the principal in an ILSC plays "as a model demonstrating personal commitment". This leadership practice in the development of an ILSC is demonstrated when the principal advocates the role of the teacher librarian in the curriculum, encourages teachers to discuss information policy, and visits the library to observe the work of the teacher librarian.

Inspire a Shared Vision

This leadership practice involves the leader in helping others to envision an exciting future and to work together towards that future. This practice is very similar to the role the principal in an ILSC plays "as a supervisor working directly with teachers". In the development of an ILSC, this leadership practice is demonstrated when the principal helps teachers to see how they might improve student learning by using a wide range of resources and by collaborating with the teacher librarian. The principal also facilitates the development of the school library media centre program through staff development activities that expand and enhance the potential of the program.

Challenge the Process

This leadership practice involves the leader in finding opportunities for change, growth and improvement and in experimenting and taking risks in order to progress. This practice is part of the role the principal in an ILSC plays "as a manager enabling the program". In the development of an ILSC, this leadership practice is demonstrated when the principal challenges teachers to infuse information literacy into the instructional program and challenges the teacher librarian to develop the school library media centre program and services to meet school goals.

Enable Others to Act

This leadership practice involves the leader in fostering collaboration and in giving others the power and resources needed for their work. This practice also is part of the role the principal in an ILSC plays "as a manager enabling the program". In the development of an ILSC, this leadership practice is demonstrated when the principal provides the resources of time, staff, and funding necessary for success of the school library media centre program.

Encourage the Heart

This leadership practice involves the leader in recognizing individual contributions and celebrating the values and successes of the community. This is very similar to the role the principal in an ILSC plays "as a mentor providing visibility and importance" for the teacher librarian. In the development of an ILSC, this leadership practice is demonstrated when the principal makes time to meet with the teacher librarian on a regular basis, acknowledges his or her achievements, and encourages him or her to take calculated risks and to continue to grow personally and professionally.

Shared vision is an essential ingredient of successful leadership. The potential influence of the teacher librarian and principal partnership should not be underestimated. The partnership will blossom under conditions of mutual respect and professional credibility. Credibility grows out of effective and accountable professional practice. Credibility must be earned. Principals come to their positions with a history and reputation that can be further developed after appointment. Teacher librarians may not have this privilege. A principal who appoints an inexperienced teacher librarian, where the school has one teacher librarian, must consider how the teacher librarian can be mentored. Direct supervision of the teacher librarian by the principal may be an important administrative arrangement to achieve this and it is an arrangement that has the added benefit of allowing the teacher librarian direct access to the principal's vision.

Expanding Understandings of the Leadership Role

To expand understandings of the leadership role of the principal in developing ILSCs, we now turn to two aspects of the results of the international study: (a) those Present Perceptions items that generated the most disagreement between principals and teacher librarians about the appropriateness of the amount of time being spent currently by the principals on those items, and (b) those Future Perceptions items that generated the highest level of agreement between principals and teacher librarians about the need for more attention to be given in the future to these items. These Present Perceptions "disagreement" items and Future Perceptions "agreement" items present fruitful areas for analysis. Because they represent areas for which either or both respondent groups see a need for change, these are areas that offer possibilities for rethinking and expanding understandings of the ILSC leadership role of the principal, using another leadership framework such as the Kouzes and Posner leadership model.

Present Perceptions "Disagreement" Items

Principals in the six countries viewed themselves as spending more time, or slightly more time, than did the teacher librarians on tasks that supported the development of an ILSC, and principals and teacher librarians in all countries but one differed significantly on the amount of time they perceived the principal to spend on these tasks. The four Present Perceptions task statements with a significant amount of disagreement were:

- advocating and facilitating the development of an ILSC
- demonstrating support for collaboration among the teacher librarian and teaching staff
- ensuring that the teacher librarian has an appropriate allocation of support staff
- allocating adequate, flexible time for the teacher librarian to administer the library

Future Perceptions "Agreement" Items

The top five tasks identified as requiring significantly more principal attention by principals and teacher librarians across the six countries in the study were:

- informs new teaching staff about the importance of collaborating with the teacher librarian
- encourages the teaching staff to invest time in cooperatively planning and teaching with the teacher librarian
- actively seeks outside school funding possibilities that can be used to supplement the library resource centre budget
- seeks feedback from staff about their impressions of the quality of library resource centre services
- works with the teacher librarian to develop the teacher librarian's personal professional development plan

These items identified for possible change by the study participants are distributed across each of the leadership frameworks, whether one is using the Oberg (1995) framework (Table 7.1) or the Kouzes and Posner (2002) framework (Table 7.4). Therefore, it would appear that an expansion of the understandings of the role of the principal in developing an ILSC is what might be needed, rather than a complete rethinking of that role.

The Present Perceptions "disagreement" items and the Future Perceptions "agreement" items offer topics that might be explored by teacher librarians and their principals as they work together in the development and enhancement of an ILSC. In relation to the Present Perceptions "disagreement" items, it might be that the teacher librarian and principals have different ideas of what the principal's work in advocating, facilitating and supporting the ILSC might involve, or it might be that the principal does not have access to the data that shows the need for resources to be devoted to library management in order to enable or enhance instructional programs. In relation to Future Perceptions "agreement" items, it might be that neither the principals nor the teacher librarians had thought of these ways to support the development of information literate school communities. For example, the Future Perception item, "The principal informs new staff about the importance of collaborating with the teacher librarian", was identified by eleven out of twelve of the respondent groups across six countries as a task requiring significantly more attention by principals in the future.

Conclusion

The themes emerging from research on the role of the principal in developing information literate school communities have been analyzed in two ways in this chapter: (a) in terms of the Five Practices and Ten Commitments of the Kouzes and Posner (2002) leadership model, and (b) in terms of opportunities for expanding our understandings of the role of the principal in developing the ILSC, in both theory and practice. The first analysis showed the role of the principal in developing an ILSC presented in the Oberg (1995) framework to be consistent with general leadership framework of Kouzes and Posner (2002). The second analysis showed that the some of the findings from the international study of the role of the principal in developing ILSCs present opportunities for expanding the understandings of that role by principals and teacher librarians as well as by researchers. These analyses also offer implications for teacher librarians in relation to the leadership role that they play in the ILSC.

Kouzes and Posner (2002) point out that credibility is the foundation of leadership. Balancing their research with leaders is their research with constituents, that is, the people who are the followers of the leaders. Kouzes and Posner surveyed over 75,000 people around the world to get the answer to the question, "What values (personal traits or characteristics) do you look for and admire in your leader?" They have distilled the many words and phrases they got in response to their earliest surveys down to twenty qualities from which they ask respondents to choose the seven that are most important to them. Only four of the qualities have consistently, over time and across continents, received over fifty percent of the votes from respondents: honest, forward-looking, competent and inspiring. These values that followers most look for and admire in their leaders are core to credibility, and credibility is established when people do what they say. Both the doing and the saying, Kouzes and Posner point out, are critical: leaders must make it clear what they believe, what they stand for, and leaders must act on those beliefs in their practice. Teacher librarians must be clear about what they stand for, they must communicate their beliefs clearly, and they must act on those beliefs. If teacher librarians believe in the values that underpin the ILSC, they must communicate those beliefs and values to others – especially to their principals – and they must act on those beliefs – in concert with their principals.

If teacher librarians expect to have their principals' support in developing an ILSC, they should be prepared to work to advance these broader goals for the school. Teacher librarians should begin by knowing their principal's views of school goals and how those school goals can be accomplished. Knowing and promoting the principals' views of school goals with others builds the teacher librarians' credibility with their principals and helps their principals see the strong connection between library program goals and school goals. A close alignment between the principal's vision and goals and the teacher librarian's vision and goals is of benefit to both of them; together the teacher librarian and the principal can form a strong team. A good start on the road to developing an ILSC might be for the teacher librarian to ask the principal how he or she might help the principal to move forward on one or more of the principal's school-wide initiatives and concerns. As Lance (2001) has pointed out, teacher librarians who contribute as school leaders build their credibility as educators and also increase the willingness of others to work with and to support them.

Acknowledgements

The ideas in this paper come from sources too numerous to list, but the authors wish to acknowledge the many researchers who have investigated the role of the principal in the school library media centre program, in particular their colleagues in an international study of the role of the principal in an ILSC, and also those researchers who have studied leaders in many fields, most notably, James M. Kouzes and Barry Z. Posner. The authors also wish to acknowledge that they have explored the ideas in many previous papers which they have drawn on in the preparation of this chapter.

Policy, Social Justice and the Information Literate School Community

Laurel Anne Clyde

What is social justice? What does it mean for the information literate school community (ILSC)? Why is it important that the school and the school library media centre be involved in social justice issues? The concept of social justice has been variously defined but it encompasses, according to the header of the *Social Justice E-zine* (Goforth & Goforth 1999), gender equality, democratic government, economic opportunity, intellectual freedom, environmental protection and human rights for all people. Article 19 of the Universal Declaration of Human Rights expands on the idea of intellectual freedom: it is "the right to freedom of opinion and expression; this right includes freedom to hold opinions without interference and to seek, receive and impart information and ideas through any media and regardless of frontiers". The implications for information literacy education are clear; if people are not information literate, then they will find it difficult to exercise these basic human rights. In addition, as Article 26 says, "everyone has the right to education… Education shall be directed to the full development of the human personality and to the strengthening of respect for human rights and fundamental freedoms". Schools, among other institutions, are charged with the responsibility for being proactive in relation to social justice. The Preamble to the Universal Declaration of Human Rights states that "every individual and every organ of society … shall strive by teaching and education to promote respect for these rights and freedoms and by progressive measures, national and international, to secure their universal and effective recognition and observance…"

If the ILSC is a school community that places a high priority on the pursuit of teacher and student mastery of the processes of becoming informed, then human rights and social justice issues will be of enormous importance for that community. Indeed, these issues could be said to underpin the whole notion of the ILSC, since an emphasis on social justice helps to ensure that all teachers and all students have the same opportunities to master the processes of becoming informed. Further, since one cannot master the processes of becoming informed without having access to a range of information sources representing different viewpoints and without having the opportunity to acquire the skills necessary to use the information in those sources, then the ILSC needs to be aware of the social justice issues raised by documents such as the Universal Declaration of Human Rights. School policies and school information (or library) policies are an important strategy for creating an environment in which human rights are respected, social justice is furthered, and all students have the opportunity to learn more about both. This chapter will first discuss the documentary support for the involvement of the school and the school library media centre in social justice issues, then discuss the function of policy, at a number of levels, in supporting social justice in the ILSC, and, finally, provide information about developing school information policies and monitoring their effectiveness.

The Documentary Support

The Convention on the Rights of the Child supports the Universal Declaration of Human Rights. The Convention was adopted by the United Nations General Assembly in 1989 and after just five years, it had been ratified by 176 of the world's (then) 191 countries, making it the most widely ratified of the United Nations conventions (UNICEF 1995). Echoing Article 19 of the Universal Declaration of Human Rights, Article 13 of the Convention guarantees each child "the right to freedom of expression; this right shall include freedom to seek, receive, and impart information and ideas of all kinds, regardless of frontiers, either orally, in writing or in print, in the form of art, or through any other media of the child's choice". Article 17 requires that the governments that sign the Convention "shall ensure that the child has access to information and material from a diversity of national and international sources…".

Professional documents in the field of teacher librarianship reflect and provide support for these ideas. The *School Library Manifesto* (International Federation of Library Associations and Institutions 2000) states that access to school library media centre "services and collections should be based on the United Nations Universal Declaration of Human Rights and Freedoms, and should not be subject to any form of ideological, political or religious censorship, or to commercial pressures". In addition, "school library media centre services must be provided equally to all members of the school community, regardless of age, race, gender, religion, nationality, language, professional or social status". This should be true regardless of the state, province, or region of a country in which the child happens to live. The *Manifesto* has been officially recognized by a number of other organizations, including the International Association of School Librarianship (IASL), whose 2002 Annual General Meeting endorsed it. The *IFLA/UNESCO School Library Guidelines* (International Federation of Library Associations and Institutions 2002) support the *Manifesto.* The *Guidelines* recommend that the "school library media centre should be managed within a clearly structured policy framework" (p. 3) that includes, among other things, a collection management policy that reflects "the diversity of society outside the school" (p. 9) and carries statements about intellectual freedom and freedom of information. The *IFLA Internet Manifesto* (International Federation of Library Associations and Institutions 2002) presents school library media centre staff with another responsibility: "Users should be assisted with the necessary skills and a suitable environment in which to use their chosen information sources and services freely and confidently".

The statements in these international documents are supported by documents at the national level (and in some countries at the state/provincial level as well). The American Library Association's *Library Bill of Rights* (1996) says that "libraries should provide materials and information presenting all points of view on current and historical issues", regardless of the age of the users, though there is evidence that the events of 11 September 2001, and the passage of the USA PATRIOT (Uniting and Strengthening America by Providing Appropriate Tools Required to Intercept and Obstruct Terrorism) Act of October 2001, have created tensions among the library profession in the United States over the ideals expressed in the *Library Bill of Rights* (Estabrook 2003). Nevertheless, "students and educators served by the school library media program [should] have access to resources and services free of constraints resulting from personal, partisan or doctrinal disapproval", says the American Library Association's statement on *Access to Resources and Services in the School Library Media Program* (American Library Association 2000).

The Australian Library and Information Association's *Statement on Freedom to Read* says that material should not be rejected for a library's collection "on the grounds that its content is controversial or likely to offend some sections of the library's community". In addition, "a librarian should uphold the right of all Australians to have access to library services and should not discriminate against users on the grounds of age, sex, race, religion, national origin, disability, economic condition, individual lifestyle or political or social views". In the Australian School Library Association (ASLA) *School Library Bill of Rights,* teacher librarians are required to "place principle above personal opinion and reason above prejudice" in order to "provide materials on opposing sides of controversial issues so that young citizens may develop under guidance the practice of critical reading and thinking". The Western Australian Department of Education's curriculum materials *CMIS Selection Policy* statement specifies that information resources should be "selected according to the principles of intellectual freedom and provide students with access to information that represents diverse points of view" on as wide a range of topics as possible.

Thus teacher librarians are challenged to support the rights of members of the school community, including students of all ages, to have access to materials representing different viewpoints, including minority viewpoints, on social and other issues. The school library media centre not only has a responsibility to develop policies and procedures that enhance all students' access to a wide range of information; it also has a responsibility to provide support for the furtherance of social justice in the ILSC, even if some of the materials provided by or through the school library media centre are controversial.

The Reality: The School Library Media Centre and Social Justice

On an international, national or local basis, the record of school library media centres today in responding to the needs of teachers and students for information about social issues, and providing access to information sources that reflect a wide range of viewpoints and the varied needs of the school community, is not as good as we might like, given the statements in our professional documents. Problems have been identified in relation to a number of issues and groups, for example, the availability of HIV/AIDS information for young people (Baffour-Awuah 2002); the provision of appropriate information and services for gay, lesbian and bisexual young people or information for young people about homosexuality and bisexuality (Clyde & Lobban 2001); "closing the disparity gap" between the level of access to reading materials enjoyed by children in middle- and high-income neighbourhoods in countries like the United States and the influence of this on school achievement (Duke 2000b, Neuman & Celano 2001); and equity of access to resources available via the Internet (Farmer 2002). Two of these examples are discussed below.

The availability of HIV/AIDS information in secondary school library media centres in Botswana has been studied by Margaret Baffour-Awuah. She found that "there is insufficient provision of HIV/AIDS information in the school libraries" (Baffour-Awuah 2002, p. 338), "in many cases, there was an average of one HIV/AIDS book to over a hundred students" (p. 335), the few books were shelved in various parts of the library because of the way they had been classified (p. 335), and "school library policies need to address HIV/AIDS resource acquisition" (p. 338). Yet as she points out, Botswana has one of the highest rates of HIV/AIDS infection in the world, with one in five community members infected on average, and with the infection rates for some groups (such those aged 15 to 49) as high as fifty-five percent (p. 332). The effect has been that many of the economic gains made by Botswana over the years since independence in 1966 have been wiped out. Thus it is important for national development, as well as in terms of social justice and individual quality of life, that issues of youth sexuality and HIV/AIDS prevention be addressed through appropriate and appropriately organized school library media centre resources, amongst other strategies.

The American Library Association's position statement on *Access to Library Resources and Services Regardless of Sexual Orientation* (2000) states that "libraries and librarians have an obligation to resist efforts that systematically exclude materials dealing with any subject matter, including ... sexual orientation". Further, all members of the library's community have a right to appropriate library materials and services, regardless of their own sexual orientation. This "includes providing youth with comprehensive sex education literature". However, while human rights issues related to race, culture, religion, and gender are often written into the documents of education authorities, the issue of sexual orientation of students is not (Murphy 2000). This means that the information needs of gay, lesbian and bisexual young people may be ignored. Lobban and Clyde (1996) found that an increasing number of fiction books are being published for young people in which there are homosexual characters or in which homosexual issues are discussed. Nevertheless, their research (Clyde & Lobban 2001) shows that in relation to meeting the needs of their gay, lesbian and bisexual users, or in relation to meeting the needs of users for realistic representations of homosexuality in our society, it is clear that school library media centres generally have a long way to go, despite some outstanding examples of good service. Even when school library media centres provide adequate collections of appropriate material, "school library media centre catalogues may not identify the books with appropriate subject headings, and there seem to be few libraries that are providing any special services based on the books. Censorship attempts and challenges have resulted in further restrictions on access" (Clyde & Lobban 2001, p. 28).

Freedom of access to information and literature for young people, freedom of expression, access to information and books reflecting a diversity of views and lifestyles, freedom from the restraints of unnecessary censorship, equitable access to resources and services that will promote their welfare and personal development as citizens – these rights, enshrined in the Universal Declaration of Human Rights and the Convention on the Rights of the Child, and in important professional documents, are beyond the experience of many users of school library media centres. Further, the position statement on *Access to Resources and Services in the School Library Program* (American Library Association 2000) identifies "major barriers" that separate students from resources; these barriers "include but are not limited to: imposing age or grade level restrictions on the use of resources, limiting the use of interlibrary loan and access to electronic information, charging fees for information in specific formats, requiring permission from parents or teachers, establishing restricted shelves or closed collections, and labeling".

Information Policy and the ILSC

The IFLA/UNESCO *School Library Guidelines* state that "The school library provides information and ideas that are fundamental to functioning successfully in our increasingly information- and knowledge-based present day society. The school library media centre equips students with lifelong learning skills and develops their imagination, thereby enabling them to live as responsible citizens". Social justice is served not just by ensuring free and equitable access to information, but also by providing opportunities for students to develop the information skills that will enable them to function effectively in an information society, and by meeting the special needs of particular groups. In addition, the members of the ILSC should be aware of the existence and needs of special groups within their own community and elsewhere. Not only does this require the provision of resources and services, but those resources need to be accessible (for example through the school library media centre catalogue or the school library media centre web site).

Policies can be seen as a way of ensuring that resources and services will be provided that meet user needs in this context, and that those resources and services will be accessible to those who need them. Policies also help to ensure that people in the school community are not discriminated against in terms of access to resources and services, and that people in the school community have access to information related to social justice issues. Policies can indicate goals for the ILSC, set directions, and provide guidance for decision-making. They can assist in the development of quality library and information services that meet the needs of members of the school community within the context of national and international guidelines. "Policies, procedures and rules related to the use of resources and services support free and open access to information", says the position statement on *Access to Resources and Services in the School Library Media Program* (American Library Association 2000). However, there is another side to this. Care needs to be taken so that policies do not become a form of social control – a way of protecting the library staff rather than protecting the rights of users. Policies should not be seen as a way of forcing teachers and students into conformity to a rigid set of requirements for use of the school library media centre and its services, regardless of their needs.

"The school library should be managed within a clearly structured policy framework. The library policy should be devised bearing in mind the overarching policies and needs of the school and should reflect its ethos, aims and objectives as well as its reality", according to the IFLA/UNESCO *School Library Guidelines*. The Canadian Library Association's *Statement on Effective School Library Programs in Canada* (2000) says, "the school library exists within a particular context and is shaped by policy set at national, provincial and local levels, by professional standards and research, by educational objectives and curriculum requirements, and by the expectations of the administration, the staff and the community". The ASLA *Policy Statement – Resource Provision* (1994) confirms this: "…the development of the school library resource centre is the responsibility of the teacher librarian working in collaboration with all staff and within a framework of broader school policies". Although these documents refer to a "library policy", in fact many schools now feel the need for an "information policy" that encompasses what would formerly have been the library policy. The school's information policy should not be written by the teacher librarian alone, but in collaboration with the school administration and teaching staff (and in some cases, working also with the school board, representatives of the school district, and/or representatives of parent groups), and in the context of wider policies. The information policy is likely to have the support of the school community only if the school community knows about it, contributes to it, and understands its provisions. The final policy document should be the result of wide consultation and discussion within the school community.

Contents of the Information Policy Document

The content of the school information and library policy should reflect information policy at what Lyn Hay (1999) has called the macro and the micro levels. The macro level includes international standards and guidelines, national documents, public policy issues, legislation, and social issues. These might include such things as international conventions and national laws on copyright, legislation related to intellectual property and fair use, freedom of access to information, the right to privacy, data protection requirements, and the provisions of legislation such as the Americans With Disabilities Act (and similar legislation in other countries). In addition, the reported results of major research projects may help to inform information and library policy in a school. At the micro level, the teacher librarian and others who are drafting the school's information policy, need to be aware of the information flows within the school, the needs of particular groups within the school, the ways in which information and resources are used in teaching, the characteristics of the information users in the school, and the existence of other school policies such as an information technology policy or plan, among other things.

A number of professional organizations (among others) make recommendations about what should be included in a school's information or library policy, for example:

- The document "should be developed and implemented within the legal framework that applies to the library"; it should cite the laws or ordinances or regulations "upon which the authority to make that policy us based, when appropriate"; "it should be developed within the framework of the *Library Bill of Rights* and its Interpretations" or equivalent documents in other countries; and "it should be based on the library's mission and objectives" (American Library Association 1994).

- "The document will specify the role of the library in relation to the following aspects: the school curriculum; learning methods in the school; satisfying national and local standards and criteria, students' learning and personal development needs; staff's teaching needs; and raising levels of achievement" (*The IFLA/UNESCO School Library Guidelines* 2002, p. 3).

- A policy document should identify "the purpose and the intended outcomes of resource provision and relate these to the school's philosophy and goals"; it should describe the scope of the school's information resources including the availability of resources outside the school; it should indicate the extent of the information that can be accessed through databases and networks inside and outside the school; it should outline the "equity and social justice considerations of relevance to the school"; it should identify priority areas for development and indicate targets for growth; it should provide information about criteria used in information resource selection and the ways in which challenges will be handled; and it should address funding implications of the policy. (Australian School Library Association & Australian Library and Information Association 1993, p. 19).

Gay Tierney and Morag Whitney of Western Australia have provided a "policy writing framework" for teacher librarians (Tierney & Whitney 1993 and 1998) based on a series of questions. They begin with "What is the purpose of the school or institution?", followed by "What is the purpose of the school library resource centre?". The following questions relate to identifying the users of the school library media centre, the roles and responsibilities of relevant committees and school library media centre staff, the educational outcomes of the school library media centre program, and the ways in which performance of the library and its staff will be monitored and evaluated. The final questions relate to the priorities for the present year, and the ways in which resources will be allocated to the various stated programs and priorities. Tierney and Whitney stress that questions can and should be modified to meet the needs of particular schools or school systems.

In most schools, the general information policy will be supported by a number of more specific policies covering particular services, groups, or situations. These might include any of the following, among others:

- *The Collection Development (or Information Access) Policy,* which will be discussed in more detail later, along with associated policies and procedures for dealing with requests for additions to, and removal of items from, the school library media centre collection.

- *An Acceptable Use Policy,* designed to cover issues raised as a result of students' access to the Internet in the school, to protect their rights as information users, and to promote safe use of the Internet.

- *The Copyright Policy,* which should be based in copyright law and should cover both the principles to which library users should adhere in using copyright material, and copyright as it applies to materials created by the school and the school library media centre (such as web pages).

- *The Information Literacy Policy,* which indicates the skills that students are expected to acquired, how this will be achieved, and who bears responsibility for the development of this key skill within the school community.

See "Resources for Policy Development" at the end of this chapter for examples of school library media centre and information policy documents.

The Collection Development (or Information Access) Policy

Sandra Hughes and Jacqueline Mancall (1999) indicate that the way in which teacher librarians develop and manage what is usually referred to as "the library collection" is influenced by a number of factors. Among these factors are the enormous increase in the amount of information available in recent decades and the proliferation of formats in which information is now available. Another is developments in learning theory that influence the ways in which information is used in the educational process and the types of resources that are needed within schools. Hughes and Mancall suggest that school library media centres should now be focusing not on collection development *per se,* but on creating "access environments that reflect the characteristics of the learner, the teaching/learning context of the school, changes in the knowledge base, and partnerships with the broader learning community" (Hughes & Mancall 1999, p. 233). The traditional collection development model used by school library media centres is, as they point out, a "just in case" model, often based on the idea of "ownership" of resources that can be provided for users as and when needed. Newer models focus on access to information and resources rather than on ownership; providing facilities for access thus takes the place of some aspects of collection development. Further, the process of locating information, whether or not it is held within the school, is now an accepted part of the information skills process, and a skill that students are expected to master. This has implications for what has become known as "the collection development policy", a document that should probably be renamed an "information access policy" or an "information resource policy".

Censorship is a particular issue in terms of information access policy or collection policy. Censorship can take many forms, but, as Claire Louise Williams and Ken Dillon (1993) suggest, it is fundamentally moral, authoritarian and negative in that it seeks to "regulate the behaviour of others in accordance with fixed ideas of right and wrong". It is most clearly manifested as conscious, deliberate behaviour, though it may also take the form of unconscious behaviour – as when a teacher librarian claims to be open to purchasing a wide range of materials for the school library media centre collection but deals only with familiar bookstores in the same part of town. Attempts to remove materials from school library media centres, or to restrict access to those materials, are usually referred to as "challenges", though most of these are, in fact, attempts to censor. Peter Williams (1998) analyzed the legal and regulatory framework governing censorship in Australian schools, and found that it was two-tiered: first, government restriction of access to certain materials for the whole community or for some members of the community (usually juveniles); and secondly, local regulations which generally place responsibility for school administration in the hands of the school principal. It is at this lower level, however, that the situation is most unclear, with few local decisions tested through, for example, appeals to ombudsmen or courts. This situation is one that will be familiar to people in many other countries. It is a situation in which the "law of the land" restricts access to certain books or films or other media (for example, for national security reasons, or because they are regarded as obscene), while at the local level, challenges are mounted against library books for other reasons (because it is claimed that they support "disobedience", for example, or that they don't fit in with the "family values" of the local community; see Schrader 1995). Williams says that "it seems crucial that teacher librarian and principal work hand in hand to develop and implement school policies and guidelines, based upon clear and relevant criteria, that will govern the matter of censorship of books in the school library" (1998, p. 20). The same advice would also apply to the use of other media in the school, for example, films shown in the classroom, or links made from the school library media centre web sites to Internet resources outside the school. Any information access policy or collection development policy should reflect this, and the policy should be backed up with resource selection procedures (with selection criteria) and procedures to be followed when materials are challenged.

Relationship of Policy to Procedures and Rules

The school's information and library policy is implemented through procedures and rules. In general, policies are "statements of principle" (Debowski 2001, p. 123) which provide a basis for decision-making. Procedures are derived from policy and may be presented as a formal procedures manual, covering all aspects of information and library provision in a school, or as separate sets of procedures for different functions. The written procedures should describe current practice in the school and should refer back to the policies. In general, procedures are written for the school and school library media centre staff; rules or regulations are created for users. A focus on social justice suggests that regulations should be written in a positive way, to promote and assist access to information and resources rather than to indicate restrictions on the users of resources. Rules and regulations should tell information users what they *can* do, rather than what they *cannot* do.

The school's information policy document may state, for example, that disabled members of the school community will have equal access to information resources that are made available within the school, whether or not those resources are held within the school or are external to the school. This will mean ensuring that the library is wheelchair accessible, that library furniture such as the circulation desk has at least a section that is low enough for users in wheelchairs, and that at least some of the online catalogue terminals are accessible for users in wheelchairs. It will mean establishing work procedures for staff that ensure that in users in wheelchairs are assisted when resources are physically out of reach (and that this assistance is readily available) and that wheelchair accessible facilities, such as a section of the circulation desk, are staffed whenever a user in a wheelchair is in the library. It may mean the implementation of regulations that give wheelchair-bound users priority access to facilities that were designed primarily for them, such as catalogue terminals set at a low level or laptop computers that provide access to the library catalogue.

Monitoring the Policy

The writing of a policy document is not the end of the process, nor is the acceptance of the policy by the school community. The policy needs to be publicized, and decision-makers need to be reminded of its existence. A policy that sits in a filing cabinet represents a waste of time. Whenever there is a discussion within the school community about information-related issues, the policy should be brought out and its provisions checked. If the policy is found to be inadequate as a basis for dealing with an information issue, then it may be time to review and revise the policy.

However, it is not enough to just bring out the policy when an information-related issue arises. There will be changes over time, at both the macro level and the micro level, that affect policy. The school's population changes over time; the curriculum changes; the needs of teachers and students change; information sources change; international conventions and national or state/provincial laws change. Further, social justice is not a static concept. Any information policy document should be reviewed regularly and revised as necessary. Good policies incorporate statements about regular review and updating, and procedures should be established to ensure that this happens.

Resources for Policy Development

A number of print and web-based resources provide support for the process of policy development. They include the following:

American Library Association, Intellectual Freedom Committee (1998) *Workbook for Selection Policy Writing*. Retrieved 28/07/2004 from http://www.ala.org/ala/oif/challengesupport/dealing/workbookselection.htm.

American Library Association, Intellectual Freedom Committee (1994) *Guidelines for the development and implementation of policies, regulations and procedures affecting access to library materials, services and facilities*. Retrieved 28/07/2004 from http://www.ala.org/ala/oif/statementspols/otherpolicies/guidelinesdevelopmentimplementation.htm.

American Library Association, Intellectual Freedom Committee (2003) *Dealing with challenges to books and other library materials*. Retrieved 28/07/2004 from http://www.ala.org/ala/oif/challengesupport/dealing/dealingchallenges.htm.

Australian Libraries Gateway (1998) *Guidelines for the Preparation of a Collection Development Policy*. Retrieved 28/07/2004 from http://www.nla.gov.au/libraries/resource/acliscdp.html.

Baltimore County Public Schools, Office of Library Information Services (2000) *School Library Facts*. Retrieved 28/07/2004 from http://www.bcpl.net/~dcurtis/libraryfacts/.

Bennetto, E. & Manning, M. (1995) *Learning for the Future: Developing Information Services in Australian Schools: Teacher Resource Kit*. Belconnen, ACT: Australian School Library Association.

Dartmouth College Library, Collection Management and Development Program (2000) *Guidelines for Writing Collection Development Policies*. Retrieved 28/07/2004 from http://www.dartmouth.edu/~cmdc/bibapp/cdpguide.html.

Debowski, S. (2001) Policies for Collection Management. In K. Dillon, J. Henri and J. McGregor (eds) *Providing More with Less: Collection Management for School Libraries*. 2nd ed. Wagga Wagga, NSW: Charles Sturt University, p. 115-142.

Education Queensland (2003) *Developing a Learning Resources Selection Policy*. Retrieved 28/07/2004 from http://education.qld.gov.au/information/service/libraries/resource/evalg-develop.html.

Hay, L. (1999) Information Policy Issues: Curse or cure? In L. Hay and J. Henri (eds) *The Net effect: School Library Media Centers and the Internet*. Lanham, MD: The Scarecrow Press, p. 160-174.

Iowa Educational Media Association (undated) *Model Statement of Policy*. Retrieved 29/04/2003 from http://www.iema-ia.org/IEMA115.html.

Lukenbill, W. B. (2002) *Collection Development for a New Century in the School Library Media Center*. Westport, CT: Greenwood.

Montana State Library (undated) *Collection Development Policy Guidelines for School Library Media Programs*. Retrieved 28/07/2004 from http://msl.state.mt.us/slr/cmpolsch.html.

School Library Association of Queensland (2002) *Policy Writing for Teacher Librarians*. Retrieved 29/04/2003 from http://www.slaq.org.au/SubCommittees/Murrumba/PD/whatispolicy.htm.

Tierney, G. & Whitney, M. (1993) Writing a School Library Resource Centre Policy. *Access* 7(2): 12-14.

Tierney, G. & Whitney, M. (1998) Policy Writing Framework Review. *Access* 12(3): 16-17.

Van Orden, P.J. (1995) *The Collection Program in Schools: Concepts, Practices and Information Sources.* 2nd ed, Englewood, CO: Libraries Unlimited.

Washington Library Media Association (2002) *Policies and Procedures Impacting School Library Media Centers.* Retrieved 28/07/2004 from http://www.wlma.org/WaLibraries/policyconcepts.htm.

Western Australia, Department of Education and Training, Office of Government Schools (2003) *School Library Support: Resource Selection.* Retrieved 28/07/2004 from http://www.eddept.wa.edu.au/cmis/eval/library/selection/index.htm.

Examples of School Information-related Policies

ACQWEB's Directory of Collection Development Policies on the Web. Retrieved 28/07/2004 from http://acqweb.library.vanderbilt.edu/acqweb/cd_policy.html.

Apponequet Regional High School Library (undated) *Collection Development and Mission Statements.* Retrieved 28/07/2004 from http://users.rcn.com/libra/mission.html.

Bellingham Public Schools (undated) *Board Policies.* Retrieved 28/07/2004 from http://www.bham.wednet.edu/policies.htm.

Groton Public Schools (2002) *Materials Selection Policy.* Retrieved 28/07/2004 from http://groton.k12.ct.us/mts/matselect.htm.

Palmerston District Primary School (2002) *Policies.* Retrieved 28/07/2004 from http://www.palmdps.act.edu.au/resource_centre/policies/policy_intro.htm.

St Joseph's Nudgee College, Information Resources Department (2003) *Policy: Information Literacy.* Retrieved 28/07/2004 from http://library.nudgee.com/information_literacy.htm.

University Laboratory High School Library (2000) *Collection Development Policy.* Retrieved 28/07/2004 from http://www.uni.uiuc.edu/library/policies/collectiondevelopment.html.

Wilmington School District, Vermont (undated) *Collection Development Policy.* Retrieved 28/07/2004 from http://www.dves.k12.vt.us/html/libpol.html.

Scaffolding and the Information Literate School Community: Knowledge Building

Sandra Lee

Knowledge Management and Schools

Knowledge management (KM) is a concept and management tool that has been around a long time but is still in its infancy in its application to education and schools. It is considered by some to be a management fad and by others as an effective framework for coping and thriving in the knowledge economy. The debate still rages, but it is not the focus of this chapter. The question to be addressed is whether KM holds relevance for teachers and leaders in education who are seeking to continuously improve their practice. The discussion looks at similarities between KM and knowledge building, an everyday framework for teaching and learning in classrooms.

KM has no singular definition because of the very diffuse nature of knowledge itself. As well, key concepts such as data, information and knowledge are defined very differently. Major thinkers in the area of KM, such as Nonaka, Takeuchi, Davenport and Prusak, approach these concepts differently. Their discussions provide good background to the field of KM but are not central to the topic of this chapter.

KM presumes that knowledge exists both in the minds of individuals and in external objects such as policy, documents, processes, etc. Knowledge is often described as tacit or explicit, essentially differentiated by its container. Tacit knowledge resides in the mind, and explicit knowledge resides in codified objects, whether printed or not – in documents, files and conversations. For many people the key to KM is the transformation of tacit knowledge to an explicit state. For business, this means capitalizing on informal or formal channels for staff development, communicating key processes and disseminating information so that it remains in the company, even if the staff holding the information do not remain. The process is thus communicative, and community has become a central theme in making knowledge explicit. What is central to KM is that there is great value in creating and sharing knowledge among individuals in an organization or profession. Sharing knowledge in the private sector increases competitiveness through research and development and improving work processes. For education, the value is equally about efficiencies, but is also about improving practice to build better schools and about shifting paradigms. Using knowledge can also encompass the more grand achievements of advancing professionalism and making the world a better place. KM, when it is used as a work process or tool, is thus appropriate in any environment where people work.

Davenport and Prusak's (1998) principles for KM echo a similar theme. They argue that knowledge originates in people's minds. The building of knowledge is a creative and sometimes spontaneous activity. Knowledge-sharing is encouraged by the organization so the necessary collaboration is supported by management. Technology plays an enabling role. KM can be assessed.

A central idea for all KM theory is sharing. Businesses and organizations will benefit from individuals sharing knowledge. Ideas of community, collaboration and sharing are frequently mentioned in the literature. This is perhaps beginning to sound familiar. It is hoped that obvious correlations between KM and the work of educators are jumping from the page. KM is about building knowledge and managing it. KM is about learning.

To follow ideas of learning then, a strong correlation can be made between KM and knowledge building; the idea of information literacy and related concepts – lifelong learning and, of course, the information literate school community. Henri (1999a) benchmarked characteristics of the information literate school that, significantly, include a notion of collaboration between teaching staff. A parallel can be drawn to what is called the Learning Organization, a KM concept describing organizations that are actively learning.

Educators and Their KM Progress

Influential educational leadership writers have observed that, despite the level of expertise in knowledge construction and learning theory, teachers do not follow their own practices to learn. Fullan states it best:

> Despite being in the learning business, schools and local education authorities (LEAs) are notoriously poor knowledge sharers. There are structural and normative reasons for this, built in to the history and evolution of schools: structural in that teachers have little time in the course of the day to get together to share ideas and refine their teaching; normatively because teachers do not have habits of giving and receiving information (Fullan 2002, p. 409)

Furthermore, Fullan challenges principals to break out of the pattern of thinking that only the school needs to improve. The discussion extends naturally to all educators, indicating that system-wide improvement and profession-wide improvement should be the goal to achieve his suggested "large-scale and sustainable reform" (p. 415).

Scardamalia and Bereiter (1999) have studied knowledge-building communities in schools and the application of information technology to knowledge construction and argue that schools are not Learning Organizations in the organizational sense, as examined by Senge, et al. (2000) and other writers in the KM field.

A number of assumptions are made about knowledge building in organizations in the business of knowledge creation. One particularly easy assumption to make is that those who teach, and thus seek to create knowledge among students, are themselves expert knowledge-builders. The same assumption could be made for any occupation. For example, plumbers would have fantastic bathrooms and physicians would live extremely healthy lives. Teachers, then, should excel at professional development because of their ability to understand learning theory. Unfortunately, this is not always true – professionals do not always personally apply the fundamentals of their skills to their own situation. With this in mind, it is perhaps not surprising then that, even with the abundance of literature on the topic of KM, not much is to be found, studied or known about KM in schools.

Several of the major players in KM, whose thoughts are echoed in the ideas of specialists in information technology in education such as Scardamalia and Bereiter (1999) and Heppell (2003), are focusing on the importance of community. This tendency suggests that, although the actual information receives most of the attention, it not as important as what is done with it – the sharing, shaping, reshaping and application of the information. Todd (2001a) also emphasizes KM as a process that involves people and their collaboration.

Consequently, for the purposes of this chapter, the focus is on the notion of community and knowledge-sharing and, thus, on the Learning Organization. Although schools are institutions where learning takes place, this chapter is interested in whether learning also takes place at the organizational level. The Learning Organization is not the same as organizational learning. Senge's definition is quoted by Malhotra as the organization "in which you cannot not learn because learning is so insinuated into the fabric of life" (Malhotra 1996). Senge's orientation also links an organization's ability to learn to its ability to stay competitive. He includes a definition from McGill et al. who define the Learning Organization as "a company that can respond to new information by altering the very 'programming' by which information is processed and evaluated" (Malhotra 1996).

So what does learning look like in the Learning Organization? The differences are framed well by Senge et al. and their discussion of generative learning, in which ideas born of constructivist philosophies are applied to companies who generate learning through a model of "inquiry, exploration and discovery" (Senge et al. 2000, p. 206). Malhotra contrasts this with his views on adaptive learning, which is less forward-thinking and adapts to change incrementally without questioning current practices and work processes for sustained problem-solving. Thus, adaptive organizations may only look to past successes for answers.

A shared problem between corporate environments attempting KM planning and schools is the gap between theory and practice. Many companies and organizations readily recognize the importance of KM but sometimes confuse it with information management. Schools on the other hand, recognize the importance of knowledge building in classrooms but have not consolidated these ideas for professional development.

But the KM discussion takes on new complexity in the context of schools, teaching and learning. Some experts in the field of knowledge building (Scardamalia & Bereiter 1999, Bigum 2004) are examining how students build knowledge, or knowledge building in the classroom. But true KM is not about producing knowledge in the classroom. Instead, it involves the codification and sharing of knowledge such as teaching practices between teachers, management and organizations. Some authors, such as Todd (2001a) and Petrides and Guiney (2002), see KM planning as a tool for schools to produce positive change. They state that schools "must examine the plethora of data they collect, how to transform data into meaningful information and how, or if that information becomes knowledge to sustain thoughtful educational decision making" (Petrides & Guiney 2002, p. 1703).

Table 9.1 compares approaches of schools as organizations to businesses and nonprofits as organizations. Although oversimplified, with plenty of theoretical gaps, it is important to begin a discussion about knowledge building and the relationship to KM by comparing the orientation of environments in which professionals practice. Debates about the relevance of a business model to school management are plentiful and provide some context in this discussion to support the ideas of change agents such as Senge and Fullan.

Table 9.1. *Comparison of mission for school and corporate models*

	School model	**Corporate model**
Customer orientation	Lower priority	High priority
Competitiveness	Lower priority	High priority
Knowledge building	Achieving outcomes/standards-based	Research and development; knowledge within employees can be leveraged
Place in knowledge economy	Not well-defined	Often a priority

Schools are often characterized as conservative environments in which competitiveness and securing a place in the knowledge economy has not changed models significantly. Often teaching and assessment are still very standardized and product-focused. Henri (1999a) argues that classrooms, at the time of writing the first edition of *Information Literate School Community*, had not changed much. Corporate or other organizations that compete for scarce resources recognize the need to innovate more quickly in order to survive. Staff turnover is an issue that must be met by ensuring knowledge is built and managed so it does not permanently leave the premises. Is it that schools do not have the same concerns as the private sector? Could it be that teachers think of knowledge building as a classroom exercise, not necessarily as an idea that extends beyond those walls and not modifiable for meeting professional needs? Perhaps this partially answers questions about why, as knowledge-building organizations, schools are not communities of knowledge building, and communities of practice.

Knowledge building is perceived differently by students and teachers. The application of teaching and learning methods to classrooms is based on mental models of how students build knowledge. Extensive research has been done on student knowledge building. Bereiter and Scardamalia's application of information and communication technology tools to the process has summarized seven levels of approach to knowledge and how the "progression through these levels represents an educational objective of particular significance to a knowledge society". These are:

LEVEL 0. Knowledge as equivalent to "the way things are". Thoughts are distinguished from things, but thoughts about things are not distinguished from the way things are; hence, the possibility of false belief is not recognized.

LEVEL 1. Knowledge as individuated mental states. Children realize that one person may know something that another does not. Thus, implicitly, there is some entity – a fact which a person may or may not know.

LEVEL 2. Knowledge as itemizable mental content. Children can relate things they know about a topic, and often delight in doing so. Thus, implicitly, knowledge consists of sortable items.

LEVEL 3. Knowledge as representable. In trying to communicate what they know to a reader, students take into account what the reader already knows and is in a position to understand. Thus, knowledge is no longer just something in the head to be expressed but is something to be represented, shared, interpreted by others.

LEVEL 4. Knowledge as viewable from different perspectives. Students see that the same knowledge can appear in different contexts and can be viewed from different perspectives. This is an important step toward objectification.

LEVEL 5. Knowledge as personal artifacts. Although constructivism is widely endorsed by teachers, it is not common for young students to view themselves as constructors of knowledge. Viewing oneself as constructing knowledge is a large step beyond viewing oneself as constructing knowledge representations (Level 3).

LEVEL 6. Knowledge as improvable personal artifacts. A theory or other knowledge object is viewed in terms of what it can and cannot do, what its virtues are and where it is in need of improvement, although still viewed as a personal possession.

LEVEL 7. Knowledge as semi-autonomous artifacts. Students recognize that knowledge objects, like other constructed objects, can take on a life of their own and may be considered independently of their personal relevance. Thus, at this level, knowledge objects become things that one can relate to, use, manipulate, judge in various ways, and have feelings about–just like other things in the real world.

(Bereiter & Scardamalia 1998, p. 675-676).

While the construct of knowledge building may not be consciously understood by students, it is an effective teaching approach understood well by teachers. It is often complemented by scaffolding, another teaching strategy that continues a metaphor of construction. Wood and Wood state that scaffolding "refers to the gap between what a given child can achieve alone, their potential development as determined by independent problem solving, and what they can achieve through problem solving under adult guidance or in collaboration with more capable peers" (Wood & Wood 1996, p.5). They further link the idea of scaffolding to learning situations among adult peers.

It is clear that current teaching practice embraces a constructivist philosophy recognizing that humans build on existing knowledge to form new understanding when solving problems. For those areas with a lot of new content, learners need some support, provided by teachers, facilitators or peers in the form of scaffolding. Scaffolds provide the supportive structure that keeps learners from making "fatal" mistakes and, in some applications, can be a form of support that is gradually removed once the underlying structure gains more strength and shape to stand on its own.

Van Merrienboer, Kirschner and Kester (2003) summarize well the various approaches to scaffolds, noting that they provide support for complex learning tasks that act as guidance for the learner. Many approaches to scaffolding include the fading or gradual removal of support as the learner gains more independence and confidence.

The overall goal, as described by Van Merrienboer, Kirschner and Kester (2003), is framed by cognitive load theory or the idea that what is achieved is an environment where learners tackle authentic "tasks [to] help learners to integrate the knowledge, skills, and attitudes necessary for effective task performance; give them the opportunity to learn to coordinate constituent skills that make up complex task performance; and eventually enable them to transfer what is learned to their daily life or work settings" (Van Merrienboer, Kirschner & Kester 2003, p. 5). Furthermore, these approaches are central to contemporary teaching approaches such as project-based learning, enquiry-based learning, etc.

The scaffold structure can take on a myriad of interpretations and forms, depending on the context and how the building itself is taking form. But what is significant in the literature and its application is that we believe this to be an effective way to build knowledge. Scaffolds are also relevant for building knowledge in any environment, including that demanded by KM in improving education. So what should teachers do to scaffold this learning for peers?

Scaffolding KM in Schools

Scaffold #1 Rethinking Knowledge

To preface and extend the entire analogy of construction, it is clear that building blocks are in place to manage knowledge in education. Teaching embraces a philosophy of constructivism, using methods to scaffold student knowledge building. So why is it so difficult to extend this model to KM among educators in schools? Scardamalia and Bereiter propose a shift in the way we see knowledge:

> On the face of it, it may seem strange to claim that focusing education on knowledge represents a radical transformation; yet educators in our experience invariably recognize it as radical, once they grasp the idea. But grasping the idea is not easy, and it seems to be more difficult for educators than it is for people in knowledge-based businesses, for instance. The reason, it seems, is that in the educational context people tend to think of knowledge exclusively as content residing in people's minds. The conception of knowledge as resource or knowledge as product, as something that can be created and improved, bought and sold, discarded as obsolete, or found to have new uses–this conception is commonsensical to people in knowledge-based businesses. (Scardamalia & Bereiter 1999, p. 276)

Hanson (2000) has also emphasized a move away from conceptualizing knowledge as a product residing in a person's head or in a printed document. The basic scaffold is then rethinking knowledge and moving on to meaningful KM planning.

Scaffold #2 Using Assessment

Self- and peer assessment is another key to reflecting and sharing to build new knowledge, and, again, teachers are well-equipped with these techniques in the use of assessment in the classroom. Sims, Dobbs and Hand (2002) cite Eastmond who uses Scriven's analogy of a cook's assessment. A cook tasting the soup is doing formative assessment; when the guests taste the soup, their assessment is summative. But the idea of self-assessment takes on a completely different form when they extend this imagery to discuss proactive evaluation. Sims, Dobbs and Hand suggest a situation where teachers, in designing curriculum and learning environments, have a "shared understanding of the ingredients and recipes to ensure that the soup is appropriate for online consumption" (Sims, Dobbs & Hand 2002, p. 136).

This analogy could be extended even further to represent an approach to best practice in general. Are teachers able to modify recipes according to understood principles of what works with what? Can we innovate and develop new recipes? And where do we acquire this knowledge to equip us with the skills to "cook" up best practice? Knowledge building and sharing would begin with the participants, possibly within a very large community of practice, what has been identified by Sims, Dobbs and Hand as "shared understanding of ingredients and recipes" (2002, p. 136). They propose evaluation as a design tool, not in a post-development instrument, and the components echo very closely what many teachers and teacher librarians would use in the evaluation stage of any information-processing model. Their five components of evaluation include assessing if project planners met their goals and outcomes and if they had any impact. Furthermore, they state that by using summative self-assessment effectively, teachers focus the process of decision-making on the intricate interaction between created content, student learning outcomes and integrating technology in teaching and learning. Better understanding of these relationships is a key source for improved teaching and learning resources.

Scaffold #3 Using Technology

There is a tendency to use information technology inappropriately in building knowledge in the classroom just for the sake of using technology. Skipping the critical process of collaborative learning makes the use of information technology extraneous and is not true integration of information technology. KM also leads to the temptation of throwing technology at a problem without planning. A focus on people, change and community create sustained structures of knowledge building, sharing and storage so it can be further reused and recreated. Change management, instilling some ideas from Fullan and Senge, are first steps, culminating in applying technology creatively as part of the scaffold.

Fullan outlines key leadership roles for the principal, but he adds that all educators are leaders and they have a "moral purpose…in making a difference in the lives of students…[and playing] a role in transforming and sustaining system change" (Fullan 2002, p. 414).

Scaffold #4 Using KM Planning

Drawing from KM plans in business models, Petrides and Guiney (2002) outline four steps to implement what they call an "ecological framework for KM" (p. 1702). They suggest that further assembly of scaffolding for teachers and schools would include auditing sources and generation of information, identifying information needs with a goal to improved work processes and aligning key processes to mission and visions – all within a construct of teamwork, collaboration and sharing culture.

Scaffold#5 Research Priorities and Personal Vision

Research must focus on the gap between teachers' knowledge of learning in the classroom and the application of these theories to their own professional development. Research should identify the barriers to transforming knowledge, and practitioners must adopt a more proactive understanding of knowledge, one that revolutionizes practice and advances the profession. What knowledge do teachers want to construct and what scaffolds are available to them? Undoubtedly, this will demand some soul-searching. Skeptics who find this approach too subjective may encounter some difficulty but in order to determine how best to apply skills in knowledge construction, we must decide what our purpose is through some personal vision. Open-minded reading of Fullan and Senge would help build foundations in these discussions.

Scaffold #6 Sustainable Changes are the Goal

To create sustainable change there must be serious dialogue. Disregard the philosophical debate and simply focus on community-building and knowledge-sharing. Diversity is going to mean some schools have an easier time in this sharing. Use whatever tactics work for the situation. Although many writers suggest offering homemade cookies as bribes for colleagues to attend meetings and to read articles, serious change agents are going to need heavier ammunition. Enlist support from influential people who may or may not be senior people. Identify colleagues who have personal or professional presence and win them over.

Build your networks and identify an arena in which you can enhance this community. Once you have the attention of more colleagues, use a framework that suits your circumstances. Scenario planning is a model that encourages focused discussion on issues identified by the group. It is also a model that looks at long-term planning. Scenario-planning books and Web resources are easy to find. Research could investigate barriers to change that are unique to educators and identify good examples of community-building where roadblocks were smoothly dismantled.

Conclusions

The myriad of KM theories and models adopted in the corporate world has relevance in schools because KM is about learning. It is worthwhile for educators to begin modifying approaches from the corporate world for suitable application in schools. Conversely, learning theory – the expertise of educators – can be applied to KM. Reluctant participants will find frameworks developed for schools by educators easier to accept. Here research is needed to determine what models or approaches are most appropriate to modify for schools, based on practitioner needs. Practitioners can then apply these models, auditing what and how knowledge is generated, shared, stored and reused in their schools and beyond. KM is part of the information literate school community.

Senge et al. (2000) state small changes are most effective. Realistic, incremental changes build on each other to equal more global change, minimizing peer alienation. The scaffolding process itself encompasses this approach, so that teachers can begin to model what they teach – constructing knowledge as lifelong learners using authentic learning tasks – in their own continuous improvement.

Teacher Librarians: Mirror Images of Teachers and Pioneering Voyagers

Jean Brown and Bruce Sheppard

Introduction

It was in the context of current reform efforts and the emerging concept of schools as learning organisations that the Toronto elementary and secondary school teacher librarians (1996, p. 2-3) asked an essential question related to their future role:

> Are teacher librarians becoming irrelevant stage magicians whose ultimate trick will be to make themselves disappear? Or are they pioneering voyagers, reshaping library information centres by engaging future technologies with critical expertise and imaginative joy?

Within the last decade, reform efforts have dominated the educational landscape throughout the world (Cousins 1996, Fullan 1993, Sheppard & Brown 1996). In spite of such emphasis on reform, research suggests that these efforts may not result in the improvements in student achievement that are anticipated by reformers (Berman & MacLauglin 1976, Deal 1990, Cranston 1994, Fullan 1993 and 1995, Murphy & Hallinger 1993, Sarason 1990, Sergiovanni 1995, Sheppard & Brown 1995). Murphy and Hallinger's research indicates that "at neither the theoretical nor the conceptual levels was there much evidence to link... restructuring efforts with changes in classrooms, relationships between teachers and students, and/or student outcomes" (1993, p. 254). Similarly, even though theories of leadership are moving away from technological, rational planning models, toward cultural, collaborative approaches in which teachers are viewed as partners (Blase 1993 and 1987, Evans 1993, Griffiths 1988, LaRoque & Coleman 1991, March 1988, Pellicer et al. 1990, Weber 1989), Clark and Clark's research reveals that "In spite of the many benefits of working in collaborative environments, there is considerable evidence that many teachers still work in isolation" (Clark & Clark 1996, p. 2).

Learning Organisations

In light of the uncertainty of reform efforts, "the generative concept of the learning organisation" (Fullan 1993, p 6) provides the basis of a promising theoretical framework for the development of better schools. Handy argues that:

> In an uncertain world, where all we know for sure is that nothing is sure, we are going to need organisations that are continually renewing themselves, reinventing themselves, reinvigorating themselves. These are the learning organisations, the ones with the learning habit. Without the habit of learning, they will not dream the dream, let alone have any hope of managing it. (Handy 1995, p. 45)

While the concept of the learning organisation has developed outside of the school setting (Senge 1990), research within education (Fullan 1993, Leithwood et al. 1993, Louis 1994) supports its meaningfulness in the school context. Fullan contends that if we are to succeed in bringing about meaningful improvement "schools must become learning organisations" (1995, p. 234). Louis, Kruse and Raywid contend that:

> The current reform movement focuses on structural and curricular changes as the main ingredients of effective schools, but pays less attention to altering the day-to-day work of teachers. When schools are seen as learning organisations and professional communities, however, attention is focussed on teachers' work as the key instrument of reform. By emphasising needed changes in the culture of schools and the daily practice of professionals, the reform movement can concentrate on the heart of the school–the teaching and learning process (Louis, Kruse & Raywid 1996, p. 7)

The concept of the learning organisation is grounded in the learning disciplines expounded by Senge (1990):

> personal mastery – learning to expand our personal capacity to create the results we most desire, and creating an organisational environment which encourages all its members to develop themselves toward the goals and purposes they choose
> mental models – reflecting upon, continually clarifying, and improving our internal pictures of the world, and seeing how they shape our actions and decisions
> shared vision – building a sense of commitment in a group, by developing shared images of the future we seek to create, and the principles and guiding practices by which we hope to get there
> team learning – transforming conversational and collective thinking skills, so that groups of people can reliably develop intelligence and ability greater than the sum of individual members' talents
> systems thinking – a way of thinking about, and a language for describing and understanding, the forces and interrelationships that shape the behaviour of systems. This discipline helps us to see how to change systems more effectively, and to act more in tune with the larger processes of the natural and economic world (Senge et al. 1994, p. 6).

While some practitioners and researchers found these five disciplines somewhat abstract (Senge et al. 1994), they and others have attempted to identify other somewhat more concrete characteristics, consistent with these disciplines. Redding and Catalanello (1992) envisage four defining characteristics of the learning organisation: constant readiness, continuous planning, improvised implementation, and action learning. Similarly, Marsick and Watkins (1996) identify seven action imperatives for building learning organisations: creation of continuous learning opportunities; promotion of dialogue and inquiry; encouragement of collaboration and team learning; establishment of systems to capture and share learning; empowerment of people toward collective vision; connection of the organisation to its environment, and leaders who model and support learning at the individual, team, and organisational level.

Organisational changes needed in the development of schools and districts as learning organisations require a major transformation in models of leadership and teachers' roles (Fullan 1995, Sheppard & Brown 1996). However, it is not surprising that leadership patterns and professional practices in schools and school districts are deeply engrained features of the educational culture that cannot be changed by simply declaring new values. "Deep beliefs and assumptions change as experience changes, and when this happens culture changes" (Senge et al. 1994, p. 20-21). If we are to develop learning organisations, the professional leadership of teachers must be developed. The required professional development cannot be delivered through traditional models of professional development that are dependent upon the one-day workshop delivered by an "expert". Ryan (1995, p. 279) contends that learners in this expert model are generally assumed to be "ignorant, passive, empty vessels who can be effectively filled up by the expert expounding knowledge". As a consequence of such inadequate professional development, "many teachers and others say they do not want to "be developed". In other words, they are not looking for other people to be responsible for their learning ... [In a learning organisation], ultimately everyone, supported by colleagues, is responsible for their own learning" (Stoll & Fink 1996, p. 164).

In like manner, Sparks (1996) contends that while professional development is essential if teachers and administrators are to avail themselves of the findings of research on teaching, learning, and leadership, it must be considerably different from past practice. It must not only affect "the knowledge, attitudes, and practices of individual teachers, administrators, and other school employees, but also the culture and structures of the organisations in which those individuals work", in other words, a major paradigm shift:

> This new form of professional development represents a "paradigm shift"... Some of the most important of these shifts represent: an increased focus on both organisational and individual development; staff development efforts driven by clear and coherent strategic plans; a greater focus on student needs and learning outcomes; an inquiry approach to the study of the teaching/learning process by teachers; an inclusion of both generic and content specific pedagogical skills; and greater recognition that staff development is an essential and indispensable part of the reform process. (Sparks 1996, p. 260)

Similarly, Cousins (1996, p. 31) states that the redefined leadership role for teachers goes beyond their involvement in school wide activities, that it requires a focus on the classroom and "students' rights to a learner-centred pedagogy". He further observes that if such leadership is to exist, teachers must have opportunities for professional development that needs to take place within the school, rather than in locations outside it.

A major component of professional development in learning organisations occurs as teachers engage in action research which requires them to gather and use new information to challenge the status quo. Sparks (1996, p. 262) states that "to become learning organisations schools must engage in organisational development activities... based on continual data collection, analysis, and feedback, focusing on the development of groups and individuals to improve group functioning". If schools are to engage in such activities, teams may find some of the information they need in the school, but they will also need to look beyond their school for information (Vail 1996). For that purpose, Cousins (1996) suggests that, if schools and school districts are to be learning organisations, there should exist a strong research department that would not only collect and analyse data on the school, but would also compile literature reviews, and routinely scan news media. While the primary base for such a department would exist at the district level, there would also be a team that would carry out a similar set of tasks at the school level.

Galbraith and Lawler provide an image of role structures in decentralised and lateral work environments such as the learning organisation. That image is quite useful as a guide to reflection regarding the role of teacher librarians in the context of the reforms and emerging paradigms of organisational leadership described above. They note that "more companies are creating matching, mirror image structures across as many functions as possible" (1993, p. 48). These mirror-image structures require that there exists a specialist who is a mirror image of another in each division of the organisation or on each team. For example, in each division there would be those with matching skills in specialised areas which would enable each team to have the expertise they need to make site-based decisions. However, we recognise, as do Galbraith and Lawler, that this sometimes presents a problem, since there may not be enough work in the area of the specialised function to support a full-time specialist. To deal with that efficiency problem, these organisations have organised into groups which include members who are mirror images of each other or generalists, but in addition, members have their areas of specialisation. This allows employees to work laterally with their mirror-image counterparts in many aspects of their work; however, the remainder of their work remains specialised. Galbraith and Lawler argue that in the future greater numbers of organisations will be structured in this way, so that most employees will be mirror images of each other, but able to add expertise as part of their work when it is required – in other words, act as mirror images plus when needed.

Galbraith and Lawler contend that increasingly much of the expertise required by the generalists will be accessible through improved information technology:

> Already, electronic mail (E-mail), conferencing on personal computers (PCs) and fax machines, and video-conferencing can connect every person in a company with every other person. Fiberoptic networks and next-generation PCS will permit video calls from anyone to everyone. The technology removes some barriers by providing connection between people. Whether connection leads to communication and then to co-ordination depends on the organisational design. (Galbraith & Lawler 1993, p. 49)

If teacher librarians wish to be pioneering voyagers, or even to be effective team players in schools that are learning organisations, they need to be mirror images of other teacher leaders, while also bringing added value as leaders in teacher librarianship. To meet this demand, teacher librarians will need a unique blend of characteristics in the following four categories: knowledge base, technical skills; personal, interpersonal and team skills; and a particular system of values and beliefs. Some characteristics within each category will be shared by teachers and teacher librarians, which is to say that they will be mirror images of each other. However, teacher librarians will also be expected to possess added qualities – the "plus" of the "mirror images plus".

This mirror image plus concept is consistent with the position articulated by the International Association of School Librarianship (1993) that "school librarians be qualified teachers who have, in addition, completed professional studies in librarianship". It is also supported by the statement from the Association for Teacher Librarianship in Canada (1996, p. 8) that "the teacher librarian needs to be a highly skilled teacher as well as a librarian, able to function on the school team as a professional with competencies from teacher education and classroom experience as well as from library and information studies".

The American Association of School Librarians (AASL) recognises that the educational landscape is changing and that "research on the restructuring of schools calls for the teacher's role to change from a textbook lecturer to that of coach. Students become active learners who create their own knowledge after interacting with information from a variety of resources... often referred to as resource based learning" (AASL 1996a, p. 1). Such an approach requires that members of the educational community "become partners in a shared goal, providing successful learning experiences for all students" (AASL 1996a, p. 2). In this role the teacher librarian works with the teacher to plan, design, deliver, and evaluate instruction; serves as teacher and consultant; provides leadership, expertise, and advocacy in the use of technology and resources; encourages students to accept responsibility for their own learning; manages personnel, resources, facilities, and services that assist students to learn how to learn. The teacher librarian is viewed as the essential link to connecting students, teachers, and others with the information resources that they need and therefore, plays a unique and pivotal role in the learning community. The Association describes this role as follows:

> School library media specialists are an integral part of the total educational team
> which prepares students to become responsible citizens in a changing global society.
> In today's information age, an individual's success, even existence, depends largely
> on the ability to access, evaluate and utilise information. Library media specialists are
> leaders in carrying out the school's instructional program through their separate but
> overlapping roles of information specialist, teacher and instructional consultant.
> (AASL 1996b)

In site-based managed schools the AASL contends that teacher librarians are important members of the decision making team. They act as partners in instruction, budgeting, program planning, and collection development; they collaborate with teachers in designing, implementing, and evaluating instruction; and they access information sources within and outside the school to guide the staff in decision-making (AASL 1996c). Vail (1996) argues that in such learning environments, teams need to look beyond their school for information, and that one critical source, still not available to many teachers due to limited technical expertise, is the World Wide Web. An essential role of the teacher librarian, then, would be to assist others in accessing available sources such as those available through the World Wide Web.

This position is consistent with that taken by the Toronto Board of Education teacher librarians (1996, p. 2) who view themselves as providing educational leadership in a manner that will "encourage and support all students in becoming life long learners and agents of change, who are self motivated, thoughtful, and literate". This educational leadership will take the form of collaboration with teachers; sharing professional expertise in curriculum design, learning and teaching strategies, and resource materials; serving on various committees; seeking opportunities for professional growth; extending professional growth of administrators, teachers, and support staff, especially in technology; and facilitating the sharing of information with other agencies.

The demands placed on schools today, urban and rural, are intensified by globalisation, declining resources, greater calls for accountability, and the impact of information technology. The roles of teachers and administrators are in transition, as all must be leaders within learning organisations and effective users of information technology. As a consequence of these role changes, the role of the teacher librarian as one of the school's leaders in accessing all forms of information required in teaching and learning, is also in transition. Like other teachers and educational leaders, teacher librarians need be leaders in this new environment and they must develop a specialised expertise to facilitate organisational learning within their schools by placing a priority on staff development and school wide improvement initiatives. The research reported here will show how some principals, teachers, and teacher librarians are facing this challenge and help us better understand how to move in this direction.

Methodology

The findings reported in this chapter represent a synthesis of four different but related studies investigating leadership for change in schools and districts. Study One began with eight schools, 139 teachers, and 2623 students from one school district in one Canadian province, but was extended to include a total of four districts, twelve schools, 254 teachers, and 4566 students. The twelve schools are located in both rural and urban centres and range in size from 50 to 870 students. Study Two is a case study of two large secondary schools, in two different school districts in the same province. Both have been recognised provincially and nationally for outstanding leadership in dealing with change and in the implementation of leading-edge technology throughout the curriculum. In both these studies, data were collected using survey instruments, interviews, document analysis (curriculum documents, departmental guidelines and policy documents, school profile information, committee papers and records), observations, and teacher journals. Study Three was conducted in seven schools from Study One and one of the schools in Study Two, and focussed on the role of, and expectations for, the teacher librarian. The schools were visited and interviews were conducted with the principal and the teacher librarians in each school. As part of the interview, each person was asked to sketch a diagram illustrating how leadership occurred in his or her school. Study Four focussed on a provincial school improvement project. Qualitative data for this latter study were collected in eight districts and 19 schools, while insights were also gained from survey data obtained from 19 districts, 155 principals, 279 teachers, 223 parents, and 69 students.

Teacher Librarians as Mirror Images of Teachers and Mirror Images Plus

Our findings reveal that all professional staff (administrators, teachers, and teacher librarians) in the schools in our studies are driven by a moral commitment to help students. Their talk and interests reveal their practice of and interest in pedagogy. They are knowledgeable about the changing economic times, the movement towards a new post-industrial society, and the impact that has on the skills and knowledge students need. Although individuals emerge as strong leaders in their own right, they are also aware of the need for staff to work together, and to collaborate with parents, community members, and other professionals. For example, in one district (in Study One), fifty-four percent of the 122 staff members in seven schools identified the whole staff as providing leadership for school improvement.

The unique role of teacher librarians, in our research, was difficult to distinguish. We found that there is an overlap, instead of a sharp division, between the roles of the teacher and the teacher librarian. This overlap in roles is readily revealed in Table 10.1, which provides examples of the qualifications and work assignments of the teacher librarians studied. For example, all four of the teacher librarians in Table 10.1 have extensive experience as teachers, and three are currently assigned classroom teaching responsibilities in addition to their role as teacher librarian.

Table 10.1. *Teacher librarians: examples of qualifications and work assignment*

Sue	She is a full-time teacher librarian, in her twentieth year of teaching, in an urban school which has a French Immersion stream. She is also responsible also for the school's computer lab which adjoins the learning resource centre. She has a Bachelor of Music degree and a B.Ed. (Elementary Education). In addition, she has completed the undergraduate Diploma in School Resource Services. She is bilingual and provides all services in English and French. She is self-taught in computers and, although she does not see herself as having an aptitude for the technical side of computers, she has learned to install software and be the main troubleshooter for technical problems in the school.
May	15 years teaching experience as a high school teacher, 12 of which were as a guidance counsellor. Currently she is one of two full-time teacher librarians in an urban secondary school which is on the leading edge of technology. She has a B.Ed, a M.Ed. in School Counselling, and a second M.Ed. in Learning

Resources (teacher librarianship). She and the second teacher librarian work as a team and are responsible for a compulsory language course which focuses on the research process, taken in the second year of high school (equivalent of grade 11). This course ensures that all students are taught research skills in a curricular context, including the skills of Internet searching for information. Of her role in a dynamic learning environment, she stated, "I couldn't tell you what my role is because it changes every day". She sees herself as a lifelong learner and commented: "I have never felt so ignorant and yet I never felt so accomplished in learning. I have never felt more of a problem solver than since I have taken this [job] on". She concluded: "You can never master it [all the skills you need as a teacher librarian], you are only going to be evolved to the next level. You are not going to master everything".

Ruth	Over 20 years teaching experience. Currently teaching in a rural school. Her teaching assignment for the current year is: 25% teacher librarian, 50% kindergarten, 25% grade six classroom teacher. She has a B.Ed degree in primary education, a second B.Ed degree in special education, and has completed six of the ten courses for her undergraduate Diploma in School Resource Services. Although she has not completed formal courses in computers in education, she is self-taught with a computer and Internet access at home. She shares responsibility with another teacher for the school's computer facilities. She has taught kindergarten, primary grades, grade four, grade six and special education.
Jim	High school science teacher with 16 years experience, currently in his first year as a teacher librarian. Jim has completed all course requirements for his M.Ed in School Resource Services except for his final project (which is near completion). Jim has developed considerable expertise in cooperative learning and is a school leader in working collaboratively with others using cooperative learning strategies. He became interested in becoming a teacher librarian after working cooperatively with the school's teacher librarian. Although he has assumed a major role in teaching colleagues to use new technology in the classroom, and is responsible for much of the school's computer resources, he admits that "I am mainly self-taught". He adds, however, that "I want to know it" and that has motivated him to keep ahead of the technology.

In spite of the fact that there was no clear "dividing line" between roles of teachers and teacher librarians, our study revealed the need for the teacher librarians to have a "plus" (See Table 10.2). They need to be knowledgeable about recent research and developments in teacher librarianship, have advanced skills in instructional development and information technology, and in accessing information and learning resources. They also need an understanding of staff development and adult learning and training so that they can be school leaders in providing training to their colleagues in this area. One teacher librarian saw the task as "building a fire truck as opposed to putting out the fire", and that the aim was to share expertise with the classroom teachers, so that, in some respects, "every single teacher in the school is becoming a Learning Resources teacher". This teacher librarian has made staff training and development a priority. His school was a national leader in piloting new information technology throughout the curriculum, and most classroom teachers were using computers in their classrooms. As he explained, his role is to learn the new ways of accessing resources, and then train teachers so that they are comfortable using it in the classroom. The teacher librarian is then free to investigate other emerging technologies which can help teachers teach and students learn.

Table 10.2. *Mirror images and mirror images plus of the work of the teacher and teacher librarian*

Teacher and teacher librarian mirror images of each other	Teacher librarian: mirror images plus
Knowledge base (Resource-based learning)	
• The practice of pedagogy	• National and Provincial Standards and Guidelines for Teacher Librarianship
• Instructional strategies	• Advanced training in instructional development
• Child development	• The teaching of independent learning skills
• Learning theory	• Access to information/ Information networks
• Instructional development	• Validation of appropriate learning resources to meet learning objectives
• Curriculum knowledge (Theory and Practice)	• Broad range of instructional strategies
• Learning resources – access and use	• General overview of the school-wide curriculum and grade levels
• Children's literature (Primary and Elementary)	• Leadership and change theory
• Educational change process	• Staff development and adult learning principles
• Interactive professionalism	
• Action research	
• Leadership (not management)	
• School and society	
"Model of good teaching practices"	"Credibility as a good teacher plus added

value as a teacher librarian"

Technical skills (resource-based learning)

- Use of appropriate technology (including current and traditional technology and computer technology)
- Up-to-date knowledge of current technologies

- Library user and basic technical skill

- Trainer of technical skills

- Selection and operation of automated library systems, technical hardware and software
- Advanced skills in information technology
- Awareness of emerging technologies
- Operation of a learning resources centre

"Integrating current technology in the curriculum"

"Learn it – then give it away and move on!"

Personal, interpersonal and team skills

- Likes working with kids
- Leadership skills
- Collaborative team player
- Flexible and open to ideas of others
- Pleasant, friendly personality

- Assertive but not threatening
- Approachable and collegial
- Coach and peer tutor

- Good communicator
- Good presentation skills

- Risk taker
- Group facilitator and trainer
- Instructional leader
- Creator of a collaborative culture
- High tolerance for change and innovation
- Entrepreneurial/ business skills
- Advanced presentation skills
- Transformational leader/leader as servant
- Delegation and time management skills
- Management skills

"A spark in the eye for kids and teaching"

"A spark in the eye for independent lifelong learning"

Values and beliefs

- Equality of educational opportunity

- Moral commitment to improving children's learning experiences and meeting students' needs
- Resource based learning philosophy

- Commitment to collaborative school cultures
- A love of learning and the value of education

- The value of the research process and systematic instruction integrated into curriculum for all
- The right of all students to be taught to access, retrieve and use information technology
- Commitment to independent, lifelong learning
- A commitment to the intellectual and physical access to information for all

"Preparing students for a new age"

"Building a fire truck as opposed to putting out fires"

Additionally, while all teachers must have strong interpersonal and team skills, if you are a teacher librarian, as one principal stated, you "may need better interpersonal skills because not are you only going to work with other kids in the library, you have to work with the teachers as well." In fact many principals, when looking for a teacher librarian, place at least as much emphasis on personal, interpersonal, and team skills as they do on specialised knowledge or technical skills. One principal commented:

> We all have knowledge of the library, we've all used books all our lives and in our training, so that's the narrow based part. It is the leadership and drive you have that makes the library program work or not. I've had people know about the resources but if they can't make people and the children want to go there, then they're useless to me
> .

Another personal attribute that set teacher librarians apart from their mirror images was the need for them to be risk takers. One teacher librarian observed that to live life on the edge of new and emerging technologies means that there is a need to take chances, to constantly upgrade one's skills, and to keep current. Teacher librarians must be committed to lifelong learning and must exhibit a high tolerance for change and innovation.

Teacher librarians must also have the "plus" in respect to their values and beliefs. We found that there is no distinction between teachers and teacher librarians in their primary motivation in teaching – the love of children. Teacher librarians, however, must also have what one principal referred to as "the spark in the eye" in this respect.

This caring for students, at the high school level, is revealed in this comment from a high school teacher librarian, Jim (Table 10.1):

> I believe in people, and helping people. I believe in showing them the way and holding their hand until they get so far and then letting them go. There is an extreme satisfaction already in this position from watching somebody light up when they see the information they are looking for.

Similarly, Ruth (Table 10.1), a primary teacher librarian, articulates the joy she experiences in helping students learn:

> We were doing an activity today and a little boy, it was the first day he wrote down a sentence by himself. Well that made my day! He was so excited and pleased with his work. It's just this kind of every day thing that I value.

Discussion of our finding to this point has been developed through an analysis of four categories of essential characteristics of the work performed by both teachers and teacher librarians: knowledge base; technical skills; personal, interpersonal, and team skills; and values and beliefs (Table 10.2). This analysis reveals clearly that within schools as learning organisations, teacher librarians must not only possess the expertise required of teacher librarians but they must be mirror images of other teachers if they are to have credibility with them. This issue of credibility is also critical to gaining the support of school principals who are extremely influential in school wide leadership. Without that credibility, teacher librarians cannot successfully perform their specialist role–that of the mirror images plus.

In all the four studies that we used in our analysis for this work, the principals were identified by all stakeholders as the primary source of leadership for the school. In Study One with eight schools and 139 teachers, seventy-five percent of the teachers rated the principal as 4 or 5 on a Likert scale of 1-5 ranging from providing "little leadership" to "a lot of leadership" for school improvement. In Study Four with 19 districts, 155 principals, 279 teachers, 223 parents, and 69 students, the most consistently high rating (on the same Likert scale described above) for leadership contribution to school improvement was afforded to school principals by all groups. Interview data from all studies clearly indicate that most of the leadership is school based and that, indeed, the principal is the primary source. Even in one school that was struggling with school improvement and where the principal's abilities were questioned by the staff, most recognised that leadership for school improvement came from the principal. One teacher commented, "The principal is attempting to lead the process and is attempting to empower people and to identify strengths and weaknesses, but I don't know how seriously this is being taken".

These studies reveal that principals have a major role to play in the success of the learning resources program. The principals we studied are committed to resource based learning, are student focussed, and eager to engage in initiatives which provide students with lifelong independent learning skills. All eight principals interviewed in Study Three see the integration of computer technology in the curriculum as a priority, and all have made considerable gains in obtaining access to the Internet. The schools range from one of the most advanced in the use of computer technology to ones where it is just beginning, but it is a priority for all, and all have access to the Internet.

Principals have a major influence over the decision to hire and retain a teacher librarian on staff. One principal was allocated a half-time teacher librarian by the school board, but had made it full-time by reducing the music teacher to half-time and using the other half for the teacher librarian's position. She justified her position this way: "there is absolutely no comparison in the value. The school can't function without the teacher librarian in my estimation"; and she described her work as the "very key" to the improvements in teaching in the school. Principals also have a key role to play in the selection of the type of individual hired in the school. One principal mentioned how they had actively lobbied to obtain the type of teachers (including the teacher librarian) they needed and how this was not an easy task: "I'm putting a lot of effort into trying to orchestrate getting people I want here... you have no idea how hard it is... it would take some lobbying". The characteristics principals look for in both teachers and teacher librarians are similar. They want strong teachers who will make a difference in students' learning in the school. Type of degree or certificate (for example, a Master's degree or a diploma), even technological ability (which was seen by all as important), are much less significant than the qualities of a good teacher.

Our research shows that the principal's support can enhance or destroy the teacher librarian's relationship with the staff, and thus success in the job. As part of Study Three, principals and teacher librarians sketched an illustration of their perception of leadership in their own schools. These diagrams (Figures 10.1 to 10.4) are very revealing. For example, Figure 10.1 reveals that Principal One saw school leadership in a traditional, hierarchical model. In her interview, she made it very clear that she saw high school teachers as specialists and as quite different in training and orientation from primary or elementary teachers:

> I've always found that high school staffs were different. Their courses are their speciality, they are the experts. Joan is doing global issues which is resource based learning but she is doing all the footwork herself. She has the background, the research, and the education, so she does it herself.

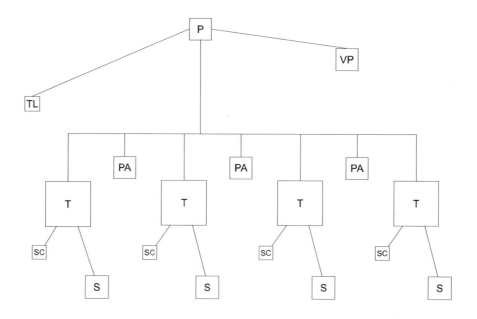

Figure 10.1. *Principal one's leadership chart*.

Codes for Figures 10.1 to 10.4 are as follows:

P	Principal	SC	Student Council
TL	Teacher Librarian	PA	Parents
VP	Vice-Principal	S	Students
T	Teachers	PL	Public Library Board

She then commented, "The library teacher we used to have would go to the teachers and offer assistance." It is significant she used the term "library teacher", for it was clear that she expected the elementary trained teacher librarian to help them use the library and little else, and that high school staffs had to be treated differently from elementary school staffs:

> Our last two librarians were trained in primary, and they expected to see a carry-over from one school to the other but it doesn't happen. It's not that the staff is being malicious, it's just their way of doing things. To force them to do a planned unit won't work for the teachers. It may make the librarian happy. So I told her it's her job to make the teachers happy. If they are happy with the information they are getting, I appreciate it. If she offers help – I may not ask for it – but I appreciate it when she does it. Or if she offers to put up a display, or put something on the bulletin board, I appreciate the helpful but non-obtrusive assistance. I think the teachers feel this way as well.

It is not surprising that Principal One's leadership chart (Figure 10.1) reveals that the teacher librarian is off to one side, insignificant, not connected to teachers or any one else except the principal (the "boss"). Her box was the smallest one drawn, and it was added only after Principal One was asked where the teacher librarian fitted in the diagram. Teacher librarian One is in Principal One's school, and her drawing (Figure 10.2) corroborates the interpretation of the principal's view, and illustrates how she perceives her role as one of insignificance in a crushing bureaucracy. She is not even in the hierarchy; instead, she is a tiny dot outside it. Trapped in such a situation, Teacher librarian One is well aware that she does not have the respect and support of her principal. When asked what is required in order to be an effective teacher librarian, it is hardly surprising that her first comment was: "knowing that the principal backs you is one of the important things."

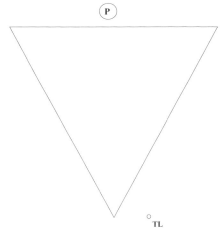

Figure 10.2. *Teacher librarian one's leadership chart.*

The situation described above exists in none of the other seven schools in Study Three. In all other instances, the teacher librarians, regardless of their qualifications (all teacher librarians were trained, either having an undergraduate diploma [after degree] or a M.Ed. in School Resource Services), are seen by the principals as school leaders. Within the interviews from Study Three, there were comparisons made to the similarity of the role of vice-principal and teacher librarian; in fact, Teacher librarian Two (Figure 10.4) is also the vice-principal. Several principals indicated, on their leadership charts, that the role is very similar to that of the vice-principal in that it is a key leadership role in the school; and several teacher librarians compared their position to the vice-principalship, explaining that they work with all staff and are the ones that staff members come to for resources and assistance. In those schools where comparisons were not made to the role of the vice-principal, the teacher librarian's role was compared to that of a department head. In the schools in which there is a definite effort being made to develop strong collaborative cultures, the teacher librarian is seen as a strong teacher-leader, one of a number on the staff. The diagram drawn by Principal Two (Figure 10.3) illustrates a school in which the principal, vice-principal, and teacher-leaders (including the teacher librarian) work together.

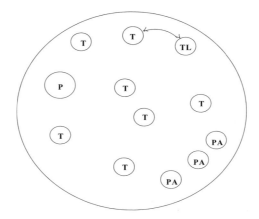

Figure 10.3. *Principal two's leadership chart.*

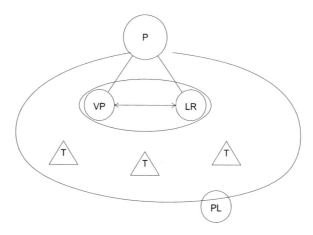

Figure 10.4. *Teacher librarian two's leadership chart.*

The diagrams and comments of Principal One (Figure 10.1) and Principal Two (Figure 10.3) provide an interesting contrast. Principal One believes that teachers have interests quite different from hers:

> One of the things I find is that at some schools the teachers share the workload of building the school profile, but I find with my staff, they like to focus on their teaching subjects and don't like to have that interfered with. So, they want me to do it, which is fine because if I make them do it they tend to get rebellious... They want to teach. They want to be left alone to teach... they want to focus on their subjects and they don't want to be sitting around until six or seven in the evening, talking theory or writing mission statements.
>
> She believes that the school is a hierarchical structure with her as "the boss":
> I view it [leadership in the school] as a hierarchy, which isn't necessarily as I would like to see it, but I still see me as the centre of movement, forcing the staff to take action. They learned last year that I wasn't going to back off. If things had to be done, I was going to do it. I still see myself as being a pusher even when the staff doesn't want to be pushed. If I have a strong vision of something I believe in, I might go ahead with it even if the staff doesn't agree with it. Simply because I believe sometimes they don't make decisions that might be best for the community, but might be best for themselves... My vision is to get Stemnet [computer Internet access] in this school, and whatever I have to do to get it, I will do it.

Being at all times the formal leader, she cannot change roles and become at other times a committee member, a team player. She observed of committees:

> I told the technology committee I didn't even want to be on it, but the committee didn't move it for a year, so I gave it another push. So even though I've attempted to set up these committees, they haven't worked in the sense that they haven't taken ownership of it.

Principal Two, on the other hand, recognises that at times he must assume a formal leadership role, but in his role as instructional leader, he sees himself as a leader among leaders. The diagram of leadership he drew (Figure 10.3) reveals that he is comfortable being a team player. The hierarchy is not totally gone, as he revealed in his interview and as he explained his diagram. In his interview he comments:

> I'm plant manager, to a certain extent; and I think I am seen as the person with the final authority. Any problems that they bring to me, we discuss them, and finally I have to make the final decision on what is to happen... The collaboration takes place but I think they do expect me to have some vision, to spark some thoughts–where from here, that sort of thing. We all bring suggestions, and then we explore them–is this a good idea or is it not a good idea? It's not me bringing my vision and imposing it, it's brought in the form of a suggestion and we look at the advantages and disadvantages and collaboratively we make a decision on it. The teacher librarian fits in as one of the other regular teachers in that group. It's got to be a collaborative process for teachers and teacher librarian to develop resource based learning.

This view helps explain why the teacher librarian in Principal One's school felt so defeated (Figure 10.2) and why the teacher librarian in Principal Two's school, who is also the school's vice-principal (Figure 10.4), feels so empowered. There is a marked difference in the acceptance and support in the two schools. The problem is that teacher librarians may find themselves in either type of situation. Although new models of educational leadership are emerging, in our research we can see the difficulty some principals have in moving towards the collaborative model. It is also clear that, although the new work of the teacher (and teacher librarian) has been identified, administrators and teachers have different ideas on how this work can be best accomplished. It is not difficult to find principals like Principal One who view the school as a formal hierarchy, with the principal being the "boss" and teachers being subject area experts with minimal interest or involvement in school-wide matters outside their classrooms. However, it is becoming more common to find principals like Principal Two who has reduced the hierarchical structure of the minimum and is striving to build a sense of community. It is easier for teacher librarians to work collaboratively in this kind of school; but, although it is more difficult, it is not impossible for them to work successfully in a school with a hierarchical structure. In all four of our studies, we have observed teacher librarians (and other teacher leaders) who are successful in schools where administration still clings to formal leadership roles and lines of authority.

Our evidence leads us to believe that teacher leaders (including teacher librarians) within a hierarchical system first of all need to understand how the principal operates and must work at developing a relationship with him or her. The support discussed earlier, which is so critical to the success of the teacher librarian's work, won't come automatically. Teacher librarian One (Figure 10.2) became a victim, as her diagram of leadership illustrates. Yet, our interview with Principal One reveals that she values expertise. In describing the characteristics she would look for in a teacher librarian, she said:

> I would look for a person who accepted the fact that the staff viewed themselves as their own experts, and would be able to infiltrate that, and have techniques to reach the teacher, to sit down with them and be persistent in reaching the staff, to show them the value of his or her assistance.

In fact, the main problem that Teacher librarian One encountered was lack of credibility as a high school teacher (the mirror image of the other high school teachers). This was based mainly on the fact that her initial teacher training was in elementary education (so she was not expected to be a good secondary teacher) and she also made it clear to everyone, including the principal, that her experience and preference was in elementary school teaching. To command the respect and the support of Principal One she needs to do two things: first, show that she is capable of teaching high school students; and second, that she has the competencies that the principal wants.

The importance of credibility as a teacher was reinforced in observations and data from other schools as well. Another teacher librarian, who is a full-time teacher librarian shared between an elementary and a junior high school, is trained as a secondary teacher with most of his experience in the junior high grades. He is an acknowledged leader in his school district (described as "one of the best" by an assistant superintendent) and running successful programs in both schools. Yet, even he reflected on the problem of establishing credibility in the elementary school. He attributed his success at the junior high school partially to his training and background experience:

> I came into this as a junior high school teacher where I knew the curriculum well and I could make connections where even people in the subject areas never saw them. I could make suggestions based on this knowledge, and the teacher would probably agree with me.

He has progressed in this school to the stage where teachers initiate activities with him and there is joint planning and teaching. However, in the elementary schools, it has been a greater struggle to obtain the same degree of acceptance with teachers:

> There is more reticence. I don't know if it was because I was a junior high school teacher, and they knew it. I certainly had to take some time to get to know the curriculum, to figure out how elementary school worked and how people worked together.

He concluded that the elementary school and the junior high school are "two distinctly different cultures", and that as a teacher librarian he needed to become part of both.

Teachers (including teacher librarians) and principals can and do move from the levels where they were initially trained and become teachers or administrators at other levels. However, they all have to prove themselves as teachers within the particular school setting in which they are working before they can hope to establish credibility and contribute in a mirror images plus role. Successful movement across different levels of the school system requires what the teacher librarian above did: taking time to understand the school, its curriculum, and its special needs. Only then can teacher librarians have the credibility that will allow them to assume a leadership role and influence what is happening in schools. Their relationship with the principal must be built on an understanding of the importance of credibility. Only if the teacher librarian is perceived to be credible by colleagues in the school will he or she receive the support of the school principal. Without that credibility and support, as one principal commented, "The teacher librarian is dead in the water!"

Conclusion

The research reported in this chapter clearly indicates that teacher librarians should be leaders of organisational learning in schools. As leaders they must serve as models of "life long learning", exemplars of personal mastery. Also, they will need strong personal, interpersonal, and team skills in order to engage in and lead the team learning required if old assumptions are to be challenged and new mental models explored. They must demonstrate that they are passionate about the development of a shared vision that is based in deeply held values and beliefs regarding the enhancement of learning opportunities for all students. Finally, if teacher librarians are to successfully fulfil their specialised role, they must have the credibility that comes from being the mirror image of other teachers. This issue of credibility is critical to gaining the respect and support of the school's most influential leader, the principal. Without such support teacher librarians will not be able to function as leaders and will become "irrelevant stage magicians whose ultimate trick will be to make themselves disappear".

Acknowledgement

This chapter is a reworking of a paper presented by the authors at the 1997 IASL Conference which appeared under the title: Teacher librarians in learning organizations, in: Lighthall, L. & Haycock, K. (1997) *Information Rich but Knowledge Poor; Emerging Issues for Schools and Libraries Worldwide* (pp. 197-216) Seattle, WA: IASL.

The Teacher Librarian Toolkit for an Information Literate School Community

Sue Spence

Introduction

If an information literate school community (ILSC) is one that places a high priority on the pursuit of teacher and student mastery of the processes of becoming informed, the teacher librarian must play a vital role in this community. In order to enact that role effectively, the teacher librarian needs to use a range of tools and strategies. This chapter examines the changing community contexts, the tools that are available and presents some strategies that have been used effectively by the author.

Changing Contexts

I can recall, some twenty years ago, struggling to read SAERIS (South Australian Education Resources Information System) microfiche when ordering catalogue records and attempting to manage circulation using a single Apple IIe computer and a homegrown program. Teacher librarians have been at the forefront of using information and communication technologies (ICT) in schools and today the use of these technologies is ubiquitous. In the 21st century, the conditions of this Information Age that argue the case for developing an ILSC also provide the means by which we can achieve this, to the extent that teacher librarians without the skills to use technology as a tool are an endangered species. As the latest edition of *Learning for the Future* states:

> Schools operating as strong learning communities are characterized by distributed ICTs and are underpinned by learning models that incorporate information and ICT literacy (Australian School Library Association &Australian Library and Information Association 2001, p. 9)

Yet technology alone is not enough. As McKenzie so rightly said, in 1998:

> Networked schools quickly learn that their investments in technology will pay off
> most handsomely when they focus on the formation of an information literate school
> community. (McKenzie 1998)

Someone said to me recently that teacher librarians, more than any other group of teachers
she has worked with, have accepted the use of email and the Internet. Most teacher
librarians have accepted the use of technology as a tool; and why wouldn't we, if our brief
is to develop an ILSC? Teacher librarians were talking about information literacy before
the Internet hit schools, when information came in book form. We are all too aware that the
Internet creates as many information problems as it solves.

Online services are a powerful pedagogical tool that can provide an individualized learning
experience – self-paced, with time to engage and interact, to resolve cognitive conflicts and
reexamine information if necessary. While I firmly believe that the Internet will never
replace books or teacher librarians – how many times have I shown students a book in
thirty seconds that provides information they have spent a whole lesson trying to find on
the Internet? – ICT are tools that we must optimize the use of. To students, the multimedia
effects of CD-ROMs and the Internet are enthralling "edutainment", but we need to make
them skilled, as well as enthusiastic, users. I see part of our role now as "harnessing" the
power of the Internet. In submission to the Australian Senate's Inquiry into the Role of
Libraries in the Online Environment, of which I was co-author (Spence & Mitchell 2002),
we pointed out that teacher librarians' expertise in "choreographing the chaos" (Laforty
2001) of the Internet has gained even more significance in the digital environment. Any
effort to create an ILSC must use ICT as a tool.

The plethora of information formats and sources can only be effectively harnessed when
driven by constructivist pedagogy, to create and guide learners through an online learning
experience. Of course the idea of using many different resources and sources of
information to construct one's own knowledge will be quite familiar to those of us who
have been using, and encouraging our colleagues to use, resource-based learning (RBL)
over many years. In South Australia, constructivist learning theory and the implementation
of a new curriculum framework, the South Australian Curriculum Standards and
Accountability Framework (SACSAF), as well as the increasing impact of the Internet and
multimedia, have led educators to revisit the RBL methodology.

> The model of Essential Learnings is part of a growing national and international trend
> to organize Curriculum around constructs designed to meet current educational needs
> by making legitimate connections between disciplines. (South Australia Department
> of Education and Children's Services 2001)

I saw those "legitimate connections" come to life at my own school when a colleague
developed an integrated unit for Year 8 students across English, Maths and Science. The
unit, in which students devised a Web Quest, "Design a zoo enclosure", for younger
students at a nearby primary school, covered virtually all the Essential Learnings required
by SACSAF – and the students had great fun doing it. That colleague was putting into
practice what she had learnt about Web Quests from a course which I presented (Spence

2002b). The same course, which was a South Australian Quality Teaching Project, enabled a Year 12 Science teacher to develop an Inspiration (software for developing concept organizational forms) template as a scaffold to improve his students' lab reports. By helping teachers integrate ICT with a range of methodologies, the teacher librarian supports the attainment of student learning outcomes.

Similar curriculum reforms are occurring worldwide, even if the terminology varies. The e-learning report by Spender and Stewart (2002) predicts that "project-based learning will be absolutely central" to education in the future. Whether you call it project-based, problem-based, inquiry-based or resource-based learning, these paradigm shifts have important implications for teachers and teacher librarians.

The ability to learn anywhere and at any time has meant rethinking how education is delivered and assessed. The "one size fits all" approach, with standardized delivery and assessment in a linear progression through prescribed content, is now redundant. I have observed some teachers react to these changes with cynicism, but such curricular and methodological changes are a golden opportunity for teacher librarians to influence the practice of their colleagues, through the provision of professional development (PD) to support and implement those changes.

One example of this is the "RBL revisited package" which I presented with another teacher librarian to our colleagues as part of a larger Learning to Learn project in 2000 (Spence 2000a). This has since evolved into a "Welcome Pack" that is part of the induction process for new teachers and student teachers at my school. Establishing that collaborative relationship early and effectively is very important.

The Colorado Study (Lance, Hamilton-Pennell & Rodney 2000) has correlated higher academic achievement with state of the art technology being integrated in the learning/teaching and information seeking processes. It has also provided evidence of the importance of collaboration between teachers and teacher librarians. As can be seen from the many workshops published on my web site, leadership in ICT and proactive collaboration with teachers are key strategies in my efforts to create an ILSC.

There have been some who try to argue that, with all this new technology, especially the Internet, we don't need libraries any more, let alone librarians or teacher librarians. As one response to such a view pointed out,

> The Internet is like a library with all the books on the floor. There are no standards, no librarians. The key isn't libraries; it is the librarians. (Kahn & Mallette 2002, p. 4)

However light-hearted this response is, the need to advocate our role in creating an ILSC is a serious one. Yes, anyone can publish anything on the World Wide Web, so why not you or me? As I point out on my welcome page:

> … I seem to be spending more and more of my time at a computer and on the Internet ... so why not combine the best of both, for my own convenience and to share with others? ... Teacher librarians are very good at that – sharing with others! (Spence 2003b)

We can leaven the bread that is the Internet with materials that guide learners to use the Internet, and other resources, including traditional print materials, effectively and ethically. Who better than a teacher librarian to create and/or organize those materials to suit their own learning community?

Scaffolds for Learning

My own foray into web authoring began with Netscape Composer, which remains one of the simplest WYSIWYG (what you see is what you get) or "point and click" web authoring tools. While step-by-step instructions for using Composer are still available on my web site, I have since progressed to using Microsoft FrontPage and am learning to use Dreamweaver. It is even possible to create simple web sites using Microsoft Word or Publisher. Other glitzy web sites may dazzle with special effects, but I believe my knowledge of educational theory and pedagogy, my librarianship skills of cataloguing, indexing and information management, and, above all, my knowledge of the learning needs of my own school community, more than make up for any technical simplicity. I have devised an Intranet which is available across the curriculum network within the school and I regularly update a modified version which is published on the school web site (http://www.adelaidehs.sa.edu .au/ahsintranet/Index.htm) for the community to access outside school.

A structure has been created that is used by both staff and students to support a RBL program, as well as by individuals for online help. There are reSearch pages (http://www.adelaidehs.sa.edu.au/ahsintranet/infoprocess/reSearch.htm) that provide online, self-paced and just-in-time learning support for the development of information literacy skills based on the information process. There are also information "shortcuts" for students – Pathfinders and Hotlists – so that they can spend more time "using" the information or transforming it into their own knowledge, rather than merely finding and reproducing it. More recently, as a result of collaboration with teachers, we have been adding full-blown online assignments. The Intranet is also a publishing medium for student work as seen in the Students section. The Teachers section is intended to become a "virtual filing cabinet" for each learning area.

Using an information process model as an organizing structure is not a new idea, and indeed it is relatively easy to pull together a list of links that will assist learners to develop specific skills such as note-taking or essay-writing. I have incorporated some original materials such as Bibliographies and Search Strategies, which are also published as hardcopy brochures for students to access "offline", to optimize accessibility. Most recently I have developed several templates that are simple Word documents that students can open up, fill in as appropriate, then save under their own name elsewhere on the network e.g., webliography template (http://www.adelaidehs.sa.edu.au/ahsintranet/infoprocess/portablebkmarks.doc).

The concept of templates is not new either. I am simply using the technology as a tool for greater efficiency and accessibility. Having set up this scaffolding and core reference, based on the information process, now, when we publish online assignments, it is an easy matter to insert hyperlinks at appropriate points that direct students to this online help (e.g., if the assignment requires students to include a bibliography, or to evaluate their sources), should they need it. This point-of-need feature shows how technology can be a tool that helps us cater for a range of abilities at once.

Alongside these reSearch help files is a subject index to an ever-growing collection of Hotlists, Pathfinders and Online Assignments. Hotlists are simply previewed and preselected lists of useful Internet sites on a given topic. These, of course, offer many advantages. One my first hotlists was to ensure students accessed appropriate, educational and safe sites when investigating sexually transmitted diseases. Again Pathfinders are not an original idea; just doing a search for "library pathfinders" will reveal there are many different versions out there on the World Wide Web. Some are only lists of links and the relevance and quality of those sites can be quite variable. The Internet Public Library (University of Michigan 2003) provides a wide range of Pathfinders that refer to print sources as well as Internet sites. The Education Department of Western Australia also provides several good examples aimed at teachers and points out that

> In a school, a teacher or teacher librarian can create a Pathfinder to guide students and other teachers to resources that support the achievement of identified outcomes. (Western Australia Department of Education 2003)

On the Adelaide High School Intranet, the Pathfinders are compiled for specific topics, on request and in consultation with subject teachers. As mentioned later, they coincidentally act as a "hook" to encourage teachers to engage in collaborative program planning and teaching with the teacher librarian. Pathfinders provide learners with subject headings to use in a catalogue search in any library, a range of relevant Dewey numbers to browse on the shelves, and point searchers to the Vertical File, videos, and magazines as well as previewed web sites. The intention is to make students and staff aware of the increased range of resources available. This is "RBL revisited" (Spence 2000a) in action. We ensure they have a consistent format for easier access. As the Intranet has grown, and it does so surprisingly quickly, it has become possible to cross-reference related Pathfinders e.g., "Australian Mammals", "Arid Land Adaptations" and "Endangered Species". Quite often as we develop online assignments, we are able to link out to a range of existing Pathfinders and/or Hotlists.

The format of Online Assignments is less consistent, as it varies with teacher input. I make no apology for using technology as a "hook" to encourage teachers to collaborate with the teacher librarians when setting research assignments. I am happy to publish their assignments on the Intranet, if teachers are willing to discuss their objectives and modify, if necessary, to assess process as well as product. I freely use ICT as a tool to reinvent the notion of Collaborative Programming, Planning, and Teaching. The teachers concerned seem more than happy with the end result, with minimal techno-stress on their part, and certainly the students appreciate such readily accessible resources. Every collaboration is an opportunity to influence the teaching practice of our colleagues, to help build an ILSC. My input might be to suggest using Bloom's Taxonomy to redesign the question, or to suggest including an assessment rubric (Schrock 2003), or even to point them to an existing Web Quest (Spence 2000b) on their topic. Teachers are even more amenable when you point out that such efforts will reduce the risk of plagiarism.

As one example, I collaborated with an art teacher to design a carefully-structured research task on Baroque art. Students followed explicit step-by-step instructions (saving and inserting images, electronic note-taking, bibliographic record-keeping etc) online, in order to complete an artistic analysis of a selected image of Baroque art, all on screen. Only the completed analysis was printed out for assessment. The students then used their newfound *knowledge,* not mere information, on Baroque art techniques to create their own Baroque-style portraits, including the picture frame. These students became *knowledge makers* rather than *information finders.* This also illustrates that not all online assignments have to be full-blown Web Quests, which can be quite time-consuming.

It is amazing how big things grow from small beginnings. We have just renamed the Intranet, *The Virtual Library,* because it now allows users to navigate between the Amlib library catalogue (which now includes direct access to catalogued web sites), the Intranet (with all its Pathfinders and online assignments), their Internet and email accounts, and networked CD-ROM resources, as well as a variety of other programs. This infrastructure effectively provides an information portal customized to our school community.

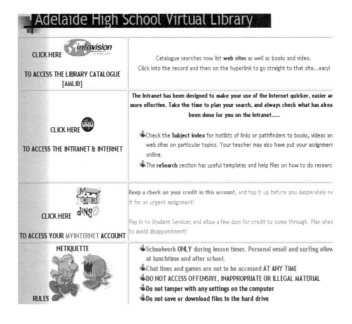

Figure 11.1. *Splash screen when the Adelaide High School Virtual Library is launched*

As Todd points out:

> Focusing on enabling library users to actively engage with ease in this complex, dynamically changing information environment should be a fundamental direction of information literacy initiatives … There is some clear evidence that information searchers are facing some real challenges and barriers to effective information seeking in digital environments. It is an important time for those engaged in formation literacy instruction to respond collaboratively, creatively and transformatively, based on an understanding of information needs and learning design, to ensure information seekers are able to engage meaningfully and purposefully in their information world. (Todd 2000).

Using technology as a tool to repackage information to suit your own learning community maximizes the accessibility of your expertise as a teacher librarian. It may appear that it places greater demands on your time and energy: you need extra training to use web-authoring programs; you need extra time to create such an intranet. Some handy hints on building an intranet and other practical suggestions have been posted on my web site. But once the groundwork has been done, it can be used over and over again, with minimal maintenance. You don't need to be the only one to do the work – your IT coordinator should be of assistance here. Train others to help, or even allow teachers to self publish, perhaps using templates that you create. Provided you employ appropriate backup procedures, valuable material will not be lost but will grow into a rich accumulation of knowledge and expertise; this is what knowledge management is about. When a teacher leaves the school, their materials and assignments need not go with them. Each year new assignments can be added or existing ones adjusted to suit new teachers and new classes. I see this function as the equivalent of any other collection development process, and just as essential. We select books to put on the shelf; in this digital age we must also select digital information and maximize its accessibility. The bonus is that in the process we have the opportunity to significantly influence the practice of our colleagues and to build an ILSC.

Teacher Librarian as PD Provider

Unless you are in a very small school with a well-staffed school library media centre (an unlikely combination), it is not feasible for the teacher librarian to work directly with every student, or even every class, in order to develop their information literacy skills. We must work with and through our fellow teachers. By collaborating on instructional design and by providing relevant PD for teachers, teacher librarians can affect the learning outcomes of far more students than by working as an individual with a few classes. Not only is that approach a more efficient and pervasive use of your expertise; as a bonus it can earn you the gratitude of your colleagues, as they come to appreciate your efforts in easing their workload and enhancing their practice. This approach works towards an ILSC that includes staff as well as students.

I am neither the first nor the last teacher librarian to move beyond planning units of work collaboratively to offering PD activities to my colleagues. Again, becoming a PD provider for groups of colleagues maximizes the accessibility of your expertise as a teacher librarian. One of the main reasons I developed my own web site was to share my PD materials with other teacher librarians and educators. It is through PD activities such as these that the culture of a school can come to take for granted the use of ICT as tool, and come to value the expertise of the teacher librarian; all to achieve improved student learning outcomes.

If we keep up-to-date with our own PD, teacher librarians can be several steps ahead of other teachers. We are at the leading edge of curriculum reforms because we want our collections to be relevant. We know that computers appeared first in many school libraries. We are no longer bedazzled by the technology; we view it as a tool and are familiar with all its shortcomings as well as its potential effectiveness. We are also well aware of how the learning and teaching context has changed. This requires us to reshape, not reinvent, what we do. Equally we can see how some things don't change – classroom teachers are still overworked and underpaid and deserve our support. I believe a very important part of our role is a support service for our colleagues. By working with them we are also working indirectly to improve the learning outcomes of our students.

Working on committees and projects, as I did with a Learning to Learn project, hones your teamwork and collaborative skills, while also boosting your confidence to speak up in larger groups. It also raises your profile with other teachers. Speaking to large groups may be intimidating initially but it does become easier with time and practice. Try "practising" on student teachers – I present an resource-based learning seminar for all new student teachers entering my school as part of their induction – and have an important influence on our future teachers. You can also "recycle" presentations for different groups. I don't believe in "reinventing the wheel", which is why I offer my PD materials to other educators on my web site. And we can offer such a wide range of PD to any audience of educators: teaching information skills, integrating ICT, how to reduce plagiarism, constructing Web Quests etc. I invite you to adopt, adapt and share what I have published on my web site provided you seek my permission beforehand.

It is not that big a step to move from collaborating with individual teachers … to small groups, on committees or in faculties … to larger, maybe whole staff groups … then even to a world wide audience via your own web site. It is not a huge leap, but a series of small steps. Remember that the ILSC includes teachers too!

Investing some of your time and energy into PD also has the effect of considerably raising your profile with the staff at your school, especially the principal. Your proactivity will not go unnoticed, especially when it also raises the profile of the school. When the Adelaide High School Intranet won an award for the school, for leadership in ICT, the award was given pride of place in my principal's office. Letters from conference organizers sent to my principal thanking me for my contribution were more than ego-boosting. Such feedback increases my influence and people are more prepared to listen to my other ideas for creating an ILSC.

Advocacy and Professional Networks

Advocacy is an essential ingredient in the creation of an ILSC. If we don't believe in our mission and our ability to carry it through, then how can our community? The American Library Association reminds us that:

> Technology is changing how we live, learn, work and govern. Library advocates must speak out for the importance of information literacy and the critical role of libraries and librarians. (American Library Association 2001, p. 2)

Before you can create an ILSC you must be part of that community. "Classroom refugees" who treat the school library media centre like their own personal palisade are nonstarters in this quest. The school community is however a dynamic organization. Staff turnover alone requires you to constantly induct new staff. A constant stream of new students, changes in curriculum, shifts in departmental goalposts: these all demand flexibility, adaptability but above all persistence, patience and a passionate belief in your own role and mission within that community.

That belief, that passion, enthusiasm and energy can only be maintained if you become part of the teacher librarian professional community. Many teacher librarians work as single entities in their schools and that can lead to feelings of isolation and possibly perceptions that they are ineffectual. The enormous value of our professional associations and related listservs like oztlnet or lm_net lies in their capacity to provide perspective, to make us realize that we are often grappling with the same issues in different schools, different states, different countries. Such support systems can always provide practical support and often encouragement to keep up the good fight – from supplying copies of torn pages or no longer available videos to excellent recommendations for professional reading, links to the latest research and strategies to get the principal on side.

In Australia, we have come to rely on our professional associations for PD as well as advocacy, in the face of departmental budget cuts alongside curriculum reform and other increased demands across the different education sectors. In South Australia we have recently combined the forces and energy of three separate professional associations into the School Library Association of South Australia (SLASA). SLASA's inaugural mission is, "A qualified teacher librarian in every school library". While it may not be difficult to argue the need for a school community to become information literate, unfortunately it is often far more difficult to convince the same community of the unique nature of the expertise that teacher librarians can bring to this process. SLASA are working with the Australian Education Union (AEU) to advocate the need for qualified teacher librarians in South Australian schools. As a member of a joint SLASA and AEU working party, I was involved in collating and interpreting the results of a survey of teacher librarian staffing in SA government schools in 2002. The two articles that I wrote on behalf of SLASA for the AEU journal (Spence 2002c and 2002d) enabled us to raise awareness of the issues with a statewide audience of teachers. The survey revealed a staggering eighty-nine percent of South Australian state secondary schools were understaffed by the Department's own staffing formula. Even worse, staff without teacher librarian qualifications filled forty percent of all positions. Even though

> a (qualified) teacher librarian can contribute to the school community to a significant degree, particularly with ongoing curricular changes and ICT impacting on teacher workload. Teacher librarians ease that workload, not by reshelving books but by using their expertise to collaborate with teachers; not by covering books but by providing valuable professional development in the use of ICT; not by checking books in and out but by joining committees to develop policies and practices that enhance student learning; not by chasing overdues but by working directly with students to develop their reading and information literacy skills. (Spence 2002c, p. 2)

If one teacher librarian can help to build one ILSC, how much more influence can a professional association of teacher librarians have? I have developed a deep appreciation of the collegiate support offered by teacher librarian professional networks – so much so that I initiated a local version of oztlnet for South Australian Teacher librarians, coslanet, now renamed slasanet to reflect our reconstituted professional association in South Australia. There are some listservs like aliaINFOLIT that focus specifically on information literacy. All share the same diversity of cross-cultural and cross-sectoral experience and knowledge.

Active involvement in teacher librarian professional associations offers many benefits to the individual teacher librarian, who is, more often than not the only teacher librarian in their school. A lone teacher librarian can call upon the collective power of the professional associations and use the SLASA role statement, or *Learning for the Future* (Australian School Library Association & Australian Library and Information Association 2001), when arguing staffing or resourcing issues within their school. *Learning for the Future* organizes the development of information services in schools into five domains: learners and learning; teachers and teaching; resourcing the curriculum; facilitating access to information; and developing the physical environment. I successfully used *Learning for the Future* this year to change a proposed two-hour cut in assistant hours into an increase (albeit temporary) of three hours per week.

The detailed role statement for teacher librarians from SLASA refers to six aspects of the role: Teaching & Learning; Leadership; Curriculum Involvement; Management; Literature Promotion; and Services (SLASA 2003). At Adelaide High School we have used this role statement to organize and document our team responsibilities. This has made it very clear to all team members, including support officers, how they each contribute to the goals of the learning community at Adelaide High School. Simultaneously, by submitting a copy of this framework to the school principal, we have improved his knowledge of how and why a school library media centre and its staff work as a team. We are consequently regarded as a value-added asset in the school community.

These key texts encapsulate the unique nature of the skills and knowledge teacher librarians can bring to the ILSC. These documents can be considered core reference texts and therefore essential tools for the teacher librarian. They will inform your vision and forward planning by enabling you to see the big picture and work towards it in a strategic, organized manner. By delineating the teacher librarian role and the functional services and standards for school libraries, these key documents act as both tools for your own PD and for advocacy of your role in creating the ILSC.

Are We There Yet?

Like housework, painting the Sydney Harbour Bridge or keeping the River Murray flowing, the job of creating an ILSC is never finished. There are always new students and teachers to connect with. I don't pretend to have all the answers, and I know that in some things, like implementing a formal information literacy program across the curriculum, I have yet to succeed. This year I want to focus more on reading and literacy, particularly for boys, because the promotion of reading is another important ingredient in the recipe for an ILSC.

12

Generating Change: A North American Perspective

Lesley Farmer

Introduction

It is no longer principally an issue of getting information: it's getting the right information at the right time to do things right and to do the right things. It entails keeping up with changing information. The job is tremendous, one that cannot be done alone. More than ever, schools need to carry out their missions as effective learning communities.

As the world seems to grow smaller, because of increased communication and population transience, the North American scene reflects a more interactive mode. Even when the United States appears to act alone and to seem isolationist, it cannot survive in that manner because the world is so interdependent. This changing environment affects education, and also emphasizes the need for education to prepare today's students address an uncertain tomorrow. Indeed, education is certainly a hot topic in North American politics and popular culture.

There tends to be a sense that education is not meeting the bar of excellence. National and international studies point out that North American students, with particular focus on United States youth, do not achieve as well academically as students on other continents. Literacy rates are disappointing, employment readiness is disappointing, participation in public life as active citizens is decreasing. What is the cause? Schools are not preparing students well. The reasons behind this assertion include:

- inadequate resources (both material and financial)
- inadequate facilities (both size and quality)
- inadequate curriculum
- inadequate family and community support
- inadequate teachers and administrators
- inadequate accountability: assessment, intervention, and consequences.

One factor in that analysis is inadequate teachers, which may stem from poor recruitment and retention as well as from poor academic preparation. The environment in which they teach has already been shown to need improvement. Many of these factors are beyond any one teacher's control; at the minimum, teachers need to garner support from one another to compensate for inadequacies and to optimize their strengths.

The short story is that education has to change. An interesting dynamic exists in the United States certainly, and to an extent in other North American countries. Some constituents fear change, so wish for "the good old days" of basic, protected education. Unfortunately for them, too much has happened in the world and too much new information needs to be examined for that model to function effectively. Yet schools do need to be stabilizing agencies, models for rational incorporation of change. Tearing down the walls of present-day education will not result in more fully developed individuals or better-prepared citizens either.

Fortunately, one societal and educational trend is the formation of communities of practice: making tacit information explicit, bringing in the newcomers into the centre of learning, and sharing best practice in order to improve the entire organization. With a variety of studies demonstrating the positive impact of professional development on student achievement, the implementation of communities of practice aimed at establishing a literate school community provides a unifying direction of effort. This chapter outlines some of the major agents of change affecting North American education and describes ways that teacher librarians can act as catalysts for change, with a focus on community growth.

What is Good Education?

If the underlying message is "things have to change", then the inevitable question is: "What should education look like?" Answering this question requires several steps: describing and analyzing what is now happening; determining what should be happening; determining what needs to be done; then implementing and monitoring that action. Another underlying element is the need for the entire school community to be actively engaged in this effort. Current educational thought in North America [see for example *Essays in Education*, 10 (2004)] subscribes to several beliefs about learning and teaching:

- All students can learn; the major work is diagnosing the student and implementing strategies to insure success
- Students need to be actively engaged in their learning, and should assume more control and responsibility for it
- Teaching and learning should recognize different learning styles and needs
- Learning needs to be authentic. Students need to make meaningful connections between school and their personal lives. Projects should be complex to reflect societal realities and to help students synthesize and apply their learning
- Assessment needs to be authentic and multifaceted, aligned with standards, and rubric driven.

These beliefs provide the foundation for schools as learning communities. The entire enterprise thus works to make these beliefs active realities. If traditional schools could be compared to Theory X businesses, where employees are told what to do in a highly hierarchical bureaucracy, then today's schools could be compared to Theory Y businesses, where participatory management is the name of the game. Learning communities would compare to Theory Z organizations where highly autonomous networks of teams have replaced hierarchy. In any case, the basis for these changing beliefs needs to be examined, and school improvement needs to leverage these changes constructively.

Changing Demographics

What is driving change in today's North American education? Most of the factors are external to the educational environment. Changing demographics probably tops the list. Particularly with NAFTA (North American Free Trade Agreement), business has become increasingly international. Materials and labour cross national borders constantly. Downturns in economies of other continents and worldwide political upheaval have resulted in growing immigration, especially in Canada where major cities are true cosmopolitan centres. The attitude surrounding immigration has also changed. The traditional image of the "melting pot" where foreigners became acculturated and Americanized has given way to a tossed salad metaphor. Cultural heritage has gained status throughout North America. Mexico, for instance, is realizing the need to maintain the languages and cultural identities of indigenous peoples before they become extinct. Populations of new Americans in the United States tend to join their first country counterparts who emigrated earlier, so, for instance, significant pockets of Khmer, Samoan and Hmong may be found in Long Beach, Carson, and the Fresno areas of California, respectively. In response, all California K-12 teachers need to demonstrate competence in teaching second-language acquisition skills and in working with diverse populations. Curriculum and accompanying textbooks are being modified to reflect these populations, and schools are expanding their efforts to partner with community groups that represent these constituents. These changes have not gone unnoticed by the surrounding citizenry. English-only legislative efforts continue with force; again, in California, which often serves as a cultural bellwether, bilingual education has been replaced by intensive English-language immersion programs in schools.

Within this change in demographics, teacher librarians sometimes feel in a quandary. They have to walk a fine line when developing responsive collections: Should and can they buy foreign language materials? Should library web pages be produced in several languages, or, at least, link to web sites in other languages? Should signage reflect the language backgrounds of the students, or should all efforts be made to facilitate English acquisition? Would library aides fluent in other languages undermine or facilitate student achievement? How do librarians communicate with families from other backgrounds and get them involved in their children's education? What if another culture values education – and parental involvement – differently from the school's stated mission and values? In *any* case, teacher librarians need to learn about the population they serve: their backgrounds, their interests, their needs, and their resources. It is important that librarians view these populations as educational contributors, not merely "people with deficiencies". Thus, librarians need to model positive and respectful communication and engagement. What would make another person feel comfortable in the school library media centre? What resources and services reflect their own identities and needs? What activities can librarians do together with these populations for some overarching mutual goal? Only by knowing each other, and partnering in meaningful activities, can effective service for diverse populations be possible. Indeed, it must be said from the offset, that the members of the school community need to include parents and other local stakeholders, as well as the traditional staff and student constituents.

Money Counts

The economy is a driving force that influences education in several ways. The most immediate impact is school funding. Most of the financial support for United States schools comes from local or state funding. Indeed, education began as a local activity with local control. The present federal administration has strengthened its influence on school support, and the funding base reflects that influence. Even if the federal government were not involved, the economic state of North American nations and their constituent regions would continue to impact site funding because of property tax and the wealth, or lack thereof, in the community. The last couple of years have seen the demise of overpriced stocks, especially in the technology arena. Unemployment figures have risen, and faith in the economy has dropped. Both situations have resulted in decreased funding for schools. As a result, buildings have deteriorated and resources have become scarce. Class size has increased, and "extras" in schools have been cut, including teacher librarian positions.

The economy influences education in a second, more long-term way. Increasingly, schools are seen as preparation environments for industry. That is, schools need to help students understand how curricular concepts apply to "the real world". The National Science Foundation, for example, provides grants to help teachers incorporate career preparation learning activities into the curriculum so students will be motivated and equipped to enter science, math, engineering and technology fields. Increasingly, business is partnering with schools to help students transition from schooling to employment. Service learning, in which academics are applied to community environments, and linked to volunteerism, is becoming a popular aspect of education. The underlying notion is that students will engage more actively in learning and contextualize it in concrete local action. On the economics side, service learning provides a potentially seamless way to transfer from the academic to the employment world.

In both cases, economic realities and school-to-career orientation, the message is that education functions within, and as a part of, economic realities. Many educators fear this impact and want to exist separately from such "corrupting" influences. However, structured interaction between school and business can actually strengthen learning communities. Educators, including librarians, should welcome the opportunity to tell their story to the "outside world". Increasingly, community entities are encouraging job-shadowing for educators, which helps both parties understand the realities of each other's worlds. This interaction can help teachers develop student research projects that contextualize curriculum. One activity that can help students visualize career opportunities is videotaping of local business operations. Teacher librarians can archive these videotapes to help students in their career exploration.

It should be noted that, within the United States, librarianship is often differentiated according to job setting so that public and teacher librarians do not collaborate as seamlessly as they could. Particularly in states where the public library becomes the safety net for student library services, sharing of expertise between public and teacher librarians is imperative. As public librarians better understand the mission of the teacher librarian and realize the academic preparation of teacher librarians, they are often more effective supporters for school library media centre funding. Some teacher librarians act as relief reference librarians in public libraries, which facilitates communication between libraries and also offers teacher librarians another perspective on library service – a service that is truly community-centred. In addition, school and public librarians can start discussing curricular and constituent needs. By understanding the school community's needs and norms, librarians in both settings can complement their resources and services to form their own community of practice to facilitate literacy.

Being Accountable

Related to the economy is the notion of accountability. As governments get involved with education, especially when they fund school initiatives, they look for return on investment: was the money well spent? In the recent United States Leave No Child Behind Act (http://www.cdfactioncouncil.org/act.htm), schools are required to test students annually. Those who do not meet grade level expectations must be given interventions so they will succeed. This is typically translated into summer schooling, although some schools provide tutoring services and extend school hours to help struggling students. All of these practices have the potential to impact library service, especially in terms of longer hours. Current library funding from the federal government is also linked to this Act and librarians need to document their impact with "scientific data". In short, school-wide assessment is "the bottom line".

Additionally, the Americans with Disabilities Act (http://www.usdoj.gov/crt/ada/adahom1.htm) and related legislation highlight the need for equitable education for special populations. By law, eligible students must be assessed and given accommodations so they can succeed. Books for the visually impaired need to be made easily available. Web pages must now be accessible for physically impaired, particularly for those with limited vision. Even physical access issues, such as traffic flow, adjustable furniture, and appropriate shelving, must take into account the needs of special populations. Thus, teacher librarians need to work with special educators to ensure reasonable resources and services for these students and for other members of the learning community with these needs.

The typical first step in addressing accountability is setting standards. Most states in the have developed content standards, mainly in terms of grade-level expectations in alignment with the federal education act. Increasingly, graduation outcomes are also being added to the assessment picture, with the idea that students must reach a certain level of competency before they can advance to the next stage of their education or enter the working world. However, fewer than half of the states have developed information literacy standards. In some cases, the states have melded these standards into other subject matter, usually language arts. Other states used technology standards as a means to address information literacy standards. Librarians would do well to examine content standards in an effort to "translate" information literacy standards into the language of other subject domain. Thus, defining an information task may incorporate the test of developing a hypothesis. By speaking with classroom teachers in their own lingo, librarians gain credibility and have a better chance of engaging students in information literacy activities that are contextualized in academic subjects.

Regardless of the standards, indicators must also be developed in order to ascertain if the students have *met* them; what is good enough? A variety of methods are being used: testing, presentations, products, portfolios of evidence, with an increased emphasis on authentic assessment. This term refers to complex learning tasks that approximate real-life situations. In this scenario, school library media centres play a significant role since much of these kinds of projects involve manipulation of a variety of resources. Indeed, authentic assessment and learning communities go hand in hard, especially when the learning activity is planned, implemented and evaluated collaboratively by an educational team of classroom teachers, teacher librarians, and other support professionals.

At the other end of the assessment spectrum is the increased emphasis on standardized testing. This approach is considered cost-effective and fair; individuals and schools can be compared with one another. Funding and other support is often based on these high-stakes tests, which in turn influences what is being taught. Indeed, in some cases, schools forego "extra" curricular areas such as arts to focus on test-taking skills. Typically, math and reading are given the lion's share of attention. As a result, less project-based learning occurs. Teacher librarians then may have to concentrate on reading support rather than inquiry-based research assignments. Fortunately, the library media program is diverse enough to be able to find a niche in the midst of most school assessment initiatives. The key is to find out who is determining the school's priorities and to join that committee in order to make a difference.

Some schools have transcended course or curricular change to embrace whole-school reform. A number of reform movements have gained ground over the last decade: Accelerated Schools (http://www.ncrel.org/cscd/pubs/lead12/1-2c.htm), which promotes an enriched learning environment for at-risk students; Success for All (http://www.ericfacility.net/databases/ERIC_Digests/ed425250.html), which encourages collaborative learning that leverages students' different learning styles; Coalition of Essential Schools (http://www.ncrel.org/cscd/pubs/lead12/1-2d.htm), which promotes in-depth inquiry-based learning; Back to Basics; and many others. Several models promote active learning, particularly using a constructivist approach where students create their own meaning from the discipline's resources and processes. Other models emphasize the social nature of learning, and structure schools into "houses" or "families", or group groups with similar interests and career goals into homogeneous academies. Some states are now supporting charter schools and voucher programs to foster family choice in education, and to promote competition in school governance and operation. These reform efforts provide a window of opportunity for learning communities. When school efforts are being overhauled, the entire school community should be involved in decision-making. In this atmosphere of change, teacher librarians should take advantage of the situation to make the library's case and to incorporate its programs into the rest of the school's mission.

In the best-case scenario, the school community is using data to drive decision-making about accountability by disaggregating the data according to potentially significant factors. Typically, schools look at data, especially test scores, in terms of demographics (ethnicity, economics, gender) and coursework (e.g., teaching, course planning). Now librarians are beginning to look for correlations between information literacy or library media programs and student achievement. To leverage such possible connections, the teacher librarian should collaborate with administrators and classroom teachers in order to examine the data and develop effective interventions based on that data. For instance, if the World History teacher who schedules library time for his students proves to have students who score most highly in standardized tests, then the teacher librarian might work with that teacher's counterparts to increase library use; subsequent examination of test results will uncover whether library use is a consistent factor in student achievement.

Impact of Technology

Another major factor facilitating, or even forcing, change is technology. More households have televisions than bathrooms. Telecommunications, especially via the Internet, has sped news and documentation to an incredible speed. It has also democratized communication to some degree, bypassing traditional selection and filtering processes to share all kinds of information and misinformation. Digital storage and data manipulation has transformed business practices, aiding collaboration and streamlining supply and demand processes. However, these same advances have also given rise to the digital divide (The Children's Partnership 2000). A direct positive correlation exists between household income and household computer ownership. The fact that over ninety percent of Internet content is in English and is produced largely by Caucasian adult males, points out the disenfranchisement felt by large numbers of constituents in society. Sadly, schools in lower economic areas tend to use technology in less effective ways, having students do drill and kill exercises rather than inquiry-based sophisticated projects. While some might assert that those children need the basics first, one might counter that argument by accelerating learning in the early years so that the basics would be addressed in a more timely fashion.

Technology changes the face of learning communities (International Society for Technology in Education 2000). It has the potential to collapse space and time. Thus, people can plan and develop products in cyberspace on their own time-frame. Technology can also "flatten" communication if it relies only on text; people do not have sound and visual cues to contextualize a message. Therefore, one needs to communicate more clearly and unambiguously. Technology also introduces another dimension in group learning: the need to know the technical aspects of communicating. Thus, contributions may be a factor more of software and hardware availability and protocol than of subject expertise. On the other hand, those individuals who are less verbal or have limited vocabulary may find telecommunications, particularly asynchronous systems, more amenable for discussion.

Particularly as more schools provide instructional computer server "workspace" for students, the library needs to include enough computer stations to accommodate at least one classroom, with additional stations for individuals coming independently to the library. Those stations should be networked to the rest of the school and have Internet connectivity in order to provide a seamless work environment. Likewise, the library should provide online databases that can be accessed remotely. These practices can be problematic, particularly when telecommunications are incorporated. With the societal fear of pornography and child molestation, filtering software is often required for school districts, and email/chat is prohibited. Thus, the benefits of technology for communication are eliminated. Librarians need to think creatively to provide acceptable solutions so students can collaborate educationally. Typically, the use of passwords, teacher-controlled access, and Internet monitoring minimize technological abuse. These issues also provide librarians with meaningful instructional opportunities so students, and the rest of the school community, can learn to be discerning and ethical information users.

Another important aspect of technology focuses on documentation. On one hand, if a person does not save their work or their communication, no record remains to show one's effort. On the other hand, emails and some virtual chat systems provide an easy way to archive thoughts. Threaded discussion is particularly effective at tracing group development of an issue.

This vehicle for documentation facilitates knowledge management, a current trend in learning communities. The basic tenet holds that organizations have tacit and explicit information, which may be otherwise designated as informal and formal information. To optimize learning, efficient sharing of that information is needed. Tacit information is made explicit through social channels, and explicit information is internalized by newer members of the organization. At the site level, knowledge management helps to acclimatise new faculty and facilitates consistency within a department or grade. Typically, this is accomplished through mentoring and the sharing of lesson plans files.

Teacher librarians can play a pivotal role in this function because they have the organizational skills to collect and manage this information and they have the communication skills to share the knowledge with the entire learning community. The present practice usually focuses on research projects, where the librarian collects student guidesheets and organizes them by subject and grade levels. They often develop bibliographies for these projects, which may be associated with the guide sheets; sometimes they develop online Webliographies as well. A knowledge database expands these practices, as shown in this grid:

	Guide sheet	Subject	Grade	Teacher	Content Std	Information Literacy Std	Resources	Student Outcome	Assess-ment
Project 1									
Project 2									

The database can be sorted by any of the fields, enabling the faculty to uncover patterns in instruction that can lead to curriculum mapping. If the database is built as a web site, the associated documents can be hyperlinked to capture all the information – and to facilitate their use by peers. Portions (or all) of this database can be made accessible to students so they can see how their education is being organized. Particularly in schools with outcomes-based assessment, this kind of database can help students develop portfolios of evidence that cross curricular lines. Thus, a science lab report could meet a writing outcome. Similarly, this model can help the learning community visualize how information literacy standards are woven throughout the curriculum, and help teachers build upon other course use of information literacy standards instead of repeating prior knowledge.

Change Within the School Library Media Centre Profession

Concurrent with social and education change are changes within the school library media centre profession. In North America, the United States has taken the leading role. The 1998 edition of the American Association of School Librarians' (AASL) *Information Power* expanded the librarian's instructional role from consultant to partner. With the push for reading literacy, the role of reading promoter and advocate has gained ground in importance as well. Technology has also become a way of life in teacher librarianship.

The library walls have become increasingly porous as resources and services have expanded to encompass the entire school community. In terms of collection development, access to resources has become almost as important as ownership. Instruction and reference service increasingly uses the Internet and can reach the classroom and home continuously. The opportunities for librarian networking, pooling resources and expertise, have also grown, although the implementation of such collaboration has far to go in most instances.

In terms of standards, the library profession has pushed information literacy standards for K-12 and college students, and AASL developed information literacy standards for beginning teachers and administrators in 19945. AASL also revised the standards for teacher librarianship preparation programs, which are accredited by the National Council for Accrediting Teacher Education (2002). The four overriding standards are:

1. use of information and ideas (efficient and ethical information-seeking behaviour, reading and literacy, access to information, stimulating learning environment);
2. teaching and learning (knowledge of learners and learning, effective and knowledgeable teacher, information literacy curriculum);
3. collaboration and leadership (connecting with the library community, instructional partner, educational leader);
4. program administration (managing information resources, managing program resources, comprehensive and collaborative strategic planning and assessment).

Not only are educational trends evident in these standards, but the emphasis on collaboration implicitly connotes a learning community.

The Librarians' Role in the Change Process

Teacher librarians operate from a unique position: the very middle of the school. They work daily with the entire learning community across the curriculum. As such, teacher librarians serve as an educational *lingua franca*, providing the intellectual glue for the community. Fortunately, the information literacy curriculum also bridges all disciplines and grades, which facilitates academic discussion and action by the learning community. Added to this repertoire of educational tools are the librarians' stock in trade: organization and access. Thus, teacher librarians can leverage their power base of knowledge by aligning themselves with the powers in the learning community.

Looking at the nature of change in North American education, most of that change is external, which entails an additional step. Not only does the individual have to change, but so does the organization.

Within that framework, the librarian needs to identify:

1. what change is eminent
2. where does that change originate
3. what role the library should play in the change process.

Notice that the emphasis is on prediction rather than on reacting to change. This approach provides librarians with a greater chance to help shape change. The process outlined here still applies to the librarian faced with catching up to change, but adds the other steps which one may address earlier on in a cycle of change.

First, the librarian needs to examine the library media program within the entire school system. Where the emphasis is on the learning community, the librarian should use the human part of the school system as the lens of perception:

• Who is the learning community? What role does each constituent play? Which ones: gather information, synthesize information, bring people together, make decisions?

- What is the school's mission? What does the school value and support?

- How do things get done? Is the school run by departments, by grades, by personality, by position? What is the base of power for each constituency: knowledge, influence, affiliation, charisma?

- What internal resources are available: human, material, financial, physical, temporal?

- What external factors influence the learning community? Which are obstacles, and which are opportunities? Which are controllable – and which are not?

For each of these questions, the librarian should also ask: 1) how does this factor impact the library program; and 2) how can the library program impact the learning community?

A typical scenario helps concretize this process. Central High School is comprised of 75 faculty, 1500 students, 4 administrators, 1 librarian, 6 other support professionals (reading specialist, special education specialist, technical specialist, 3 counsellors, nurse). The department chairs tend to run the school and senior faculty are highly regarded. The younger teachers are building strength, particularly in the area of technology. The principal is a convener and facilitator rather than a traditional leader. The school's mission is to prepare lifelong learners who contribute to society; traditional academics are valued, and several Advanced Placement courses are offered. Sports is also highly valued by the school old guard, a strong parent-community booster club. The school's financial base is beginning to drop as local businesses have faced economic setbacks and a manufacturer has left. Fortunately, a competitive technology grant has been announced. Unfortunately, the school itself is getting crowded, so while another computer lab would be welcome, space is limited. The community is middle-class and blue-collar, with about half Anglo, third Latino, sixth Asian and African American. The neighbourhood is becoming more diverse, with a sizeable population of new Americans. Standardized reading scores have decreased the last two years. The library is mainly used for research papers, and leisure reading is limited. The collection is sound, and six computers have Internet connectivity.

With this scenario, the librarian might well predict that the school will focus on reading. She could work with new teachers (Farmer 2001), particularly in using technology to facilitate reading: a library Web page with book links and interactive reading testimonials; workshops that show how to use the Internet and multimedia authoring programs to help students investigate topics of interest, and so on. She could identify the key grant-writer, and help get a mobile computer lab, with the added benefit of checking out laptops overnight. The librarian could also work with departments to address reading issues, particularly for English-language learners, and coordinate a database of reading-based lessons. She could join an action research committee to develop reading interventions based on disaggregated data. She might also work with an influential teacher to start a faculty book club. She could brainstorm with the sports booster club about ways to link sports and reading – such as buying sports-related reading and having athletes share their favourite reading materials. The librarian could reach out to the public library to see if they could co-sponsor family reading programs. Potentially, by working with the various members of the learning community, the librarian can facilitate a school-wide reform for reading.

Of course, these perceptions and efforts have to be assessed from the start. Learning communities including librarians, should prioritize needs, determining what initiatives will create the greatest impact, using available resources. To aid in this part of the process, librarians need to be ready with a list of assessment instruments, appropriate for different purposes. The typical tools include:

- statistics garnered from circulation programs
- schedules and calendar of use; use counter hits for Web pages
- surveys and questionnaires
- student projects, products and tests
- library documents: reports, lesson plans, handouts, guide sheets, flyers, bibliographies,
- observations
- individual and group interviews

Not only do librarians need to have the tools, they need to know how to use these tools to assess their own practice – and have improved their own programs in the process. With this kind of grounding, librarians can be prepared to contribute significantly to the learning community, linking tools and analysis expertise. Especially since organizational change requires personal as well as group change, librarians should assess their own needs, and develop professional goals to address those needs. They need to be ready to accept change and to lead in the change effort.

From the starting inquiry to the finishing touches of evaluation and improvement, librarians' knowledge and spirit of collaboration offers a unique perspective, an ability to bridge the various agendas of the learning community membership. Moreover, as librarians network with each other, they establish a library-centric learning community that spans school sites. As such, they can extend their influence across districts and, potentially, throughout the profession of librarianship and related educational groups. Particularly in Canada and the United States, where regional and national teacher librarianship associations offer a strong voice for action and student achievement, teacher librarians can act as effective change agents to foster effective literate communities.

13

Generating Change Through Professional Development: A New Zealand Perspective

Linda Selby and Maureen Trebilcock

Introduction

The purpose of this chapter is to describe how Infolink, a professional development (PD) course for teachers, has provided the catalyst for change in schools in New Zealand. The larger social and educational context of New Zealand is described in order to explain the ways in which information literacy has emerged as a concept and as a framework for learning and teaching. This chapter is organized to provide a brief overview of PD for teachers; a discussion about school library media centres and the development of information literacy skills; and finally, presentation of results from two recent projects that were undertaken to evaluate the Infolink course.

Professional Development for Teachers

In New Zealand prior to 1989, PD for primary and secondary teachers was provided by colleges of education, the Ministry of Education, the New Zealand Education Institute (NZEI), the Teachers Refresher Course Association, and through courses for individual teachers from universities (Poskitt 2001). Schools did not have a direct relationship with PD providers and opportunities to make their own choices concerning their PD needs were rare. However, with the advent of *Tomorrow's Schools* (New Zealand Department of Education 1988), schools became independent and self-managing.

The present New Zealand Ministry of Education (MoE) was created out of the old Department of Education as a policy-only body and other statutory bodies were created to deal with important functions devolved from the MoE, for example, the Education Review Office (ERO) became responsible for quality assurance of schools, the New Zealand Qualifications Authority (NZQA) became responsible for secondary and tertiary level qualifications, and all schools were made responsible for their own administration and management, through single-school boards (Wylie 1997, cited Brown 2003). Fiske and Ladd (2000) provide an excellent review of the impact of this restructuring on New Zealand schools.

As a result of these administrative changes, schools now receive proportions of funding that they can use to select and deliver their own PD alongside Ministry of Education-funded initiatives. This is consistent with Rudman's view (1999) that adults are self-directed in their learning, therefore PD is more likely to bring about change if the program is inclusive and the stakeholders have some ownership of the process.

For some years there was concern that PD often consisted of a teacher going to a particular short course and picking up some useful teaching strategies. Instead, the focus should be on PD that provides the experience and understanding for teachers that actually brings about change in the ways in which teachers think about student learning. Research by Showers and Joyce (1996), suggests that coaching involving in-class observation and the sharing of best practice can be particularly effective. As noted by New Zealand researchers Hill, Hawk & Taylor (2002), teachers need to be able to learn, observe and network with their peers at both formal and informal levels. Effective PD is about improving teachers' educational practice through changing their attitudes and beliefs. The ultimate goal should be to equip teachers with the knowledge and skills to improve their practice, therefore offering better opportunities for improvement in student learning.

In order to better support work in this area the New Zealand MoE created a separate Professional Development Funding Pool to which individual schools and clusters of schools may apply to directly for funding. The purpose of this is to allow schools to develop their own models of PD that are suited to the school's individual needs. There has also been the development in recent years of more cohesive MoE-funded programs and resources for PD in key target areas, for example, information and communication technology (ICT), literacy, numeracy, and assessment.

Whole-school PD has found favour as a model recently, as more attention is being given to institutional change within schools, which is seen by many as more likely to lead to improved student learning outcomes. For example, Hopkins (1996) notes that when teachers are faced with acquiring new skills, the school itself may be faced with new ways of working that are not compatible with existing organizational structures. There is a growing expectation that PD should result in tangible benefits not only for the teacher involved in the experience, but for the whole school. Fullan (1995) makes the point that if we are to succeed in bringing about meaningful improvement, schools must become learning organizations. As noted by Hill, Hawk and Taylor, "the evidence is clear that quality PD happens onsite, where teachers have access to the ongoing support and encouragement of their colleagues" (2002, p. 15). Recent research by the New Zealand Council for Educational Research (NZCER), entitled "Teachers making a Difference", also shows that while most schools allow some personal PD for individual teachers, schools consider that whole-school PD based on identified school priorities is a more effective use of funding (Mitchell, Cameron & Wylie 2002). Developing a culture within schools where staff feel supported, encouraged and expected to extend not only their own teaching practice but also their own professional learning, is increasingly seen as fundamental to good school management.

The impact of new information and communication technologies has been felt in New Zealand, as it has in other countries worldwide. This impact has resulted in an increasing demand for education that is relevant to life in a technologically advanced society. While presenting many challenges for educators and information professionals, it is apparent that to integrate new technologies effectively in teaching and learning, a grounding in information literacy is essential (Probert 1999, Todd 1999, McKenzie 1998). New Zealand education has also experienced a number of curriculum reforms, the latest being the introduction and implementation of the National Certificate in Educational Achievement (NCEA). This new secondary school qualification places a heavy demand on information literacy and research skills across a number of curriculum areas.

These reforms together with the impact of technology have led to a closer examination of the process of learning and teaching and what we should expect from an education system. While much has been said in the literature about technological transformations that are taking place, less has been written about the educational transformations that are needed to create capable thinkers and learners who can not only acquire information, but also actively transform it into personal knowledge (Selby 1999). Despite the emphasis that is being placed on the development of a "knowledge economy" in New Zealand and elsewhere, this will remain a vacuous notion unless we can understand what kind of education will best prepare students for life and work within this "knowledge society". Typical answers to this question suggest that education should foster "flexibility, creativity, problem solving ability, technological literacy, information-finding skills and above all a lifelong readiness to learn" (Scardamalia & Bereiter 1999).

It is reasonable to assume that teachers make a difference, however recent research by Bond, Smith, Baker and Hattie (2000) suggests that the most relevant features related to student learning (other than those the students bring to the classroom) are controlled by the teacher. There is evidence that up to sixty percent of variance in student performance may be attributable to differences between teachers and classes, while as much as twenty percent has been found to be attributable to school level variables (Baker 2002). Therefore PD for teachers in New Zealand is seen to be of prime importance and increasingly individual teachers have to meet PD goals as part of ongoing performance appraisals within their schools. This PD usually encompasses the areas suggested by Scardamalia and Bereiter (1999), with the addition of higher order thinking skills, metacognitive skill building, and the meaningful integration of ICT into teaching and learning. Inquiry learning approaches, including resource-based learning (RBL), are finding increasing favour in an educational climate that has for many years been based on constructivist theories of learning. As a consequence of this focus, information literacy is gaining a high profile as being of central importance to education in New Zealand.

Information skills have been identified in the New Zealand Curriculum Framework (New Zealand Ministry of Education 1993) as being one of the essential skills that all students are to be taught and it is intended that students will learn these skills in an integrated fashion as they work through the eight essential learning areas of the curriculum (Brown 1999). However, underlying the drive for the development of information literacy in schools is an assumption that teachers are themselves information literate, that information-processing models or approaches inform their teaching, and that they understand how to apply higher order thinking skills when undertaking information tasks. However, Henri (2001, cited Moore & Trebilcock 2003a, p. 10) found that practising teachers and trainee teacher librarians in Australia "demonstrated much of the impoverished information behaviour" shown by senior school students. Further, a study by Moore (1998) found that primary school teachers do not necessarily agree on what information literacy skills are. If we are to be successful in teaching students in our schools to become information literate, there is some urgency for teachers to improve their own level of information literacy and for some agreement to be reached about what information skills actually are.

In a case study of one school's journey towards information literacy, Moore (2000) reported on four months of intensive PD and research in one primary school. Teachers identified concerns about students as information users and went on to conduct small-scale research projects with the aim of improving student learning outcomes. This intensive PD initiative provided an opportunity for teachers to focus on information literacy, to make manageable interventions in a supportive environment and to share their combined knowledge to build on information literacy insights across every level in the school. Moore's model in this study emphasizes the "thinking, questioning and mental monitoring" (Moore 2000, p. 2) needed to work through an information problem.

The National Education Monitoring Project (NEMP) started in 1993 with the aim of assessing and reporting on the achievement of all primary school students in all areas of the curriculum. In 1997 and 2001 NEMP reported on the development of students' information skills as outlined in the New Zealand Curriculum Framework. Over this period there was little evidence of change in Year 4 and Year 8 students' ability to find and gather information (Flockton & Crooks 2002).

School Library Media Centres and Learning

School library media centres in New Zealand are well-developed and well-established and there is evidence that some school library media centres appear to be highly effective in supporting student learning. As a further indicator of progress, the School Library Association of New Zealand/Aotearoa (SLANZA) was established in May 2000 and currently it has over 600 members. The Education Review Office states that

> Most schools have good reading resources … Schools in which there is a universally high level of teacher skill in reading across the curriculum and resource-based learning and which have complementary library facilities, provide their students with the best opportunities for literacy learning (New Zealand Education Review Office 1997, p. 10).

Schools have operated for many years with a pedagogical emphasis on constructivism and RBL, particularly in the primary schools (Moore & Trebilcock 2003a). However few schools employ qualified teacher librarians because these positions are not part of the regular staffing allocation. Unless school principals are aware of the strategic importance of this position and the special skills teacher librarians have to offer, school library media centres are generally staffed by a variety of different personnel, including teachers with library responsibility, librarians and/or library assistants, parent and student helpers. There are also many small schools in New Zealand for whom funding a full-time teacher librarian position would not be an option. Moore suggests that because of these factors, it is important to find "complementary methods of developing information services in schools and to promote information literacy through continuing professional education of teachers themselves, as well as that of the information specialists who can support them" (Moore & Page 2002, p. 81).

Many school library media centres have been renamed as Library and Information Centres to better reflect the teaching and learning activities carried out by the library staff, the teachers and the students who use the space. While it does appear that library staff, where supported by the principal, are usually highly committed to learning through the library and have developed effective strategies for supporting students and teachers, the connection between the library activities and student learning is not always explicit. Moore noted

> the links between learning theory, students' development and the curriculum have been difficult to expose in the context of the library, partly because of people's perceptions of the role of the library and the difficulty of actually monitoring the learning that libraries support (Moore 1995, p. 140).

In a more recent study of the role of the school library media centre team and its influence on learning and teaching, Moore & Trebilcock (2003a) concluded that while there were some aspects of an ideal school library media centre instructional program present in the three schools that participated in the study, information skills tended to be fragmented rather than systematically taught. Overall, the schools lacked tools for evaluating the connection between the educational activities of the school library media centre team and student learning.

The National Library and the MoE have recently published guidelines for school library media centres. This document, *The School Library and Learning in the Information landscape: Guidelines for New Zealand Schools*, identifies six key principles which offer a range of perspectives and options rather than setting down a blueprint for the ideal school library media centre or making any definite statements (2002, p. 16). The six guiding principles of the document are as follows:

information literacy: the school library media centre is a learning environment central to the development of an information literate school community (ILSC)

service:	the school library media centre is a managed centre of professional expertise and support for the school community
reading:	the school library media centre is a foundation for the school's literacy programs and a catalyst for the development of lifelong readers
access:	the school library media centre is a hub and an interface with organized systems for accessing and managing information resources
information resources:	the school library media centre is a provider of information resources
resources:	selected to meet the curriculum and information needs of the school
place:	the school library media centre is a student-centred facility designed to play a key role in the intellectual, educational, and cultural life of the school.

These guidelines state that

> The schools information literacy program is essential to learning across the curriculum: all teachers are responsible for implementing this program with their students ... the success of a school's information literacy program depends on the school's commitment to effective school library media centre staffing and ongoing teacher professional development (New Zealand Ministry of Education & National Library of New Zealand 2002, p. 19).

These guidelines also state "people are the key to the library's role in raising students' achievement" (2002, p. 23). These statements seem to reinforce the view that it is knowledgeable people and the relationships they form by working together that is of the greatest importance, together with library systems and structures.

In evaluating the implementation of the National Library of New Zealand's Focus Programme, designed to support school library media centre development, Slyfield (1997) noted that the teaching of information skills was at a developmental stage. Her subsequent report (Slyfield 2001) included a focus on information literacy and reported that information skills were taught in many places in the school curriculum, particularly Social Studies, English and Science. She also noted that almost all schools were taking some actions relating to the teaching of information skills and the models of information skills used most were Action Learning (Gawith 1987a) and a school-developed model. She found that, although over half the schools in the study had teachers who had taken some form of PD relating to information literacy, only a small percentage of teachers within each school had actually been involved.

It is within this larger social and educational context that the need for PD in information literacy as a concept and framework for teaching and learning has emerged in New Zealand. The next section of this chapter examines the Infolink: Information Literacy Skills For Teachers course offered by Auckland College of Education. Infolink is the largest PD course in information literacy in New Zealand and it has been flexibly delivered to a large number of trained teachers throughout the country for at least a decade.

Infolink: A Change Model for Schools

Infolink: Information Literacy Skills is the foundation course for the Graduate Diploma of Education specialisms in teacher librarianship and information technology offered by the Auckland College of Education. The course was designed as a mediated distance-delivered course for practising teachers throughout the country who wished to gain a specialist qualification in the area of teacher librarianship. It was later extended to also become the foundation course for a specialist qualification in information studies and information technology. The aim of the course is to introduce teachers to a process approach for designing, monitoring and evaluating a RBL unit of work emphasizing the development of information literacy in different areas of the curriculum. It is based on a six-stage process model called Action Learning (Gawith 1987a), which provides an approach to learning for both teachers and students. Teachers enroll in the course at school-based sites throughout New Zealand and meet fortnightly to work with a lecturer who guides them through the content using a mixture of study guides, workbooks, readings and audio-conferences. The course is also available to teachers online (Hunt & Trebilcock 2003). Teachers are expected to practise their skills with their own students between sessions and record and reflect on their experiences. During the course, the different sites from across the country join together for the purposes of teaching and sharing experiences either by teleconference or Internet discussion. More than 5000 New Zealand teachers have taken the course since it began and in the last two years it has also been offered to teachers in Beijing, China. The course content focuses on the following:

1. teachers identify and teach the information skills needed by students to undertake a RBL unit in a selected area of the New Zealand curriculum;
2. teachers design, introduce, monitor and evaluate an RBL unit as part of their classroom program and;
3. teachers discover the relationship between information skills, information literacy and contemporary learning theory.

One of the major strengths of the course is that it provides teachers and students with an information process model that is transferable across all levels and curriculum areas within the context of the New Zealand Curriculum Framework.

In a recent study Vine (2003) investigated the impact Infolink has had on teaching practices. The key research questions for her study were:

1. How do school management teams and teaching staff collaborate in terms of their roles in the development of information literacy in classroom programs?
2. What aspects of this collaboration could be attributed to the Infolink course?
3. What, if any, educational activities that school library media centre teams, ICT specialists and curriculum teams have initiated could be attributed to the Infolink course?
4. How is the effectiveness of these activities evaluated in terms of student learning?

The researcher used a random sample of schools that have been involved in the course on a regular basis. The schools taking part in the survey were two elementary schools and one junior high school. All three schools were within the Auckland metropolitan area, although they represented different socioeconomic levels. Semi-structured interviews and focus group discussions were conducted with principals, PD coordinators, teachers, and teacher librarians from the three schools. All the participants had taken part in the Infolink course as part of their PD. The study reported that the course had impacted on the teaching practice in schools in the following ways:

- Enhanced the development of a shared understanding of pedagogy and best teaching practice for information literacy
- Developed closer working relationships between classroom teachers and library teams in the development of student library and information skills
- Developed a clear understanding of RBL for library staff who are now able to support students through the research process
- Produced a paradigm shift in the way ICT is used in teaching practice. ICT specialists are no longer viewed as being responsible for teaching technical skill development but they have an active role in meaningful integration of ICT into the curriculum
- Encouraged more cross-curricular approaches
- Increased collaboration between teaching staff and management concerning planning, policy and vision
- Produced a sense of a shared experience and feeling part of a team that learns and solves problems together
- Created a power shift between senior and junior teachers that led to the development of a mentoring approach to supervision
- Developed a recognition of the importance of teachers continuing to improve their own information literacy skills
- Allowed teachers to develop professionally at various stages of their career in a supportive environment
- Improved coordination and access to the schools resources
- Developed shared responsibility for the selection of school resources.

The only negative impact reported was that some teachers felt resentment that participating in the course was compulsory and that it took away the aspect of choice for them.

Overall Vine reported, "the study affirms the effectiveness of the course and provides evidence that the course can bring about substantial changes to the ways in which teachers and school managers view the teaching and learning practices within their schools" (2003, p. 28).

Recently a further study was conducted by the authors of this chapter to seek information from those with experience in teaching and implementing the course in their schools. A focus group of twelve participants was set up and asked to address the following questions:

1. What are the features of the content and delivery of Infolink that make it a successful learning experience for teachers?
2. What are the tangible benefits of the Infolink course for children's learning?
3. What does Infolink contribute to overall change within the school?
4. What are the limitations and barriers of the Infolink course?

The participants were school principals, full-time course lecturers and part-time course lecturers (who were also employed in schools as teachers/teacher librarians and often members of the school senior management team). One of the participants was a teacher librarian with considerable experience in schools, now employed by the National Library of New Zealand.

The use of a modified Delphi technique allowed for this group of participants to identify and prioritize the strengths and weaknesses of the Infolink course as a PD experience for teachers. The Delphi method of data collection can use both questionnaires and interviews while ensuring the anonymity of the experts. The method employs a multistage ethnographic approach and has been used since the early 1950s, mainly by qualitative researchers. The intention of the Delphi method is to determine the level of agreement amongst experts in the field. The Delphi process requires more time than a typical one-shot survey and it draws on a broad base of people already knowledgeable in one particular field. The choice of the participants in this method is based on their relative expertise, rather than on the need to represent a larger population. The participants are often more actively involved in the research process as they contribute to the development of a dataset that has been generated by their own responses and the responses of other knowledgeable colleagues (Doyle 1993).

The information summarized through the use of the Delphi process provided some answers to the four key research questions.

Research Method

Round One: Four open-ended questions were sent out to the participants via email with the request that they list their responses to the questions in short sentences or bullet-pointed lists.

Round Two: The responses were analyzed and repetitions and unclear statements deleted. The responses were then sent back to the participants and they were asked to rank the items in order of priority. The rankings from each participant were compiled into total scores and ranked from highest to lowest. Only the first fifteen ranked items were included in the analysis. The rankings from each participant were then added together to determine a total score for each item. The items were then listed from the highest to the lowest score.

Responses for Round One and Round Two were received from a total of twelve participants. The results from the study identified a consensus among the participants regarding the top fifteen responses to the questions.

Results

Tables 13.1 to 13.4 display the top fifteen items that were selected in order of the number of responses received from participants to the questions.

Table 13.1
Question: What are the features of the content and delivery of Infolink that make it a successful learning experience for teachers?

Item	Responses
It is a very workable model that provides a framework for good teaching practice across all levels and all curriculum areas.	8
The course provides time and opportunities for reflective practice. Teachers have time to think about what they are teaching and how they are doing it. Too often skill levels and the range of necessary skills are taken for granted.	8
The readings, teaching practice, workshops and reflections combine to extend and consolidate teacher's thinking.	8
Teachers have the opportunity, during the sessions, to think ahead and visualize the whole process or a part off the process, so that when they teach that stage they are well prepared and can cope with "surprises" as there will be fewer of those.	6
The information process model is taught within the context of real practice. Theory first, then followed by modeling, followed by doing.	6
Infolink provides teachers with a model to introduce resourced-based learning into their classroom.	6
The course is clearly grounded in contemporary learning theory and links this theory to classroom practice.	6
The development of new teaching pedagogy which focuses on the teaching of higher order thinking and processing skills reflects the current need for teachers to upskill in this area.	5

Strategies are introduced throughout the sessions in ways that scaffold the teachers' learning.	5
The sessions provide a forum for teachers' success. Sharing of strategies also builds a repertoire that teachers can use in their own classrooms.	5
All lecturers are experienced practitioners of this approach and so have a depth of both theoretical and practical knowledge to share.	5
It can be used immediately and provides a framework in which children learn and practice the requirements of the NZ Curriculum Framework.	4
School based delivery/online delivery saves time and stress traveling distances after a busy day and caters well to individual school needs.	4
Delivery and session structure fits nicely within the culture of NZ teachers and NZ schools.	4
The delivery actually models the teaching approach.	4

The results of this question show that the participants considered that the course provides a framework for good teaching practice to all levels of students across all curriculum areas. There was also importance attached to the close links made between theory and practice and the opportunities provided within the course to relate theory to practice within the context of the New Zealand school curriculum. The key aspects valued by the participants were the ways in which the course stresses the importance of directly teaching skills, introduces RBL and is well grounded in contemporary learning theory. Directly engaging teachers in the skills of reflective practice, scaffolding student and teacher learning and teaching higher order thinking skills were also considered to be important aspects of the course. The fact that it provided a forum for teachers to share ideas and successes was also highly rated by participants.

Key aspects of the actual course delivery were the skills and experience of the lecturing staff, the convenience of school-based or web-based delivery, and the fact that the structure and delivery of the sessions matched well with the culture of New Zealand teachers and schools.

Table 13.2
Question: What are the tangible benefits of the Infolink course for children's learning?

Item	Responses
Helps them to acquire skills they can build on and use for the rest of their lives.	10
Provides many strategies, which are transferable to other learning activities.	7
Supports ownership of the learning – and developing independence as the students gain control and connect purposefully with the learning task.	7
Children learn to think about the process of thinking and learning (metacognitive development).	7
Assists with the development of questioning skills.	6
Provides a defined process for students to follow.	6
Gives students a framework within which to complete research tasks.	5
Shows students how tasks can be broken down into manageable steps.	5
Success and ownership equal fun and enjoyment in learning which in turn sets up life long learners.	5
Provides scaffolding for the seemingly difficult aspect of learning, i.e., the cognitive processes.	5
Much of the extra skill development is done on the job, at a point of need and therefore seems to "stick" with them.	5
The ability to analyze, synthesize and evaluate the quality of information which is essential to learners becoming critical members of society.	5
Develops skills of self-evaluation and decision-making about their learning.	5
It provides opportunities for child-centred learning with skilful teaching that is relevant to needs.	4
No assumptions are made about children's learning.	4

The tangible benefits for student learning gained from the Infolink course were considered to be many. They included the acquisition of lifelong learning skills, transferable learning strategies, feelings of ownership of learning and the development of independence as the student gains control and connects purposefully with the learning task. Participants also rated very highly the opportunity the course provides for students to learn about the process of thinking and learning. Other tangible benefits included the development of questioning skills, the understanding of a defined process to follow with tasks broken down into manageable steps and the success and ownership which leads to fun and enjoyment of learning which in turn hopefully leads to students becoming lifelong learners. Gaining skills of self evaluation and decision-making were also valued along with the ability to analyze, synthesize and evaluate the quality of information.

Table 13.3
Question: How does Infolink contribute to overall change within the school?

Item	Responses
It can be used as a key element in driving pedagogical change within the school.	9
When it is school-based and a majority of teachers use the strategies within their classrooms the common approach supports children's learning at all levels As each student meets the strategies along the continuum they are able to work at an increasingly sophisticated level.	8
As a school-based activity this collegial/cooperative approach can lead to the development of school-wide philosophy in practice. It becomes part of the "way we learn things here" …part of the learning "culture" of the school.	8
The development of a common approach to teaching the Essential Skills, which are often left to chance.	8
All staff and students use the same processes and language in RBL leading to greater knowledge and understanding of information literacy.	8
All teachers are using common methods that help students develop skills so they won't find each teacher expecting them to work in different ways. A common thread will run through the school.	8
Helps to create an ILSC.	7
Teachers and students are able to support each other emotionally as they implement a common approach – more collaboration less isolation therefore increased chance of improved learning outcomes.	6
Continuity of skill development across the curriculum at all levels.	6

Gives value to the library and place of library in an information literate community.	6
Development of a shared language and shared concepts gives a unity of purpose to the staff.	5
It facilitates/improves reflective practice in a school both individually and collectively.	5
Contributes to the information literacy level of all teachers.	5
Provides an opportunity for inquiry learning.	4
Staff work co-operatively and support each other in using Infolink which has a positive effect on collegiality and provides opportunities for incidental PD.	4

Participants considered that there were many connections between the Infolink course and overall school change, in particular that it could be used as a key element in driving pedagogical change within the school. The establishment of a common approach to student learning at all levels in the school and the collegial/cooperative approach of the course was considered by participants to lead to a shared philosophy and school-wide understanding of the importance of information literacy. The implementation of this common approach was also seen to provide emotional support for teachers and students, to have a positive effect on collegiality and to have continuity of skill development at all levels across the curriculum. The course was seen to contribute to school change by placing value on the library, on the development of an ILSC and it was considered to contribute to the information literacy skills of all teachers.

Table 13.4
Question: What are the limitations and barriers of the Infolink course?

Item	Responses
Some teachers don't understand the importance or significance of this process so they are reluctant to take part.	9
The success of the course is dependent upon senior staff commitment.	9
Sometimes staff are told they have to attend which can lead to reluctance to "join in" and it can make for a difficult atmosphere for teachers and lecturers.	8
Some teachers think they already know about information literacy.	8
Teachers from countries where teaching tends to follow a "transmission mode" often have difficulty with both the concepts and structure.	7

Teachers sometimes feel it will be an added chore – they won't have time.	7
Timing is a huge issue. Teachers are busy people with huge workload and commitments. This course is worthwhile but it does demand time and energy. It cuts across existing programs sometimes.	7
In our efforts to scaffold teachers in their learning of the process we can sometimes increase their stress in the meeting of deadlines.	7
The level of lecturer training. Are we really all saying, believing, teaching the same things?	7
Some staff find it difficult to cope with the many interruptions during term time.	6
Timing with other school commitments. Time to fit it into an already busy timetable.	6
Teachers require practical teaching experience and knowledge of how schools operate. First year teachers shouldn't be expected to take this course.	5
The timing of training has not always aligned with the cycle of development in our school.	5
Not as well known in secondary schools so continuity of understanding broken as students move from elementary to secondary.	4
Inconsistent profile nationally e.g., very strong in the Auckland region while not so well known in other parts of the country.	4

In discussing the limitations and barriers of the course, participants did not always confine their remarks to the actual course itself. It appears that some teachers do not understand the importance or significance of the course and that some teachers believe they already know about such things. The course is very dependent upon support from senior staff in the school if it is to be run successfully. Another highly-rated item suggests that if attendance is compulsory for all staff there may be a reluctance to join in, which in turn makes a difficult atmosphere for the course lecturer. Time-related issues also appeared high in the ratings. Busy teachers had to take the course amidst interruptions, it was demanding and time- consuming and it sometimes cuts across existing programs and initiatives adding to the already high stress load of teachers. The level of lecturer training was also presented as a possible limitation, as was the fact that Infolink is not so well known in secondary schools so continuity of understanding could be lost as students move from elementary to high school. An interesting response centred around two items concerning teacher skills and experience. Respondents felt that it was not a suitable course for inexperienced teachers and they also noted that teachers with a "transmission" approach to teaching had particular difficulties with the course concepts and structure.

Discussion

The results of these two studies indicate that Infolink continues to be a workable model that provides the framework for good teaching practice across all levels and curriculum areas. It is highly successful, not only because it teaches teachers and students a process for developing information literacy skills, but also because of the advantages it brings as a school-based activity. This collegial and cooperative learning approach can lead to a common direction and philosophy of learning that is evident at every level of the school. As noted by Kulthau (1993b), a shared educational philosophy centred on inquiry learning provides an appropriate and common climate for engaging teacher librarians and school staff in collaborative, integrated learning opportunities.

The course provides teachers and students with a process approach taught within the context of real practice in which they are able to decide, find, analyze, synthesize and evaluate both process and product. As noted by Todd

> the systematic and explicit development of students' abilities to connect with, interact with, and utilize information to construct personal understanding, results in more positive attitudes to learning, increased active engagement in the learning environment, and more positive perceptions of students themselves as active, constructive learners (Todd 2001b, p. 10).

Participants in both research studies found that the course assisted with the development of both teachers and students' information literacy skills. This addresses some of the concerns expressed by Henri (1999a) concerning the lack of teachers' skills in information literacy and Doyle's (1994) comments that teachers are the most critical key to student attainment of information literacy skills.

A feature of the course is the emphasis placed on linking contemporary learning theory to current classroom practice. This is reflected in comments concerning "reflective practice", "scaffolding learning", "child-centred learning" and "learning to think about the process of thinking and learning". The emphasis on reflective thinking processes is not unexpected as New Zealand primary schools have for a long time been influenced by constructivist learning theory (Moore & Trebilcock 2003a). A notable point is that teachers following more of a "transmission approach" to teaching reportedly had more difficulty with the course. This is a significant finding as Infolink, along with many other PD initiatives for teachers, assumes some knowledge and understanding of constructivist learning and teaching approaches. Kember suggests that there are three main approaches to teaching. The first is a teacher-centred transmission approach and the second is a student-centred conceptual approach. Kember has argued that these conceptions are not hierarchical but rather "an ordered set of qualitatively differing conceptions" ranging along the axis from teacher-centred to student-centred (1997, cited in Brown 2002, p. 263). It is suggested that because of the complexity of teachers' mental realities many teachers' conceptions of teaching actually lie between, as much as at either end of the continuum, hence giving rise to the third approach. Given the diverse population and recent arrival of teachers to New Zealand from a variety of cultures and teaching environments it may be that PD initiatives need to be more cognizant of these differences in approaches to teaching. It appears that

Infolink is particularly valuable as a vehicle for shifting the thinking of the middle group towards more active collaborative student-centred approaches, however the group of teachers firmly embedded at the teacher-centred end of the continuum could be much more difficult to shift.

Time constraints were noted as a problem because of the busy, stressful working conditions of teachers. Staff teaching on the program have taken this into consideration as much as possible and experimented with a range of delivery modes, streamlined the course, adjusted the timing, and where possible tailor-made options for delivery to individual schools. It does take time, however, for teachers to absorb and understand new teaching strategies and to ensure that they are successfully embedded into classroom practice. If new teaching strategies are simply skimmed over, then desired changes to teaching practice will not occur.

One of the most significant problems identified by the participants in both research studies concerned the nature of whole-school PD. While it was recognized that this critical mass approach had many benefits, there was recognition also of limitations. Some teachers felt resentment when participating in a course that was mandatory. Making the course compulsory for teachers who did not, for whatever reason, wish to be there often caused problems for the lecturer and the rest of the group. As Fullan and Hargreaves (1996) note, teachers at different points in their career vary in their needs and attitudes toward change and improvement. For this reason they bring to any PD program their personal characteristics, histories and beliefs. Therefore it is important that the PD activity integrates both individual needs and school-wide goals with a view to improving both individual and organizational performance.

Some participants in the research felt that inexperienced teachers should not attempt this course. This could be because it was felt that new teachers should first come to grips with the basic requirements of teaching, or it could be that they are perceived to have an insufficient understanding of information literacy. Moore (2002) makes the point that preservice teacher education programs should include more emphasis on information literacy and school library media centre services. Preliminary results from studies (Asselin & Doiron 2003) show that teacher educators do not address the role of the school library media centres in teaching and learning and that preservice teachers are not being taught how to teach information literacy. If this teaching occurred as part of teacher training, then inexperienced teachers would probably have sufficient understanding to benefit from the Infolink course along with their more experienced counterparts.

Conclusion

The Infolink course has evolved and developed over the years into a very successful model that provides a framework for good teaching practice across all levels and all curriculum areas. It systematically teaches information skills to teachers and students and, in doing so, acts as a catalyst for pedagogical change in schools. This onsite practice-linked PD initiative involving all staff within a school has enabled the development of a shared understanding of pedagogy and best teaching practice for information literacy. It also provides a forum for teachers to share and reflect on their teaching practice and help and support each other in the process. When timed in such a way that it fits into the life of the school, and when supported and encouraged by the principal and senior staff, it can provide a catalyst for change. It also plays an important role in giving focus and value to the place of the library and the work of teacher librarians.

Infolink continues to play an important role in providing teachers with a framework that they can use to create better conditions for learner-centred, enquiry-based forms of education. Through systematically teaching skills of thinking and problem-solving, the content and the organization of the Infolink course offers an infrastructure that teachers and students alike can adopt to enhance their effectiveness as active thinkers and learners. It is important to bear in mind however, that no one particular course, whether Infolink or another approach, can serve as a prescription for effective development of information literacy. As the findings from the studies reported in this chapter indicate, it is the fundamental principles and practices that underpin the formation of an information literate school culture that are so essential. The best and most effective approaches will be those that serve to empower and up-skill teachers so that they can actively engage their students in the process of creating their own knowledge and understanding.

14

Systems Issues and the Information Literate School Community

Ken Haycock

Introduction

Developing a high quality, integrated school library media centre program as a critical ingredient of the information literate school community is a partnership, a partnership of the school principal, the classroom teacher, the teacher librarian and the education authority – whether at the school district, provincial/state or national level, or any combination thereof. This chapter focuses on the unique role and responsibilities of the state agency as a support for the development of school library media centre programs and information literate school communities. The examples provided here are common in many jurisdictions and are thus reasonable expectations of these agencies.

Organizational structures vary considerably in the English-speaking world, from national agencies that direct and closely supervise educational policy and school level services to highly decentralized schools that operate autonomously with only broadly stated policy direction or intended learning outcomes. The issues and recommendations outlined here need to be addressed somewhere in the system, but the appropriate agency and level will be different for each jurisdiction.

The research evidence makes it clear that teacher librarians and school libraries have a positive impact on student achievement, on motivation and ability to read, and on the teaching and learning climate in the school. These effects are achieved with *qualified* teacher librarians who *collaborate* with classroom colleagues to *integrate* those skills and strategies that enable students to access and use information effectively. The resulting units of study are team-taught by the teacher and teacher librarian in *flexibly scheduled* resource centres. The availability of support staff free the teacher librarian to plan and teach with colleagues.

The Policy Framework

State the Purpose of the Program

School systems, with the support of the state government and school communities, invest millions of dollars each year in school libraries, in terms of facilities, personnel and resources. Nevertheless, there is often no clear understanding by the various stakeholder groups as to the purpose of the program and its intended outcome. Systems require an overarching statement of intended outcome in order to evaluate fully and fairly whether the investment justifies the return.

An example: The purpose of the school library media centre program is to assist students to become informed decision-makers and lifelong learners.

Or: The school library media centre program ensures that students and teachers become effective users of information and ideas.

Define the Roles of the Partners

The next responsibility of the district or state agency is to articulate inherent roles and responsibilities of partners in program development and delivery. Each partner in the school resource enterprise has a unique but critical role in program development.

The development and implementation of the school library media centre program thus involves specific partners:

- The Province/State, which provides an overall framework and funding;
- The District, which provides specific direction and personnel and resources to achieve stated goals;
- The Principal, who establishes clear expectations and provides instructional leadership in a collaborative work environment;
- The Classroom Teacher, who bears specific responsibility for implementation of the curriculum and information literacy and the students' overall program;
- The Teacher librarian, who provides specialized support for the classroom teacher through knowledge of resources and their effective use by students; this is accomplished as a collaborative and equal teaching partner working in flexibly scheduled programs; and
- Parents and Students, who are both funders and consumers of the service.

The focus here is on the district/state agency. At the very least, the state Ministry of Education will acknowledge the research base and best practice for school library media centre libraries through references in curriculum documents. The Ministry of Education will contemplate the role of the teacher librarian as collaborative program planning and teaching in resource-based learning environments. The state agency will also typically fund facilities to accommodate multiple classes, groups, and individuals in flexible groups and on flexible schedules. Regrettably, recent actions by government do not match these policies and guidelines.

The issue of congruence and alignment is pervasive – program goals, appropriate staff and roles, facilities, resources, funding all need to be aligned with policy statements and support.

Define the Terms

The simple definition of terms in policy and curriculum documents provides guidance for program development. For example, these terms are defined by the Association for Teacher Librarianship in Canada and the Canadian School Library Association (1997) and have been adopted by many school systems:

Information literacy: The ability to: recognize the need for information to solve problems and develop ideas; pose important questions; use a variety of information-gathering strategies; locate relevant and appropriate information; access information for quality, authority, accuracy and authenticity. Includes the abilities to use the practical and conceptual tools of information technology, to understand form, format, location and access methods, how information is situated and produced, research processes, and to format and publish in textual and multimedia formats and to adapt to emerging technologies.

Teacher librarian: A professional teacher with a minimum of two years of successful classroom experience and additional qualifications in the selection, management and utilization of learning resources, who manages the school library media centre and works with other teachers to design and implement resource-based instructional programs.

School library media centre: The instructional centre in a school that coordinates and provides on-site and off-site access to information, resources, services and programs that integrate information literacy, the intellectual access to information, with teachers, to develop independent learners who are effective users of information and ideas and committed to informed decision-making.

School library media centre program: The collaboratively planned and taught units of study developed through the shared expertise and equal partnership of classroom teachers and teacher librarians, based on the principles of resource-based learning and designed to achieve the educational goals of the school.

The relatively simple task of defining and using common terms makes implementation clearer and easier to deliver.

Clarify Roles and Expectations

If professional staff are to be engaged, the funding agency or employer has a responsibility to clarify the role and responsibilities of the teacher librarian, including appropriate qualifications, evaluation measures and processes, a role statement with professional and personal competencies, minimum qualifications required, and a recruitment plan needed. The Association for Teacher Librarianship in Canada and the Canadian School Library Association, in consultation with teachers and administrators across the country, developed a statement of competencies for teacher librarians in 1997. This has been adopted by many school systems as a model. Competencies are defined as follows, with several examples, a program framework and context provided in the original.

Professional competencies

The teacher librarian:
1.1. places a priority on staff relationships and leadership in the implementation of change.
1.2. provides leadership in collaborative program planning and teaching to ensure both physical and intellectual access to information and commitment to voluntary reading.
1.3. knows curriculum programs mandated by the province, district and school.
1.4. understands students and their social, emotional, and intellectual needs.
1.5. has expert knowledge in evaluating learning resources in different formats and media, both on-site and remote, to support the instructional program.
1.6. develops and promotes the effective use of informational and imaginative resources in all formats through cooperative professional activities.
1.7. provides appropriate information, resources or instruction to satisfy the needs of individuals and groups.
1.8. uses appropriate information technology to acquire, organize and disseminate information.
1.9. manages library programs, services and staff to support the stated educational goals of the school.
1.10. evaluates program and services.

Personal competencies

The teacher librarian:
2.1. is committed to program excellence.
2.2. seeks out challenges and sees new opportunities both inside and outside the library.
2.3. sees the big picture.
2.4. looks for partnerships and alliances.
2.5. creates an environment of mutual respect and trust.
2.6. has effective communications skills.
2.7. works well with others in a team.
2.8. provides leadership.
2.9. plans, prioritizes and focuses on what is critical.
2.10. is committed to lifelong learning.
2.11. is flexible and positive in a time of continuing change.

The state or district can also ensure that partnerships are in place with universities to deliver the courses and programs in teacher librarianship.

Following a clear role, support needs to be provided for school principals to ensure, through fair and objective measures, that each teacher librarian is capable of fulfilling the approved role or encouraged to seek an alternative teaching assignment. The role of the teacher librarian, expectations, criteria for assessment and evaluation procedures should be reviewed with school administrators and incorporated in administrator leadership preparation programs.

State agencies and school districts need to affirm policies on minimum qualifications for teacher librarians, namely a minimum of two years of successful classroom experience, a master's degree or diploma in teacher librarianship and the ability to demonstrate the competencies outlined in the role description.

Provide Ongoing Professional Development

Districts can identify essential elements of an ongoing professional development plan for teacher librarians. Principals and teacher librarians should encouraged to develop professional growth plans to ensure that each teacher librarian can meet the stated expectations or move back to a classroom position in the system. Priorities need to be identified for professional development, including a trainer of trainer model for teacher librarians to provide leadership in collaboration, inquiry and the selection and use of learning and information technologies in all forms and formats.

Tied to this investment in staff fulfilling their intended roles, the district is the only agency in a position to provide consultative assistance in collaboration, leadership and information literacy. If necessary, this time could even come from the overall allocation of teacher librarian time.

Define Best Practice

1. *Collaborative planning and teaching*

Collaboration between teachers and teacher librarians does not happen naturally or easily. It is more readily implemented where the district has adopted a model of collaboration and ensures that its teacher librarians are trained in collaboration. This happens in courses for teacher librarianship and is reinforced and extended through ongoing staff development for teachers and, most especially, teacher librarians.

2. *Information continuum/information process model*

While information literacy is an important skill, indeed essential for students to achieve the learning outcomes prescribed in state and district curriculum, and while many teachers and teacher librarians are involved in teaching it, there is no discrete program devoted to it. Accountability for an overall system of teaching and assessing these skills is not well defined because they are integrated into many curriculum areas. Information literacy involves skills and strategies that are developmental and cross-curricular.

While integration in all curricular areas is important for the learning of information literacy strategies, implementation will be most successful where there is a school-based continuum of appropriate skills and strategies at each grade level representing a minimum level of expectation and consistency across the school. The state or district can provide examples, models and processes for developing a continuum, or scope and sequence, defined for the local school community and the unique needs of its learners.

Information literacy includes many skills and strategies, but at its core is the ability to interpret information in order to create meaning and new ideas. A school-based continuum includes basic information about the development of

- defining the need for information through asking important questions;
- information-gathering skills;
- skills in the selection, sorting and discerning use of information;
- skills that enable students to organize, translate and synthesize information;
- skills that enable students to clearly communicate the meaning of ideas they have created (written, spoken, visual and electronic communication).

Similarly, a common information-processing model for students provides a basis for instruction, for reinforcement across subject areas and for professional and staff development for teachers. The information process helps to break a complex task into smaller pieces, provides a focus for teaching, guides students and enables more specific assessment.

3. *Integration of information skills, strategies and dispositions*

There is often no common language for those abilities and skills necessary to determine a need for information, frame appropriate questions, determine sources of information and ideas, assess and process the information through reading, viewing, listening, record information in one's own words, cite the sources used, share the information through print, visuals, electronic programs, and evaluate both the process and the product. These incorporate reading, research and study skills, media literacy, language arts, social studies skills, the scientific process, inquiry, library skills (a largely discredited and dated term), information skills and strategies, problem-solving, decision-making, etc. The system can define and develop a common language that facilitates conversation and dialogue to address this cross-curricular area.

4. *Flexible scheduling*

The teacher librarian is most successful when collaborating with teachers and implementing resource-based units of study together. Through integrated instruction, students develop proficiency in the use of information and achieve better on assessment of both skills and content knowledge. Isolated instruction (typically through the provision of preparation periods for classroom teachers) and related instruction (typically through preparation periods following consultation with the teacher) do not result in the same degree of achievement. Providing preparation time for the classroom teacher to plan means that the teacher librarian is not available to plan, when collaborative planning is the foundation of the program.

The criterion for use of a teacher librarian is for those strategies that are resource-based, focus on inquiry, involve active participation and require two teachers for implementation. Other involvement that could be undertaken by the classroom teacher alone, e.g., telling or reading stories, should be determined based on available time. The state and district can provide the rationale and policy direction for flexible scheduling to ensure effective library programs and reasonable return on investment.

5. *Systematic and congruent assessment and evaluation*

Assessment and evaluation are applied to student performance through products and deliverables, through process to ensure mastery of information skills and strategies and through content knowledge. Assessment and evaluation are also applied to the resource centre program itself through periodic district reviews. Evaluation of resource centre programs should involve all the partners – principal, teacher, teacher librarian, student, district – and should be based on stated objectives and clear criteria. Evaluators operate primarily within a framework of their personal experience, training and attitude rather than of objective criteria. Assessment of the role of each of the partners is important, as is assessment and evaluation of the role of the teacher librarian.

Guidance in the assessment of school library media centre programs is appropriate from the state or district, as few superintendents or principals will have the background, experience or tools to be comprehensive and focused on best practice.

6. *Provide symbolic leadership*

Although it is a simple step, without cost, the inclusion of the word "libraries" in central office vocabulary is disappearing. Consider the different messages sent from these two examples: Information Technologies, or, Libraries, Media and Technologies, the latter more fully reflecting responsibilities for the broad range of available technologies (books, audiovisual media, electronic technologies), equipment, facilities and human and material resources necessary to fulfill broad mandates.

Resource Management

State and district agencies need to review resource selection and management, including the state of print and audiovisual collections and access to electronic information, on a regular basis to ensure that efficiencies of scale be employed wherever possible, e.g., in the acquisition, organization and processing of resources.

Efficiencies are derived from school collections being supplemented and complemented by specialized district collections such as professional resources for teachers and administrators, videos and first language collections. The State/Ministry of Education can sign statewide site licences for full-text databases appropriate for elementary schools and secondary schools in collaboration with other groups. The system can also take a district approach to identifying, evaluating and organizing web sites for student use.

Systems can encourage schools to take a broad view of resource management, including print, audiovisual and electronic resources regardless of budget area and regardless of location in the school, in order to effect better cooperation and coordination of resources. Library automation projects to include all accessible learning resources as part of an overall resource management strategy, and to ensure access to collections from terminals in school classrooms as well as across the district, requires sustained district leadership.

Districts need to explore means of using the teacher librarian's special expertise in the selection and evaluation of learning resources in the system. The district can enhance, with little cost, the management of its resources through a handbook for administering the school library media centre. A current area of duplication due to a lack of system leadership is in the area of technology. Technology is a useful tool for teaching and learning. The vision is clear and the goals important and achievable. There are limitations, however, in assuming a limited vision of "information technology" and excluding other tools (books, videos, commercial databases) that allow students to explore issues, solve problems or create meaning and new ideas.

A more integrated and coordinated approach to resource management at the school and district level is necessary to ensure that all resources are used effectively and to the fullest. Systems need to develop a holistic and integrated approach to resource management incorporating all learning resources in the school and district regardless of format, providing systematic support for the development of the typical hybrid libraries, incorporating print, audiovisual and electronic resources for use as appropriate to the intended learning outcomes.

It is also important to recognize the serious difficulties that students face in using information effectively. It is difficult to use print-based information, and computer-based information is no easier for students to use. It is critical to distinguish here between *physical* access to information, the challenging but nevertheless easiest steps in the process, and *intellectual* access to information, the ability of students to process and use information effectively, where there is a long history of poor achievement.

The system can identify the teacher librarian as the primary school contact for the selection, evaluation, management and use of learning resources in all formats and support this role through a trainer of trainers model and/or specify coordinated approaches to information technology resources and use.

In terms of coordinated approaches to technology use, the district should develop a graphic user interface connecting learning resources in the school, in the district and beyond, for use in schools consistent with a policy on the selection of learning resources. The intent here is to ensure an in-district gateway to the school's resources (e.g., library resources, school-developed web site bookmarks, other school resources), to district resources (e.g., district collections of learning resources too expensive or specialized for one school, other school resources and gateways), and beyond (e.g., the resources of other appropriate service providers, such as public libraries, reference tools, and children's information magazines, for which site licences for the district or broader community have been signed). The system can produce and mount WebQuests and Graphic Organizers for specific units of study at specific levels of difficulty as support for school libraries, develop standards for school web sites and specifically the school library media centre section and consider subscriptions for schools to databases of reviewed and recommended web sites for elementary schools. Students should be able to access electronic resources and information 24 hours a day, seven days a week. Similar to these uniquely system-level efficiencies of time and money, facilities can only be refurbished on a planned cyclical basis by the district.

Coordinate External Programs and Services

Only the district can identify mutual roles, expectations and responsibilities with other agencies, specifically the Public Library. Each agency selects and manages resources for a common client group and develops literacy programs to encourage best use of those resources. Several collaborative projects are possible, from homework centres to family literacy programs to a centre for research and professional resources. Each student should have a public library card and a visit to the public library by the end of the fourth grade.

The school district and the library board should develop and approve a policy statement on mutual expectations, which outlines both roles and responsibilities of each partner in providing access to information and ideas by young people. Each system needs to identify and acknowledge the expertise and specializations of the other partner and ensure that resources are targeted strategically to ensure maximum return on investment.

A joint advisory committee, with responsibility for liaison assigned to senior officials of each agency will better ensure cooperation and collaboration. The two systems might establish a jointly funded position of liaison librarian between the schools and public library. Contracted services, including evaluative and descriptive lists of materials for specific curriculum units and selection of learning resources within clear curriculum, course and school profiles, should be explored. Specific areas of collaboration might include:

- identification and evaluation of curriculum-related and developmentally appropriate web sites;
- homework centres;
- technology training centres;
- teachers' professional library;
- summer reading programs;
- family literacy centres;
- teen reading programs; and
- career exploration centres.

Each of these possibilities has been successfully implemented by other school district/public library jurisdictions.

To return to partnerships:

- the province/state provides overall direction and funding;
- the district provides vision, leadership and training in collaborative planning and teaching, developing an information continuum/process, support for the integration of skills, strategies for flexible scheduling and ongoing assessment and evaluation, consultative and technical services, and support for resource management;
- the principal fosters a climate for collaboration, ensures competent personnel and ensures access to the facility and resources in conjunction with all staff;
- the teacher is responsible for the full program for students and thus needs to collaborate with teacher librarians for inquiry-based programs and the best use of resources;
- parents and students are also partners as major funders, supporters and users of the service.

The roles in policy, direction, coordination and centralized support and services can be undertaken only by a central agency with authority and resources. The system is a critical ingredient to planned, deliberate and sustained services.

15

Preparing Preservice Teachers as Members of Information Literate School Communities

Marlene Asselin

Introduction

This chapter describes methods that have been used to educate preservice teachers to collaborate with teacher librarians and to extend their understandings of literacy and literacy instruction to include the literacies of information. The contexts of these preservice teacher education initiatives are first reviewed – specifically, major directions in school and teacher education reform, and the places of school libraries and information literacies within these reforms. Three models of educating preservice teachers about school libraries and information literacies are described: authentic task, integrated mentoring, and reciprocal mentoring. Recommendations for developing initiatives that prepare preservice teachers as members of information literate school communities conclude the chapter.

Neither schools, school libraries, nor information literate school communities operate in a vacuum. The first part of this chapter presents two major influences on schools and school libraries – the school reform movement and trends in teacher education. These pervasive forces are in turn deeply enmeshed in larger social, political, and economic contexts.

Educational Reform: Trends and Issues

Educational reform theorists identify the essential nature of the change process as paradoxical and complex (Bascia & Hargreaves 2000). Reform is complex because of the multiple forces that generate educational changes. Paradoxes arise from humanist or functionalist interpretations of the same phenomena. While change forces are variously labeled and enumerated in the reform literature, I have distilled them into three labels for the purposes of this chapter: a) globalization and technology; b) diversity; and c) accountability. Below, I briefly describe the complexities and paradoxes of these agents as a framework for situating efforts to prepare preservice teachers as active members of information literate school communities.

Globalization and Technology: Creating a Global Community or Foundations of the Knowledge-Based/New Economy

The humanist view of these intertwined forces emphasizes new opportunities for communicating and learning about people, places, and ideas around the world. Previously vast and impenetrable distances have dissolved and new worlds characterized by community, collaboration, and equity are possible. On the other hand, technology and globalization combine to form the foundation of the concept of a "knowledge-based economy". Propelled by the notion of the Information Age, many countries have produced visions, policies, and plans for building knowledge-based economies and societies with the new tools engendered by information, communication, and multimedia technologies. For example, *Canada's Innovation Strategy* (Canada 2002) defines the goals and means of establishing the country as a competitor in a global network of knowledge-based economies. Emanating from these directives are descriptions of employability and workforce skills necessary to create and sustain a nation's position in this global network (e.g., "manage information: locate, gather, and organize information using appropriate technology and information systems: access, analyze, and apply knowledge and skills from various disciplines" (Conference Board of Canada 2000)). Educational policy in turn mirrors these political and economic agendas, as in Canada's view of education as "a lifelong learning process (where educators) strive to create a learning society in which the acquisition, renewal, and use of knowledge are cherished" (Canadian Council of Ministers of Education 1999).

Diversity: Source of Enrichment or Impoverishment

Changing demographics accompanying globalization has meant increased numbers of students come from cultures and language groups other than the white Western mainstream. On the one hand, multiculturalism, social justice, and English as a second-language are educational responses to our diverse student populations. On the other hand, many of these new students enter schools poorly equipped to succeed in traditional teaching and curriculum cultures. The consequential declining scores on high-stakes tests, instruments that are geared to mainstream students, have propelled a political shift to test-driven teaching and curriculum (Allington & McGill-Franzen 1992), which, as explained hereafter, perpetuate divisiveness rather than support diversity.

Accountability and Outcomes-based Education: Setting Goalposts for Learners or Marginalizing Students of Diversity

Incited by the increased diversity and widening achievement gaps of today's students, the public's demand for accountability has led to development of standards- and outcomes-based education system. Many education systems throughout the world are moving towards the use of performance indicators and descriptive, multilevel standards (e.g., being below, meeting, and exceeding expectations) for evaluating learning. This approach represents a compromise about learning expectations between rigid uniformity and individuality. Other stakeholders in education, usually the public and policy-makers, support the use of standards as a means of achieving educational uniformity within and across schools. From a critical perspective, a rigid standards-based education system marginalizes the very students it purportedly sets out to assist (Lewin & Medina 2003) in two ways. First, political pressure has successfully narrowed the meaning of education to "core curriculum" and "basic skills". Second, while ideally learning outcomes should be used to determine an individual's growth and goals, in reality, over-standardization ends up penalizing many students because of their diversity and perpetuating social and economic inequities.

In sum, major themes in current educational reform can be conceived from functionalist or humanist perspectives. While neither perspective is ever represented in its purity, varying emphases on the need for schools to develop a society's citizens and workers in a knowledge-based economy on one hand, and to develop moral individuals in a multiple communities on the other hand, define main approaches to shaping schools for the future. One bright note amidst the complexities and paradoxes of educational reform is the growing research demonstrating that teachers make a difference to student learning (Rivkin, Hanushek & Kain 2000) and the need to invest in the preparation of quality teachers (National Commission on Teaching and America's Future 1996). It is within this professionalization view of teacher education that opportunities lie for cultivating preservice teachers as participants in information literate school communities.

What's a Teacher Educator to do? Teacher Education Responding to Reform

Teacher educators, like teachers, are caught in a seemingly impossible position of being responsible for supporting the complex and paradoxical aims of education described above. Ultimately, the work of educators is driven by conceptions of an educated person. The emergent view is that of a person who is both a savvy competitor in, and a humane contributor to, a global world. In what Hargreaves calls the era of "the new orthodoxy", the role of teachers in developing educated people for today's society and economy is

> to ensure that students learn how to learn. Students … will need to be much more inventive and flexible as learners and performers than were their predecessors. The continuing explosion of knowledge means that there is no single, limited body of facts to be committed to memory that will suffice for modern living. Teachers … must prepare [their students] to manage change and to maneuver information systems (Bullmaster & Darling-Hammond 1997, p.1070).

In terms of curriculum, while policy-makers push for an emphasis on basic literacy, numeracy, and science, the humanists caution that "in today's informational society, we will be poorer democracies and weaker economies if we cannot [also] educate students for the artistic, critical, and social-scientific life world" (Hargreaves et al. 2001, p. 5). To accomplish these ends, teaching must be socially rich and cognitively and emotionally engaging.

Teacher educators who are committed to a professionalization paradigm debate what exactly teachers should know and know how to do. Three universal outcomes of today's teacher education programs are:

1. *Using technology to support student learning.* Preparation in the use of information and communication technologies has rapidly become a focus of teacher education. This new emphasis includes the role of technology in both the way courses are taught and in the way preservice teachers are expected to use information technologies in the planning, preparing and presenting of their lessons. Of critical importance to all teachers is an understanding of how technology is altering conceptions of literacy and literacy instruction (Leu 2000, Reinking et al 1998). Researchers predict that workplace literacy will rely increasingly on being able to gain, transform and generate knowledge, and that "future workplaces will require the full range of multiliteracies – most especially, analysis, synthesis, and evaluation of multiple pieces and forms of information" (Kibby 2000, p. 381). Preservice teachers must learn these literacies themselves, as well as how to teach them to their students.

2. *Collaboration skills.* A collaborative school culture is a key characteristic of schools that are effective and moving forward (Hargreaves 1995). Students do better when classroom teachers, specialist teachers, and administrators regularly plan, teach, and evaluate together, each bringing specific skills to support the learner. Four types of school cultures are individualized, collaborative, balkanized, and contrived collegiality. Hargreaves distinguishes collaborative from contrived collegiality cultures this way: "If collaboration is limited to anecdotes and help-giving only when asked, or to pooling existing ideas without examining and extending them, it can confirm the status quo. …joint work embraces activities like team teaching, shared planning, mutual observation, action research, and mentoring". He continues to explain that schools with collaborative cultures move forward because the culture "implies and creates stronger interdependence, shared responsibility, collective commitment, and greater readiness to participate in the difficult business of review and critique" (Hargreaves 1997, p. 1312). With this type of culture, it is not surprising that both student achievement and educational change are positively affected.

3. *Change skills.* Given the rapidly evolving directions in technology, society and the economy, teachers must be both responsive and generative in a culture where change is the norm. New curricula, new resources, new technologies, new students, and new parent expectations all require teachers that move with the times. Thus in progressive teacher education programs, preservice teachers develop skills that enable them to focus on quality teaching and high standards of student learning in the inevitable face of chaos, complexity, and paradoxes.

Advances in teaching and learning theory have provided direction for ways that preservice teachers can best attain the three major outcomes above. Effective teacher education rests on three pedagogical principles:

Active learning and authentic learning tasks: Just as classroom learning should be grounded in constructivism, so should the learning of preservice teachers. Learners construct their own understandings by active investigation, analysis, and reconstruction of ideas. Thus past practices of information-giving are being replaced with problem-based approaches to teaching and learning in which preservice teachers apply their learning to real students, real classrooms, and real schools.

1. *Authentic learning environments*: Making the link between theory and practice is a long-standing obstacle for preservice teachers. Site-based (i.e., school-based) experiences help new teachers bring theory to life and use theory to inform practice. While the ideal learning environment for preservice teachers is entirely within schools, reality often demands compromises. However, the trend is toward integrating more authentic learning contexts into programs.

2. *Mentoring*: Related to constructivism, mentoring is a form of scaffolding. As Tharp and Gallimore explain, "For teachers to learn new ways of teaching, we must construct settings that assist teachers to perform the new skills before they are fully competent" (1988, p. 190). The complexity of excellent teaching is notoriously underestimated by preservice teachers and many others. Mentoring clarifies the complexity: "Through their joint participation in activities authentic to teaching, the mentor and novice develop shared understandings about the meaning and purposes of these activities, and the novice gradually internalizes ways of thinking, problem solving and acting needed to carry them out" (Feiman-Nemser & Beasley 1997, p. 108).

Policies, Visions, and Realities: The Current Situation in Preservice Teacher Education Concerning the Role of School Libraries

Although this is not the place for an exhaustive review of policies and visions from the school library field, I will cite two international sources to illustrate the alignment between the work of school libraries and the goals of progressive school reform. School library organizations at all levels uphold collaboration, knowledge building, information literacy and the place of the school library program in these dimensions of teaching and learning. (At the end of this chapter, I will address the issue of the particular conception of information literacy represented in current school library policy and practice. Until that time, references to information literacy are based on conventional definitions which feature abilities to access and use information, and the association of information literacy with the notion of lifelong learning.)

The *IFLA/UNESCO School Library Manifesto* synthesizes major goals of the school library program in this way:

> The school library provides information and ideas that are fundamental to functioning successfully in today's information and knowledge-based society. The school library equips students with life-long learning skills and develops the imagination, enabling them to live as responsible citizens. The school library offers learning services, books and resources that enable all members of the school community to become critical

thinkers and effective users of information in all formats and media (International Federation of Library Associations and Institutions 2000).

A collaborative school culture is critical for school library programs to thrive, as is clearly stated in the *IASL Policy Statement on School Libraries*,

> a planned program of teaching information skills in partnership with classroom teachers and other educators . . . This cooperation with teachers may concern: development of the curriculum, the educational activities offered by the school to the child, as well as short and long term planning concerning the use of materials, information technology and equipment, and development of information skills for the child's education (International Association of School Librarianship 1993).

Since development of those abilities defining the current view of an educated person is the mandate of school libraries, one would assume that some part of teacher education includes the role of the school library. However, despite calls from professional organizations that teacher education and performance expectations should be modified to include information literacy concerns and information literacy be included in preservice teacher education (American Library Association Presidential Committee on Information Literacy 1989), reviews of programs since that time show this has not been implemented.

Given this situation, it is not surprising that many teachers are uninformed about information literacy and how teacher librarians integrate instruction of information literacy into the school curriculum. A recent study of teacher librarian and teacher collaboration for information literacy instruction in the United States (Whelan 2003) found that only fifteen to twenty percent of elementary and secondary teachers collaborate with teacher librarians, and only eleven percent of teacher librarians who do collaborate do so regularly, while fifty-one percent of that group sometimes collaborate, and thirty-five percent of that group rarely collaborate. Whelan suggests that educators' lack of awareness about information literacy explains these low levels of collaboration.

Teacher Education in Canada

In Canadian teacher education programs, as in many parts of the world, opportunities for preservice teachers to gain understandings about the role of the school library and teaching information literacy are limited (Asselin & Doiron 2003). Only three school library education programs remain in the country, thereby diminishing resources for leadership and research for initiatives that would spearhead implementation of the American Library Association's 1989 recommendations to include school libraries in teacher education. Findings from the Canadian study show that preservice teachers receive little information (commonly in the form of pamphlets or guest speakers), if any, about the role of a school library and little or no practicum experience with school libraries.

As in many countries, learning outcomes representing various aspects of information literacy are embedded in major curriculum documents in each province in Canada. The concepts, attitudes, and skills associated with information literacy, such as working with the research process, are a part of language arts and social studies methods courses, but little is being done to show preservice teachers how to integrate information literacy into classroom curriculum. The emphasis appears to be on preservice teachers' own information literacy development and not enough support is given to how to teach research-related concepts, strategies, and skills to school children. The Canadian study also found that university librarians working in faculties of education help preservice teachers develop information literacy; however, they were not aware of leadership in the area of information literacy by any of the faculty or course instructors, a critical factor of effectiveness of information literacy programs in academic libraries (Ivey 2003).

Models for Introducing Preservice Teachers to the Role of the School Library and Information Literacy Instruction

If an essential role of the school library program is to work with teachers to develop information literacy across the curriculum, then how do teacher educators prepare new teachers for this collaborative responsibility? Three approaches have been developed in Canada, each in a different part of the country. Canadian teacher education programs are not accountable to a national certifying body, thus each program develops its own learning outcomes. As explained above, abilities to work collaboratively with teacher librarians and to teach information literacy are not learning outcomes in any of the programs represented in the Asselin and Doiron study. However, in the three programs described below, a faculty member has designated these abilities as learning outcomes within a course or practicum, and, drawing on principles of effective teacher education pedagogy (active learning, and authentic learning environments and tasks, and mentoring), devised means for preservice teachers to attain these outcomes. Effects on preservice teachers' understandings and abilities relating to school libraries and information literacy were tracked in each project.

The models are named according the primary pedagogical method used to work with preservice teachers. Aspects of each project are described, specifically, the context (place in the teacher education program), learning environment, leaders and team members, primary learning task and outcomes for students, and activities used to guide students through the task. Highlights of what students learned in these experiences conclude the description of each program. Table 15.1 summarizes features of each model.

Table 15.1. *Models for introducing preservice teachers*

Project features	Model project		
	Authentic task	**Integrated mentoring**	**Reciprocal mentoring**
Course level	Elementary & secondary	Elementary	Elementary
Course type	Elective	Core	Core
Subject focus	RBL	Language arts	Practicum
Learning environment	University classroom	University library School library District resource centre University classroom	School classroom and library
Leaders/Team members	Course instructor Education librarian	Education librarians Local teacher librarians Course instructor	Classroom teacher Teacher librarian Practicum supervisor from university
Learning task	Integrated, RBL unit One ICT lesson plan	Framework of integrated RBL unit One information literacy lesson plan	Experience curriculum planning with teacher librarians Take leadership role in integrating IT
Task activities/ Assignments	Immersion in resources Three mini-assignments: 1. Annotated bibliography 2. Web site evaluation Poster of community resource	Series of activities: 1. Observe school library program (research process) 2. Observe modeling of CPT 3. Unit resource selection in library 4. Collaboratively planned info lit lesson with teacher librarian	Observations and guided applications of 1. CPT 2. Integration of IT into curriculum Reflective discussions with classroom teacher, teacher librarian and practicum supervisor
Student learning	Process-based view of information literacy Richer, more extensive resource use in teaching How to integrate information literacy into subjects	Teacher librarian as teaching partner Benefits of resource-based teaching and learning Information literacy instruction as cross-curricular approach Lesson planning skills	Complexity of curriculum planning process Methods and challenges of integrating IT Complex role of the teacher librarian Concern for equity issues around IT

Model 1: Authentic Task

This initiative took place within one section of an elective course for both elementary and secondary students. The project aimed to increase preservice teachers' own information literacy and understandings of how to integrate it into their teaching. Course content focused on understanding

> how to locate, evaluate, and use appropriate teaching and learning resources in a variety of formats to develop an integrated resource-based learning unit. It also highlighted research process models, learning styles, authentic assessment, school library programs (including visits to school libraries at the elementary, junior and senior high level), inquiry-based learning, planning a resource-based learning project, and how to promote reading in schools (Branch 2003).

Through a variety of experiences and a series of assignments, preservice teachers worked toward designing an integrated resource-based unit that included instruction of learning outcomes in the province's new Information and Communication Technology (ICT) curriculum. The course instructor was a faculty member responsible for teacher librarian education but also taught courses in the teacher education program. While she was the primary instructor for this initiative, one of librarians in the Faculty library provided two workshops for the preservice teachers, one being an orientation to the library and important resources; and the other, a session on ERIC database searching. It is noteworthy that a strong collaborative relationship between the instructor and the Faculty librarian, based on shared understandings of course goals, had already been established.

The environment of the university classroom was developed to immerse the preservice teachers in the research process, information literacy, and resource-based learning. Three assignments related to resource selection led the preservice teachers toward the target task of designing an integrated, resource-based unit:

a. an annotated bibliography of relevant print and multimedia resources;
b. evaluation of a website; and
c. poster presentation of a community resource.

Other classroom experiences were designed to develop preservice teachers' understandings of and abilities in applying research-process models and information literacy concepts and outcomes to their unit plans. These included exploring their own research process based on different research scenarios and then comparing them with popular models of the research process (e.g., Kuhlthau's Information Search Process Model, Eisenberg and Berkowitz's Big Six and several academic library research models). Preservice teachers then listed the skills necessary to complete a research project and then considered how to teach each of these skills in the context of a research project and also in the context of other classroom activities. The skills listed were then compared with the provincial ICT curriculum. As part of their final unit plan, preservice teachers were required to integrate some of these skills into their unit plan and to explain how they would teach them.

Responses to pre- and post-course questionnaires about various aspects of teaching information and communication technologies showed that this project helped preservice teachers develop a process-based view of information literacy and sparked ideas for integrating it into their classroom teaching. The instructor advises that "teacher educators need to move from helping preservice teachers become more information literate to helping preservice teachers integrate information literacy skills into their own teaching" (Branch 2003).

Integrated Mentoring

This model has been in a process of refinement since its development in 1997 and as a core component of a large teacher education program in western Canada. The project has been described in detail by Asselin and Lee (2002).

This project partners teacher education course instructors, university library staff, teacher librarians from local school districts, and preservice teachers. A two-week module focused on resource-based learning and information literacy is integrated into a required language arts course. Teacher librarians from the local school districts volunteer to plan collaboratively information literacy lessons with the university students. These lessons are part of an assignment to develop an integrated unit of study.

The project began by forming a collaborative team with the provincial and district teacher librarian associations, as well as Faculty of Education librarians with major responsibilities in the teacher education program. Each year, a project team is formed consisting of two faculty librarians (who are also trained teacher librarians), one teacher librarian from the field (responsible for coordinating volunteers from the field to work with students), and two faculty members who coordinate and teach the required literacy courses for elementary preservice teachers.

A group of ten to fifteen teacher librarians also work in the project at different stages when students observe library programs in action, select resources and plan lessons in their practicum school libraries, and learn how to access and use materials at district resource centres. The project depends on volunteers from the field, usually retired teacher librarians or teacher librarians with part-time appointments, who come to Faculty libraries and work individually with students. They help students select a wide range of teaching and learning resources and plan an information literacy lesson to implement in their practicum.

During the first year, the planning team designed learning experiences that meshed with the broader course objectives and assignments related to integrating language across the curriculum. Classes for this course meet six to eight hours a week in a shortened term. Over a three-week period within this term, preservice teachers participate in several experiences and complete an assignment, one part intended to increase their own information literacy and their ability to teach information literacy. These experiences are:

a. introduction to inquiry-based teaching and integrated unit planning;
b. observation of simulated collaborative planning of an information literacy lesson between teacher and teacher librarian;
c. observation of a collaboratively taught information literacy lesson in a local school library; and,
d. one to two class periods for each student with a teacher librarian to collaboratively plan an information literacy lesson.

The assignment outcome of these experiences is an integrated unit plan consisting of a graphic organizer of unit outcomes, activities and resources; descriptions of introductory and closing activities for the unit; one information literacy lesson for use within that unit; and an annotated, critically evaluated bibliography of eight to ten print, electronic and multimedia learning resources. Students design their units and lessons for use in their upcoming practicum.

The collaborative planning sessions occur in the two faculty of education libraries where a variety of print and electronic resources supportive of unit themes are pulled or bookmarked in advance. Students work either individually or in small groups with teacher librarians with the ratio of teacher librarians to students set at one to six for the duration of each class period. Students work with the same teacher librarian each period. In some cases, students plan their information literacy lessons in the libraries of their practicum school with the teacher librarian they would be working with using the resources available in the school district. Students structure their lesson plans based on learning outcomes from an information literacy curriculum developed and used in local schools.

A variety of methods have been used to examine effects of this project over its first five years including pre- and post-questionnaires, case study, pre- and post-concept maps, reflective writing, and document collection. Students consistently shifted towards a process view of information literacy; increased their abilities to plan focused, organized lessons; increased their awareness of the difference between a textbook-based unit and a unit supported by rich and diverse resources; and revised their assumptions about teacher librarians as librarians to curriculum teachers and resource specialists. In the words of the preservice teachers:

- I have been opened up to a whole different angle of teaching by introducing the library and its resources to the kids.
- It gave me a clear understanding of what information literacy is, and that it is a part of most lessons, even though we don't realize it.

- I have become much more aware of how to critically evaluate resources through participating in the project. I have become much more aware of the age appropriateness, quality and location of useful learning resources.

- I learned so much about how to connect learning outcomes with assessment. As to learning outcomes, it is important to tell children why I ask them to do certain things.

Reciprocal Mentoring

This project was part of a research program examining effective methods for introducing educational innovation – in this case, the use of information technologies in teaching and learning. The project took place over an extended practicum period in the elementary teacher education program and involved preservice teachers, classroom teachers, consultants, and the practicum supervisor from the university – a faculty member with a teacher librarian background. The role of the teacher librarian was a special focus in two schools where students would have opportunities "to work with teacher librarians in the development of information technology projects that would model how information technology becomes integrated into learning outcomes associated with information literacy" (Doiron 2001, p. 28). The two schools with the teacher librarian focus were selected as strong models of integrated school library programs.

Goals of this part of the project focussed on ICT integration and collaboration with the teacher librarian were:

- To create authentic learning situations where preservice teachers could work along side inservice teachers to develop applications of information technology in existing curriculum;

- To create a collaborative environment for exploring the issues around integrating information technology across the curriculum; and,

- To develop effective teaching strategies for using information technology across the curriculum.

All team members actively planned, implemented and evaluated multiple ways of integrating various information technologies into authentic resource-based learning activities across the elementary curriculum. Special efforts were made to place preservice teachers and teacher librarians in collaborative learning situations. The preservice teachers observed "theory in practice", both in classrooms and the school library, and in modelled examples of collaborative curriculum planning by the faculty supervisor and the teacher librarian. Preservice teachers were responsible for examining the existing and newly implemented curriculum and learning how information technology is infused into learning outcomes. Additionally, they learned about information literacy and the process of integrating a school library program across the school curriculum. Finally, they planned and carried out learning activities using information technologies.

Regular discussion and problem-solving amongst the participants occurred at all stages. Reflective learning, in the form of journals and interviews, was an important component of this experience for both the faculty supervisor and the preservice teachers. Over the course of the practicum, it became apparent through discussions and reflections that the more typical authority relationships between inservice and preservice teachers had changed. Instead, both groups were both mentees and mentors. The preservice teachers learned management and instructional skills from the teachers, and the teachers gained support from the preservice teachers in accepting and applying information technologies in their teaching as well as how to enrich their teaching and learning by collaborating with the teacher librarian.

Interviews with preservice teachers at the end of the project indicated they had learned about the complexity of planning, implementing and evaluating curriculum, learned and tested a variety of methods of integrating information technologies and literacies into their own teaching, realized the multiple roles of a teacher librarian and the importance of teacher librarians working with teachers as educational partners, and increased their awareness of the social and economic influences on the ways information technologies can be used in schools. Preservice teachers in this project had "not only seen a teacher librarian working in the collaborative planning and teaching process, they have been part of that process and have developed a deep understanding of how the school library program is essential to the integrated use of information technology and students' information literacy" (Doiron 2001, p. 34).

Conclusions and Recommendations

Each of these approaches helped preservice teachers understand how school library programs and teacher librarians support teaching and learning in information literate school communities. Guided by teacher librarians and supported by faculty leadership, preservice teachers in these projects examined a wide range of print and multimedia resources they would use in learning activities during their practica. They came to realize the multiple skills and strategies their own students would need to effectively access and use these various and diverse information sources to learn, and they came to distinguish between becoming information literate themselves and teaching information literacy. Preservice teachers in two of the approaches learned first-hand that collaborating with teacher librarians is a powerful way to plan instruction that would help their students gain the literacies required by information texts.

In different ways, the projects supported development of the major teacher competencies of using technology to support student learning, participating in collaborative learning cultures, and teaching with and for change. The projects were designed based on principles of effective pedagogy. All of them honoured constructivism by ensuring that preservice teachers engaged in active and authentic learning experiences. While the reciprocal mentoring model applied the principle of providing an authentic learning environment most effectively, the integrated mentoring model was partially successful by having some groups plan their units and lessons in their practicum school library. The reciprocal mentoring model also effectively applied the principle of mentoring by establishing the project over a long-term practicum period with exposure to and experience with multiple types of mentoring, while the integrated mentoring model afforded preservice teachers the opportunity for collaborating with teacher librarians for several class periods. It is important to note the comparative scale (one class, multiple classes, and two schools) and contextual factors of each project that affect the potential degree of implementation of each of the three principles of effective pedagogy.

Recommendations

There is no one best method to preparing preservice teachers as members of information literate school communities. While the context for developing an initiative for this purpose will be unique, guidelines can be drawn from the three models presented in this chapter. Table 15.2 identifies the principles underlying the recommendations.

Table 15.2. *Principles for developing initiatives to prepare preservice teachers*

Principle	Application
Connections	Integral links to courses and program
Community	Project team – directly and indirectly involved
Context-sensitivity	Balance between responsiveness and generativeness
Constructivism	Learning experiences
Credibility	Demonstrate to all stakeholders
Complexity	Planning and implementing change

- Design the project as an integral part of a course or optimally, an integral component of the larger teacher education program rather than an add-on to existing structures.
- Develop a collaborative culture with all participants in the project – library staff, faculty members, faculty administration, schools, the school library community. There will be different degrees of collaboration with different participants.
- Situate your initiative in a larger educational context rather than the role of the school library and/or teacher librarian per se. For example, literacy, technology, globalization, and lifelong learning are global issues across school systems and their curricula.
- Incorporate the three principles of effective pedagogy in teacher education programs into the design of what the students will be doing.

- Explicitly identify valid and relevant teacher competencies your initiative aims to support. Explain exactly how the learning experiences will accomplish development of those competencies.

- Set high expectations for preservice teachers about the quality of: a) the resources they should use in their teaching; b) their collaboration with teacher librarians; c) the teaching competence they will gain; and d) the learning that their own students will attain when school library programs and services are fully utilized. If preservice teachers are startled by reality later (and they will be), then their understandings of the potential of school libraries will only strengthen their positions as agents of change.

- Provide valid and reliable evidence of the effects of your initiative on preservice teachers' development as defined by the competencies it sets out to support.

- Walk in with your eyes open to the dynamics of the change process. Be prepared for chaos and complexity and commit to any attempts for a sustained period in order for the project to evolve from grassroots efforts to institutionalized change.

Any initiatives must tread the fine line between being responsive to local contexts and current directions, and being generative by pioneering the application of cutting-edge theories and practices associated with information, literacy, teachers' work, and teacher education. I firmly believe that a national and international network of initiatives like those described in this chapter are necessary for teacher librarians to have a significant leadership role in education. However, future projects should go further in their conceptual and practical views of information literacy.

Assumptions about the contributions of school libraries to teaching and learning in the three projects address primarily the educational goal of developing "competitive citizens in a knowledge-based economy". As a new literacy, there is more to information literacy than mastering a scope and sequence program of skills and strategies for accessing, evaluating, organizing, and communicating information. Current critical perspectives of literacy expose the paradox of increasing inequities in the literacy instruction of culturally diverse students (International Reading Association 2003). Kapitzke (2003a) challenges the school library field to go beyond current positivist views of information literacy and seize the leadership role in the hyperliteracy or meta-knowledge of information so that students are taught not just to learn with and through information but to learn about the political, economic and cultural production and consumption of information and knowledge (see Chapter 3 in this book for practical examples). It is only when preservice teachers are prepared to partner with teacher librarians in developing students' full scope of information literacies that they will truly regard teacher librarians as key members of information literate school communities.

Bibliography

Abbott, J. & Ryan, T. (1999). Constructing knowledge, reconstructing schooling. *Educational Leadership 57*(3): 66-69.

Adams, M. (1990). *Beginning to Read: Thinking and Learning About Print.* Cambridge: MIT Press.

Adler, M. J. (1967). *How to Read a Book.* New York: Simon & Schuster.

Adolescents and Literacies in a Digital World. (2002). D. E. Alvermann, ed. New York: Peter Lang.

Alberta Assessment Consortium (1997). *A Framework for Student Assessment.* Edmonton, Alberta.

Alberta Assessment Consortium (2000). *How to Develop and Use Performance Assessment in the Classroom.* Edmonton, Alberta.

Alberta Education. (1990). *Focus on Research: A Guide to Developing Students' Research Skills.* Edmonton, Alberta.

Alberta Learning (2003). *Classroom Assessment Took Kit for the Information and Communication (ICT) Program Studies.* Edmonton, Alberta.

Alexandersson, M. & Limberg, L. (2003). Constructing meaning through information Artefacts. *New Review of Information Behaviour Research 4*(1): 17-30.

Allington, R. L. & McGill-Franzen, A. (1992). Unintended effects of educational reform on New York State. *Educational Policy 6*(4): 396-413.

American Association of School Librarians (1996a). *Information Literacy: A Position Paper on Information Problem-solving.* http://www.ala.org/ala/aasl/aaslproftools/positionstatements/informationliteracy.htm

American Association of School Librarians (1996b). *Position Statement on the Value of Library Media Programs in Education.* http://www.ala.org/ala/aasl/aaslproftools/positionstatements/aaslpositionstatementvalue.htm

American Association of School Librarians (1996c). *Position Statement on the Role of the School Library Media Specialist in Site-based Management.* *http://www.ala.org/ala/aasl/aaslproftools/positionstatements/aaslpositionstatementroleschool.htm*

American Association of Schools Librarians (2002). *ALA/AASL Standards for Initial Programs for School Library Media Specialist Preparation.* Chicago, IL: American Library Association.

American Association of Schools Librarians & Association of Educational Communications and Technology (1998). *Information Power: Partnerships for Learning*. Chicago, IL: American Library Association.

American Library Association (1994). *Guidelines for the Development and Implementation of Policies, Regulations and Procedures Affecting Access to Library Materials, Services and Facilities*. Retrieved 28/07/2004 from http://www.ala.org/ala/oif/statementspols/ otherpolicies/ guidelinesdevelopmentimplementation.htm

American Library Association (1996). *Library Bill of Rights* (Adopted 1948; amended and reaffirmed 1996). Retrieved 28/07/2004 from http://www.ala.org/ala/oif/statementspols/ statementsif/librarybillrights.htm

American Library Association (2000). *Access to Library Resources and Services Regardless of Gender or Sexual Orientation: An Interpretation of the Library Bill of Rights* (Adopted 1993; amended 2000). Retrieved 28/07/2004 from http://www.ala.org/ala/oif/ statementspols/statementsif/interpretations/accesslibrary.htm

American Library Association (2000). *Access to Resources and Services in the School Library Media Program: An Interpretation of the Library Bill of Rights* (Adopted 1986; amended 2000). Retrieved 28/07/2004 from http://www.ala.org/ala/oif/statementspols/ statementsif/interpretations/accessresources.htm

American Library Association (2001). *A Library Advocate's Guide to Building Information Literate Communities*. Retrieved 28/07/2004 from http://www.ala.org/ala/advocacy bucket/informationliteracy.pdf

American Library Association Presidential Committee on Information Literacy (1989). *Final Report* (ERIC Document Reproduction Service No. ED 315074). Retrieved 28/07/2004 from http://www.infolit.org/documents/89Report.htm.

Anderson, R. C. (1994). Role of the reader's schema in comprehension, learning, and memory. In *Theoretical Models & Processes of Reading*. Newark: International Reading Association.

Apple, M. (1996). *Culture, Politics and Education*. New York: Teachers College Press.

Arizpe, E. & Styles, M. (2003). *Children Reading Pictures: Interpreting Visual Texts*. London: Routledge Falmer.

Armstrong, T. (2000). *Information Transformation: Teaching Strategies for Authentic Research, Projects, and Activities*. Markham, Ontario: Pembroke Publishers.

Asselin, M. & Doiron, R. (2003). An analysis of the inclusion of school library programs and services in the preparation of preservice teachers in Canadian universities. *Behavioral and Social Science Librarian 22*(1): 19-32.

Asselin, M. & Lee, E. (2002). I wish someone had taught me: information literacy in a teacher education program. *Teacher Librarian 30*(2): 10-17.

Association for Teacher Librarianship in Canada (1996). *Competencies for teacher librarians: Preliminary draft.* Vancouver, BC.

Association for Teacher Librarianship in Canada & the Canadian School Library Association (1997). *Students' Information Literacy Needs in the 21st Century: Competencies for Teacher-librarians.* Ottawa. Retrieved 28/07/2004 from http://www.atlc.ca/Publications/Competencies.PDF.

Australian Library and Information Association (1985). *Statement on Freedom to Read* (Adopted 1971; revised 1985). Retrieved 28/07/2004 from http://www.ifla.org/faife/ifstat/aliastat.htm.

Australian School Library Association & Australian Library and Information Association (1993). *Learning for the Future: Developing Information Services in Australian Schools.* Carlton, Vic: Curriculum Corporation.

Australian School Library Association & Australian Library and Information Association. (2001). *Learning for the Future: Developing Information Services in Australian Schools*, 2nd ed. Carlton South, Vic: Curriculum Corporation.

Australian School Library Association (1971). *Policy Statement – School Library Bill of Rights.* Retrieved 28/07/2004 from http://www.asla.org.au/policy/p_bor.htm.

Australian School Library Association (1994). *Policy Statement – Resources Provision.* Retrieved 28/07/2004 from http://www.asla.org.au/policy/p_rp.htm.

Baffour-Awuah, M. (2002). The fight against HIV/AIDS: Are school libraries at the battle front? In Singh, D. et al. (eds.), *School Libraries for a Knowledge Society: Proceedings of the 31st Annual Conference of the International Association of School Librarianship held at Petaling Jaya, Malaysia, 5-9 August* (pp. 329-340). Seattle, WA: IASL.

Baker, R. (2002). *Teachers Make a Difference: What is the Research Evidence?* Wellington: New Zealand Council for Educational Research.

Baldwin, M. K. (1996). Enhancing Learning Through Library and Information Services in K-12 Education: A Future Search Conference. Unpublished doctoral dissertation, Seattle University. In *Dissertations Abstracts International* (A 56/08, p. 2918).

Barton, B. & Booth, D. (1995). *Mother Goose Goes to School.* Markham: Pembroke.

Bascia, N. & Hargreaves, A. (2000). *The Sharp Edge of Educational Change: Teaching, Leading, and the Realities of Reform.* New York: Routledge.

Bauman, Z. (2001). *Community: Seeking Safety in an Insecure World.* Cambridge: Polity Press.

Beane, J. A. (1997). *Curriculum Integration: Designing the Core of Democratic Education.* New York: Teachers College Press.

Beane, J. A. (1998). *Curriculum Matters: Organizing the Middle School Curriculum.* Retrieved 28/07/2004 from National Middle School Association: http://www.nmsa.org/services/cmorganizing.htm.

Beck, I. L. & McKeown, M. G. (2001). Text talk: capturing the benefits of read aloud experience for young children. *The Reading Teacher 55*: 10-20.

Beck, I. L., McKeown, M. G. & Kucan, L. (2002). *Bringing Words to Life.* New York: Guilford Publications.

Bellanca, J. (1992). *The Cooperative Think Tank II: Graphic Organizers to Teach Thinking in the Cooperative Classroom.* Palantine, IL: Skylight.

Bellanca, J. (1992). *The Cooperative Think Tank: Graphic Organizers to Teach Thinking in the Cooperative Classroom.* Palantine, IL: Skylight.

Bellanca, J. & Fogarty, R. (1991). *Blueprints for Thinking in the Cooperative Classroom.* Palantine, IL: Skylight.

Benton Foundation (1996). *Buildings, Books, and Bytes: Libraries and Communities in the Digital Age.* Washington, DC.

Bereiter, C. & Scardamalia, M. (1998). Beyond Bloom's Taxonomy: Rethinking knowledge for the Knowledge Age. In Hargreaves, A. et al. (eds.), *International Handbook of Educational Change* (pp. 675-692). Dordrecht: Kluwer.

Berman, P. & McLaughlin, M. (1976). Implementation of educational innovation. *Educational Forum 40*(3): 345-370.

Beswick, N. (1986). *Re-thinking Active Learning.* London: Falmer.

Bigum, C. (2002). Design sensibilities, schools, and the new computing and communication technologies. In *Silicon Literacies: Communication, Innovation, and Education in the Electronic Age* (pp. 130-140). London: Falmer-Routledge.

Bigum, C. (2004). *The Knowledge Producing School.* Retrieved 28/07/2004 from http://www.cite.hku.hk/events/doc/2004/ChrisBigumhksem

Bigum, C., Lankshear, C. & Knobel, K. (in process). Schools as knowledge producers. Research proposal under development. Rockhampton: Faculty of Education and Creative Arts, Central Queensland University. Cited in Lankshear, C. & Knobel, M. (2003). *New Literacies: Changing Knowledge and Classroom Learning.* Philadelphia: Open University Press.

Blase, J. (1987). Dimensions of effective school leadership: The teacher perspective. *American Educational Research Journal 24*(4): 589-610.

Blase, J. (1993). The micropolitics of effective school-based leadership: Teachers' perspectives. *Educational Administration Quarterly 29*(2): 142-163.

Bolter, J. D. & Grusin, R. (2000). *Remediation: Understanding New Media.* Cambridge: MIT Press.

Bond, L., Smith, T., Baker, W. & Hattie, J. (2000). *The Certification System of the National Board for Professional Teaching Standards: A Construct and Consequential Validity Study.* Greensboro, NC: Center for Educational Research and Evaluation.

Branch, J. (2003). Teaching, learning and information literacy: developing an understanding of preservice teachers' knowledge. *Behavioral and Social Sciences Librarians, 22*(1).

Brown, A. L. (1997). Transforming schools into communities of thinking and learning about serious matters. *American Psychologist, 52*(4): 399-413.

Brown, G. (1999). Information literacy curriculum and assessment: implications for schools in New Zealand. In *The Information Literate School Community: Best Practice* (pp. 55-74). Wagga Wagga, NSW: Centre for Information Studies, Charles Sturt University.

Brown, G. (2002). *Teachers' Conceptions of Assessment.* Unpublished PhD Thesis, University of Auckland.

Brown, G. T. (2003). Searching informational texts: Text and task characteristics that affect performance. *Reading Online, 7*(2). Retrieved from http://www.readingonline.org/articles/art_index.asp?HREF=brown/index.html.

Bruce, B.C. (2002). New technologies and social change: Learning in the global cyberage. In *Research in International Education* (pp. 171-190). New York: Peter Lang.

Bruce, C. (1997). *The Seven Faces of Information Literacy.* Blackwood: Auslib Press Pty.

Bruce, C. & Candy, P. (2000). *Information Literacy Around the World: Advances in Programs and Research.* Wagga Wagga, NSW: Charles Sturt University.

Bullmaster, M. A. & Darling-Hammond, L. (1997). Changing social context of teaching in the US. In *International Handbook of Teachers and Teaching* (pp. 1052-1079). Boston: Kluwer.

Campbell, B. S. (1995). High School Principal Roles and Implementation Themes for Mainstreaming Information Literacy Instruction. Unpublished doctoral dissertation, University of Connecticut. In *Dissertations Abstracts International* (A 56/03, p. 770).

Canada (2002). *Canada's Innovative Strategy.* Retrieved 28/07/2004 from http://www.innovationstrategy.gc.ca/gol/innovation/interface.nsf/engdocBasic/3.html.

Canadian Council of Ministries of Education (1999). *Shared Priorities in Education at the Dawn of the 21st Century: Future Directions for the Council of Ministries of Education Canada.* Retrieved 28/07/2004 from http://www.cmec.ca/reports/victoria99.en.stm.

Canadian Library Association (2000). *Statement on Effective School Library Programs in Canada*. Retrieved 28/07/2004 from http://www.cla.ca/about/school.htm.

Castells, M. (1996). *The Rise of the Networked Society*. Oxford: Blackwell.

Castells, M. (1998). *End of Millennium*, 2nd ed. Malden, MA: Blackwell.

Castells, M., Flecha, R., Freire, P., Giroux, H. A., Macedo, D. & Willis, P. (1999). *Critical Education in the New Information Age*. Lanham: Rowman & Littlefield.

Chall, J. S. (1983). *Stage of Reading Development*. New York: McGraw-Hill.

Chall, J. S. (1996). *Stages of Reading Development*, 2nd ed. Fort Worth: Harcourt Brace.

Chall, J. S., Jacobs, V. A. & Baldwin, L. E. (1990). *The Reading Crisis: Why Poor Children Fall Behind*. Cambridge: Harvard University Press.

Charter, J. B. (1982). Case Study Profiles of Six Exemplary Public High School Library Media Programs. Unpublished doctoral dissertation, Florida State University. In *Dissertations Abstracts International* (293A-294A, p. 43).

The Children's Partnership (2000). *Online Content for Low-Income and Underserved Americans*. Santa Monica, CA.

Christie, J. F. (1990). Dramatic play: a context for meaningful engagements. *The Reading Teacher 43*: 542-545.

Clark, D. & Clark, S. (1996). Building collaborative environments for successful middle level school restructuring. *NASSP Bulletin 80*(578): 1-16.

Clay, M. M. (1991). *Becoming Literate: The Construction of Inner Control*. Portsmouth: Heinemann.

Clyde, L. A. (1999). *Managing InfoTech in School Library Media Centers*. Englewood, CO: Libraries Unlimited.

Clyde, L. A. & Lobban, M. (2001). A door half open: young people's access to fiction related to homosexuality. *School Libraries Worldwide 7*(2): 17-30.

Conference Board of Canada (2000). *Employability Skills 2000+*. Retrieved 28/07/2004 from http://www.conferenceboard.ca/education/learning-tools/employability-skills.htm.

Cooper, C. & Boyd, J. (1995). *Schools as Collaborative Learning Communities*. Launceston, Tas.: Global Learning Communities. Retrieved 16/07/2004 from http://www.vision.net.au/~globallearning/pages/lfs/clc_artcle.html

Corr, G. P. (1979). Factors that Affect the School Library Media Specialist's Involvement in Curriculum Planning and Implementation in Small High Schools in Oregon. Unpublished doctoral dissertation, University of Oregon. In *Dissertations Abstracts International* (2955A, p. 40).

Cousins, B. (1996). *Understanding Organizational Learning for Educational Learning for Educational Leadership and School Reform*. Paper presented at the annual conference of the Canadian Society for the Study of Education, Calgary.

Cranston, N. (1994). Translating the 'new organization' into educational settings. *International Studies in Educational Administration 60*: 24-31.

Crawford, W. & Gorman, M. (1995). *Future Libraries: Dreams, Madness & Reality*. Chicago: American Library Association.

Cushman, K. (1993). What's essential? Integrating the curriculum in essential schools. *Horace, 9*(4). Retrieved 28/07/2004 from http://www.essentialschools.org/cs/resources/view/ces_res/171.

Davenport, T. & Prusak, L. (1998). *Working Knowledge: How Organizations Manage What They Know*. Boston: Harvard Business School Press.

Deal, T. (1990). Reframing reform. *Educational Leadership 47*(8): 6-12

Deal, T. E. & Peterson, K. D. (1999). *Shaping School Culture: The Heart of Leadership*. San Francisco: Jossey-Bass.

Debowski, S. (2001). Policies for collection management. In K. Dillon, J. Henri & J. McGregor (eds.), *Providing More With Less: Collection Management for School Libraries* (pp. 115-142). Wagga Wagga, NSW: Charles Sturt University.

Dekker, B. (1989). Principals and teacher-librarians: their roles and attitudes regarding school libraries: results of a survey of elementary schools in Ontario. *School Libraries in Canada 10*(2): 32-37.

Dertouzos, M. L. (1997). *What Will be: How the New World of Information Will Change Our Lives*. San Francisco, CA: HarperEdge.

Dewey, J. (1916). *Democracy and Education: An Introduction to the Philosophy of Education*. New York: Macmillan.

Dickinson, D. K. & Smith, M. W. (1994). Long-term effects of preschool teachers' book reading on low-income children's vocabulary and story comprehension. *Reading Research Quarterly 29*(2): 104-122.

Dizard, W. J. (2000). *Old Media, New Media: Mass Communications in the Information Age*, 3rd ed. New York: Longman.

Doiron, R. (2001). University-school library collaborations to integrate information technology into the pre-service teaching environment, *Journal of Professional Studies 8*(2): 28-35.

Donahue, P. L., Voelkl, K. E., Campbell, J. R. & Mazzeo, J. (1999). *NAEP 1998 Report Card for the Nation and States*. Washington, DC: US Department of Education.

Dorrell, L. D. & Lawson, L. (1995). What are the school principals' perceptions of the school library media specialists? *NASSP Bulletin 79*(573): 72-80.

Dovey, J. (1996). *Fractal Dreams: New Media in Social Context.* London: Lawrence & Wishart.

Dowhower, S. L. (1994). Repeated reading revisited: Research into practice. *Reading and Writing Quarterly 10*(4): 343-358.

Doyle, C.S. (1993). The Delphi Method as a qualitative assessment tool for development of outcome measures for information literacy. *School Library Media Annual 11*: 132-144.

Doyle, C. S. (1994). *Information Literacy in an Information Society: A Concept for the Information Age.* Syracuse, NY: ERIC Clearinghouse on Information and Technology.

Dressman, M. (1997). *Literacy in the Library.* Westport, CT: Bergin & Garvey.

Duke, N. (2000a). 3.6 minutes per day: the scarcity of informational texts in first grade. *Reading and Research Quarterly 35*(2): 202-224.

Duke, N. (2000b). For the rich it's richer: print experiences and environments offered to children in very low- and very high-socioeconomic status first-grade classrooms. *American Educational Research Journal 37*(2): 441-478.

Duke, N. K. & Purcell-Gates, V. (2003). Genres at home and at school: Bridging the know to the new. *The Reading Teacher 57*(1): 30-37.

Duke, N. K., Bennett-Armistead, V. S. & Roberts, E. M. (2003). Filling the great void. *American Educator 27*(1): 30-35.

Durkin, D. (1993). *Teaching them to Read*, 6th ed. Boston: Allyn & Bacon.

Education Queensland (2000a). *Literate Futures: Report of the Literacy Review for Queensland State Schools.* Brisbane.

Education Queensland (2000b) *Education Queensland Strategic Plan 2000-2004.* Brisbane.

Education Queensland (2001). *New Basics Project.* Retrieved 28/07/2004 from http://www.education.qld.gov.au/corporate/newbasics/

Ehri, L. C. (1998). Grapheme-phoneme knowledge is essential for learning to read words in English. In J. L. Metsala & L. C. Ehri (eds.), *Word Recognition in Beginning Literacy.* Mahwah, NJ: Erlbaum.

Ehri, L. C., Nunes, S. R., Willows, D. M., Schuster, B. V., Yaghoub-Zadeh, Z. & Shanahan, T. (2001). Phonemic awareness instruction helps children learn to read: Evidence from the National Reading Panel's meta-analysis. *Reading Research Quarterly 36*: 250-287.

Ericsson , K. A. & Charness, N. (1994). Expert performance: its structure and acquisition. *American Psychologist 46*(8): 725-747.

Estabrook, L. (2003). *Public Libraries and Civil Liberties: A Profession Divided.* University of Illinois at Urbana-Champaign. Retrieved 28/07/2004 from http://alexia.lis.uiuc.edu/gslis/research/civil_liberties.html.

Evans, R. (1993). The human face of reform. *Educational Leadership 51*(1): 19-23.

Fairclough, N. (1989). *Language and Power.* London: Longman.

Fairclough, N. (1995). *Critical Discourse Analysis: The Critical Study of Language.* Harlow: Longman.

Fairclough, N. (2000). *New Labour, New Language?.* London: Routledge.

Farmer, L. (1995). *Leadership within the School Library and Beyond.* Worthington, OH: Linworth.

Farmer, L. (1999). *Partnerships for Lifelong Learning.* Worthington, OH: Linworth.

Farmer, L. (2001). *Teaming with Opportunity.* Englewood, CO: Libraries Unlimited.

Farmer, L. (2002). Issues in electronic resource services in K-12 school library settings. *Education Libraries 25*(2): 6-12.

Farwell, S. M. (1999). Profile of Planning: A Study of a Three-Year Project on the Implementation of Collaborative Library Media Programs. Unpublished doctoral dissertation, Florida International University. In *Dissertations Abstracts International* (A 59/11, p. 4042).

Fielding-Bransley, R. (1997). Explicit instruction of decoding benefits children high in phonemic awareness and alphabet knowledge. *Scientific Studies of Reading 1*(1): 85-98.

Feiman-Nemser, S. & Beasley, K. (1997). Mentoring assisted performance: a case of co-planning. In V. Richardson (ed.), *Constructivist Teacher Education: Building a World of New Understandings* (pp. 108-126). London: Falmer.

Fiske, E. & Ladd, H. (2000). *When Schools Compete: A Cautionary Tale.* Washington, DC: Brookings Institution Press.

Flockton, L. & Crooks, T. (2002). *Information Skills; Assessment Results 2001.* Dunedin: Educational Assessment Research Unit, University of Otago.

Foorman, B. R., Fletcher, J. M., Francis, D. J., Schatschneider, C. & Mehta, P. (1998). The role of instruction in learning to read: preventing reading failure in at-risk children. *Journal of Educational Psychology 90*: 37-55.

Fowler, B. (1996). *Critical Thinking Across the Curriculum Project: Bloom's Taxonomy and Critical Thinking.* Lees' Summit, Miss.: Longview Community College. Retrieved 28/07/2004 from http://www.kcmetro.cc.mo.us/longview/ctac/blooms.htm.

Freire, P. (1998). *Teachers as Cultural Workers: Letters to Those who Dare Teach.* Boulder, CO: Westview Press.

Frender, G. (1990). *Learning to Learn: Strengthening Study Skills and Brain Power.* Nashville, TN: Incentive Publications.

Frender, G. (1994). *Teaching for Learning Success: Practical Strategies & Materials for Everyday Use.* Nashville, TN: Incentive Publications.

Fromkin, V., Rodman, R., Hultin, N. & Logan, H. (1997). *An Introduction to Language.* Toronto: Harcourt Brace.

Fullan, M. (1993). *Change Forces: Probing the Depths of Educational Reform.* London: Falmer.

Fullan, M. (1995). The school as a learning organization: distant dreams. *Theory Into Practice 34*(4): 230-235.

Fullan, M. (1998). Leadership for the 21st century: breaking the bonds of dependency, *Educational Leadership 55*(7): 6-10.

Fullan, M. (2001). *Leading in a Culture of Change.* San Francisco: Jossey-Bass.

Fullan, M. (2002). The role of leadership in the promotion of knowledge management in schools. *Teachers and Teaching: Theory and practice 8*(3/4): 409-418.

Fullan, M. & Hargreaves, A. (1996). *What's Worth Fighting for in Your School?.* New York: Teachers College Press.

Galbraith, J. & Lawler, E. (1993). *Organizing for the Future: The New Logic for Managing Complex Organizations.* San Francisco: Jossey-Bass.

Gallego, M. A. & Hollingsworth, S. (2000). *What Counts as Literacy?: Challenging the School Standards.* New York: Teachers College Press.

Gambrell, L. B. & Javitz, P. B. (1993). Mental imagery, text illustrations and children's story comprehension. *Reading Research Quarterly 28*(3): 264-276.

Gambrell, L. B., Wilson, R. M. & Gantt, W. N. (1981). Classroom observations of good and poor readers. *Journal of Educational Research 74*(6): 400-404.

Garvin, D. (2000). *Learning in Action: A Guide to Putting the Learning Organization to Work.* Boston: Harvard Business School Press.

Gawith, G. (1987a). *Information Alive.* Auckland: Longman Paul.

Gawith, G. (1987b). *Information Skills for Research and Reading.* Auckland: Longman Paul.

Gawith, G. (1988). *Action Learning: Student Guide to Research and Information Skills.* Auckland: Longman Paul.

Gee, J. P. (2000). New people in new worlds: networks, the new capitalism and schools. In *Multiliteracies: Literacy Learning and the Design of Social Futures* (pp. 43-68). New York: Routledge.

Gee, J. (2002). New times and new literacies. In *Learning for the Future: New Worlds, New Literacies, new learning, new people* (pp. 59-83). Australia: Common Ground.

Gee, J., Hull, G. & Lankshear, C. (1996). *The New Work Order: Behind the Language of the New Capitalism*. Sydney: Allen & Unwin.

Gee, J. P., Michaels, S. & O'Connor, M. C. (1992). Discourse analysis. In *Handbook of Qualitative Research in Education* (pp. 227-291). San Diego: Academic Press.

Gehlken, V. S. (1995). The Role of the High School Library Media Program in Three Nationally Recognized South Caroline Blue Ribbon Secondary Schools. Unpublished doctoral dissertation, University of South Carolina. In *Dissertations Abstracts International* (A55/11, p. 3338).

Giroux, H. (1981). *Ideology, Culture and the Process of Schooling*. Philadelphia: Temple University Press.

Giroux, H. (1988). *Teachers as Intellectuals: Towards a Critical Pedagogy of Learning*. Westport, CT: Bergin & Garvey.

Goforth, R. & Goforth, K. (1999). *Social Justice E-zine, 32*. Retrieved 28/07/2004 from http://www.anarki.net/abc/news/0074.html

Graves, M. & Watts-Taffe, S. (2002). The place of word consciousness in a research-based vocabulary program. In *What Research has to Say about Reading Instruction*. Newark: International Reading Association.

Griffiths, D. (1988). Administrative theory. In *Handbook of Research on Educational Administration* (pp. 27-51). New York: Longman.

Groundwater-Smith, S. (2001). *Supporting and Sustaining the Knowledge Building School*. Paper presented at the European Educational Research Association Annual Conference, Lille, France, 5-8 September 2001.

Guthrie, J., Alao, S. & Rinehart, J. (1997). Engagement in reading for young adolescents. *Journal of Adolescent & Adult Literacy 40*(6): 438-446.

Hall, S. (1996). The meaning of new times. In *Stuart Hall: Cultural Dialogues in Cultural Studies* (pp. 223-237). London: Routledge.

Hall, S. (1997). The spectacle of the 'Other'. In *Representations: Cultural Representations and Signifying Practices* (pp. 223-276). London: Sage.

Handy, C. (1995). Managing the dream. In S. Chawla & J. Renesch (eds.), *Learning Organizations: Developing Cultures for Tomorrow's Workplace* (pp. 45-56). Portland, OR: Productivity Press.

Hanson, K. (2000). Knowledge management: Interaction not transaction. In Hay, L. & Henri, J. (eds.), *Enter the Millennium: Information Services in Schools 1999 Online Conference Proceedings*. Wagga Wagga, NSW: Centre for Studies in Teacher Librarianship.

Hargreaves, A. (1995). Cultures of Teaching and Educational Change. In *International Handbook of Teachers and Teaching* (pp. 1297-1316). Boston: Kluwer.

Hargreaves, A. (1997). *Changing Teachers, Changing Times: Teachers' Work and Culture in the Postmodern Age*. New York: Teachers College Press.

Harris, T. & Hodges, R. E. (1995). *The Literacy Dictionary, the Vocabulary of Reading and Writing*. Newark: International Reading Association.

Hart, B. & Risley, T. R. (1995). *Meaningful Differences in the Everyday Experiences of Young American Children*. Baltimore: Brooks.

Hartwell, G. & Vargas-Baron, E. (1998). *Learning for All: Policy Dialogue for Achieving Educational Quarterly*. Presented at the International Working Group on Education, Munich, 23-26 June 1998.

Hauck, P. & Schieman, E. (1985). *The Role of Teacher-Librarian in Alberta Schools*. Unpublished Research Report, University of Calgary, AB, Canada (ERIC Documentation Reproduction Service No. ED262788).

Hawamdeh, S. (2003). *Knowledge Management: Cultivating Knowledge Professionals*. Oxford: Chandos.

Hay, L. (1999). Information policy issues: curse or cure? In L. Hay & J. Henri (eds.), *The Net Effect: School Library Media Centers and the Internet* (pp. 160-174). Lanham, MD: Scarecrow Press.

Hay, L. & Henri, J. (1995). Leadership for collaboration: making vision work. In *Proceedings of the IFLA Conference, School Libraries Programme Session, Istanbul, Turkey*. Retrieved from http://www.ifla.org/IV/ifla61/61-hayl.htm.

Hay, L., Henri, J. & Oberg, D. (1999). The principal's role in developing information literacy: findings from Australia and Canada. In S. Shoham & M. Yitzhaki (eds.), *Education for All: Culture, Reading and Information: Proceedings of the 27th International Conference of the International Association of School Librarianship* (pp. 69-80). Israel: Ramat-Gan.

Hellene, D. L. I. (1974). The Relationships of the Behaviors of Prinicipals in the State of Washington to the Development of School Library/ Media Programs. Unpublished doctoral dissertation, University of Washington. In *Dissertations Abstracts International* (3835A, p. 34).

Henri, J. (1995). The information literate school community: exploring a fuzzy concept. *Scan 14*(3): 25-28.

Henri, J. (1998). Developing information literate schools: findings from Australia. In *Proceedings of the IFLA Conference, Section of School Libraries and Resource Centres, Amsterdam, Holland*. Retrieved from http://farrer.riv.csu.edu.au/principal/survey/report/paper_AU.html.

Henri, J. (1999a). The information literate school community: not just a pretty face. In *The Information Literate School Community: Best Practice*. Wagga Wagga: Centre for Information Studies, Charles Sturt University.

Henri, J. (1999b). *Teachers Seeking, Using and Making Information: What do we Know?* Paper presented at the Millennium: Information Services in Schools, 1999 online conference. Retrieved 12/12/2003 from http://www.csu.edu.au/cstl/community/isis/pubs/isis99.html

Henri, J. (2000a). *The Information Literate School Community and Authentic Assessment*. Paper presented at the meeting of the Tasmanian Education Department, Hobart, Australia, May 2000.

Henri, J (2000b). *The Information Literate School Community and the Role of the Principal*. Paper presented at the WASLA Conference, Perth, Australia, October 2000.

Henri, J. (2001). Thinking and informing: a reality check on class teachers and teacher-librarians. In P. Hughes & L. Selby (eds.), *Inspiring Connections: Learning, Libraries and Literacies: Proceedings of the 30th Annual Conference of the International Association of School Librarianship* (pp. 119-128). Seattle: IASL.

Henri, J. (2004). *Building an Information Literate School Community: Putting Teachers First*. Paper presented at the ASLA Online 1: Constructing communities of learning and literacy conference 2004. Abstract retrieved 20/04/2004 from http://www.asla.org.au/online/il_abstracts.htm

Henri, J. & Hay, L. (1996). The principal's role in developing and supporting an information literate school community. In *Beyond the Horizon: Conference Proceedings of the Fourteenth Biennial Conference of the Australian School Library Association* (pp. 111-125). West Perth, Australia: ASLA.

Henri J., Boyd, S., & Eyre, G. (2002). *Sculpting an Information Literate School Community: Looking for Touchstones*. Paper presented at the Sixth International Forum on Research in School Librarianship, 31st Annual Conference of the International Association of School Librarianship, Petaling Jaya, Malaysia, August 2002.

Henri, J., Hay, L. & Oberg, D. (2002). *The School Library-Principal Relationship: Guidelines for Research and Practice (IFLA Professional Report, No. 78)*. The Hague: IFLA.

Henson, K. (2004). *Constructivist Methods for Teaching in Diverse Middle Level Classrooms*. Boston: Allyn and Bacon.

Heppell, S. (2003). *No one Ever Said This Was Going to be Easy.* Keynote address presented at the International Conference on Computers in Education, Hong Kong, December 2003.

Herz, S. & Gallo, D. (1996). *From Hinton to Hamlet: Building Bridges Between Young Adult Literate and the Classics.* Westport, CT: Greenwood Press.

Hiebert, E. (1999). Text matters in learning to read. *The Reading Teacher 52*(6): 552-556.

Hill, J., Hawk. K. & Taylor, K. (2002). Professional development: what makes it work? *SET 2*: 12-15.

Hirsch, E. D., Jr. (2003). Reading comprehension requires knowledge of words and the world. *American Educator 27*(1): 10-29.

Hoggett, P. (1997). Contested communities. In *Contested Communities: Experiences, Struggles, Policies.* Bristol: Policy Press.

Hood, D. (1998). *Our Secondary Schools Don't Work Anymore.* Auckland: Profile Books.

Hood, D. (2002). Thinking outside the boxes. *New Zealand Education Review 22*(7).

Hopkins, D (1996). Towards a theory for school improvement. In J. Gray, D. Reynolds, C. Fitz-Gibbon & D. Jesson (eds.), *Merging Traditions: The Future of Research on School Effectiveness and School Improvement.* London: Cassell.

Hopkins, S. M. (1996). The Library Bill of Rights and school library media programs. *Library Trends 45*(1): 61-74.

Houghton, J. M. & Houghton, R. S. (1999). *Decision Points: Boolean Logic for Computer Users and Beginning Online Searchers.* Englewood, CO: Linworth.

Howe, N. & Strauss, W. (2000). *Millennials Rising: The Next Great Generation.* New York: Vintage Books.

Hughes, S. M. & Mancall, J. C. (1999). Developing a collaborative access environment: meeting the resource needs of the learning community. In B. K. Stripling (ed.), *Learning and Libraries in an Information Age: Principles and Practice* (pp. 231-259). Englewood, CO: Libraries Unlimited.

Hunsader, P. D. (2002). Why boys fail and what we can do about it? *Principal 82*(2): 52-55.

Hunt, T. & Trebilcock, M. (2003). Three level learning: information literacy learning through the Internet. *Computers in New Zealand Schools 15*(1): 5-10.

The Information Literate School Community: Best Practice (1999). (J. Henri & K. Bonanno, eds.). Wagga Wagga: Charles Sturt University.

International Association for the Evaluation of Educational Achievement (2001). *PIRLS News.* Retrieved 19/10/2003 from http://timss.bc.edu/pirls2001i/PIRLS2001_news.html

International Association of School Librarianship (1993). *IASL Policy Statement on School Libraries*. Retrieved 28/07/2004 from http://www.iasl-slo.org/policysl.html.

International Federation of Library Association and Institutions (2000). *IFLA/UNESCO School Library Manifesto: The School Library in Teaching and Learning for All*. Retrieved 28/07/2004 from http://www.ifla.org/VII/s11/pubs/manifest.htm.

International Federation of Library Associations and Institutions (2002). *The IFLA Internet Manifesto*. Retrieved 28/07/2004 from http://www.ifla.org/III/misc/im-e.htm.

International Federation of Library Associations and Institutions (2002). *The IFLA/UNESCO School Library Guidelines*. Retrieved 28/07/2004 from http://www.ifla.org/VII/s11/pubs/sguide02.pdf.

International Reading Association (2003). *The Role of Reading Instruction in Addressing the Overrepresentation of Minority Children in Special Education in the United States*. Retrieved 28/07/2004 from http://www.reading.org/positions/overrepresentation.html.

International Society for Technology in Education (2000). *National Educational Technology Standards for Teachers*. Eugene, OR.

Ivey, R. (2003). Information literacy: How do librarians and academics work in partnership to deliver effective programs? *Australian Academic & Research Libraries 34*(2): 100-113.

Jackson, D. (1998). Breaking out of the binary trap: boys' underachievement, schooling and gender relations. In E. Epstein, V. H. Elwood & J. Maw (eds.), *Failing Boys? Issues in Gender and Achievement*. Philadelphia: Open University Press.

Jensen, E. (1997). *Brain Compatible Strategies*. San Diego, CA: The Brain Store.

Juel, E. & Roper-Schneider, D. (1985). The influence of basal readers on first grade Reading. *Reading Research Quarterly 20*(2): 134-152.

Kahn, C. & Mallette, M. (2002). Why do we need a teacher-librarian or a library when we have the Internet? *Teacher Librarian 29*(4). Retrieved 28/07/2004 from http://www.teacherlibrarian.com/tlmag/v_29/v_29_4_feature_bonus.html

Kapitzke, C. (2001). Information literacy: the changing library. *Journal of Adolescent and Adult Literacy 44*(5): 450-456.

Kapitzke, C. (2003a). (In)formation literacy: a positivist epistemology and a politics of (out)formation. *Educational Theory 53*(1): 37-53.

Kapitzke, C. (2003b). Information literacy: the changing library. In *Literacy in the Information Age: Inquiries into Meaning Making with New Technologies* (pp. 59-69). Newark, DE: International Reading Association.

Kember, D. (1997). A reconceptualisation of the research into university academics' conceptions of teaching. *Learning and Instruction 7*(3): 255-275.

Kibby, M. W. (2000). What will be the demands of literacy in the workplace in the next millenium? *Reading Research Quarterly 35*(3): 378-383.

Kintsch, W. (1998). *Comprehension: A Paradigm for Cognition.* New York: Cambridge University Press.

Kinzer, C.K. (2003). The importance of recognizing the expanding boundaries of literacy. *Reading Online 6*(10). Retrieved 28/07/2004 from http://www.readingonline.org/ electronic/elecindex.asp?HREF=/electronic/kinzer/index.html

Kist, W. (2001). Searching for new literacy classrooms: An invitation. *Reading Online 5*(1). Retrieved 28/07/3004 from http://www.readingonline.org/newliteracies/lit_index.asp? HREF=/newliteracies/kist/index.html

Koechlin, C. & Zwaan, S. (2001). *Info Tasks for Successful Learning: Building Skills in Reading, Writing, and Research.* Markham, Ontario: Pembroke.

Kolencik, P. L. (2001). Principals and Teacher-Librarians: Building Collaborative Partnerships in the Learning Community. Unpublished doctoral dissertation, University of Pittsburgh. In *Dissertations Abstracts International* (A 62/05, p. 1784).

Koskinen, P. S., Gambrell, L. B., Kapinus, B. A. & Heathington, B. S. (1988). Retelling: a strategy for enhancing students' reading comprehension. *The Reading Teacher 41*(9): 892-896.

Kouzes, J. M. & Posner, B. Z. (2002). *The Leadership Challenge*, 3rd ed. San Francisco, CA: Jossey Bass.

Kuhlthau, C. C. (1993a). Implementing a process approach to information skills: A study identifying indicators of success in library media programs. *School Library Media Quarterly 22*(1): 11-18.

Kuhlthau, C. C. (1993b). *Seeking Meaning: A Process Approach to Library and Information Services.* Norwood, NJ: Ablex.

Laforty, J. (2001). *Choreographing the Chaos.* Keynote address to Forging Future Directions, ASLA XVII Conference, Twin Waters, Queensland.

Lance, K. C. (2001). Proof of the power: quality library media programs effect academic achievement. *Multimedia Schools 8*(4): 14-20.

Lance, K C., Rodney, M. & Hamilton-Pennell, C. (2000). *How the School Librarians Help Kids Achieve Standards: The Second Colorado Study.* Retrieved 28/07/2004 from http://www.lrs.org/documents/lmcstudies/CO/execsumm.pdf

Langerman, D. (1990). Books & boys: gender preferences and book selection. *School Library Journal 36*(3): 132-136.

Lankshear, C. & Knobel, M. (2003). *New Literacies: Changing Knowledge and Classroom Learning.* Philadelphia: Open University Press.

LaRoque, L. &Coleman, P. (1991). Negotiating the master contract: Transformational leadership and school district quality. In K. Leithwood and D. Musella (eds.), *Understanding School System Administration: Studies of the Contemporary Chief Education Officer.* New York: Falmer.

LaRocque, L. & Oberg, D. (1990). Building bridges between the library and the principal's office. In *Proceedings of the 19th Conference of the International Association of School Librarianship, Umea, Sweden.* Kalamazoo, MI: IASL.

Learning for the Future: New Worlds, New Literacies, New Learning, New People (2002). (M. Kalantzis, G. Varnava-Skoura & B. Cope, eds.). Australia: Common Ground.

Lee, M. (1998). Learning communities: an opportunity for Australia's teacher librarians. *Access 12*(4): 17-19.

Leithwood, K., Dart, B., Jantzi, D. & Steinbach, R. (1993). *Building Commitment for Change and Fostering Organisational Learning (Final Report).* Victoria, BC: British Columbia Ministry of Education.

Lemke, J. (1996). Critical literacy for the multimedia future. *Interpretations 29*(2): 1-18.

Lenhart, A., Simon, M. & Graziano, M. (2001). *The Internet and Education: Findings of the Pew Internet and American Life Project.* Washington, DC: Pew Internet and American Life Project.

Leu, D. (2000). Literacy and technology: deictic consequences for literacy education in an information age. In *Handbook of Reading Research 3* (pp. 743-770). Newark, DE: International Reading Association.

Leu, D. (2002). The new literacies: research on reading instruction with the Internet. In *What Research Has to Say About Reading Instruction.* Newark: International Reading Association.

Leu, D. J., Kinzer, C. K., Coiro, J. & Cammack, D. W. (2004). Toward a theory of new literacies emerging from the Internet and other information and communication technologies. In *Theoretical models and processes of reading,* 5th ed. (pp. 1570-1613). Newark: International Reading Association. Available: http://www.readingonline.org/newliteracies/lit_index.asp?HREF=/newliteracies/leu

Leung, C. & Pikulski, J. J. (1990). Incidental word learning of kindergarten and first grade children through repeated read aloud events. In J. Zutell & S. McCormick (eds.), *Literacy, Theory and Research: Analyses from Multiple Paradigms.* Chicago: National Reading Conference.

Lewin, T. & Medina, J. (2003). To cut failure rate, schools shed students. *New York Times* 31 July: p. A1.

Limberg, L. (1999a). Experiencing information seeking and learning. *Information Research: An International Electronic Journal 5*(1). Retrieved 28/07/2004 from http://informationr.net/ir/5-1/paper68.html.

Limberg, L. (1999b). Three conceptions of information seeking and use. In D. Wilson & D. Allen (eds.), *Exploring the Contexts of Information Behaviour* (pp. 116-135). London: Taylor Graham.

Limberg, L. (2000). Is there a relationship between information seeking and learning outcomes? In C. Bruce & P. Candy (eds.), *Information Literacy Around the World: Advances in Programs and Research* (pp. 193-218). Wagga Wagga: Centre for Information Studies, Charles Sturt University.

Limberg, L. & Alexandersson, M. (2003). The school library as a space for learning. *School Libraries Worldwide 9*(1): 1-15.

Limberg, L., Hultgren, F. & Jarneving, B. (2002). *Informationssökning och Lärande - en Forskningsöversikt [Information Seeking and Learning – An Overview of Research]*. Stockholm: Skolverket.

Lincoln, P. (1987). *The Learning School*. Boston Spa: British Library.

Lobban, M. & Clyde, L. A. (1996). *Out of the Closet and Into the Classroom: Homosexuality in Books for Young People*, 2nd ed. Port Melbourne: DW Thorpe.

Loertscher, D. (2001). *Information Literacy: A Review of the Research. A Guide for Practitioners and Researchers*, 2nd ed. San José, CA: Hi Willow Research and Publishing.

Lohrey, A. (1998). *Critical Literacy: A Professional Development Resource.* Melbourne: Language Australia.

Louis, K. (1994). Beyond managed change: Rethinking how schools improve. *School Effectiveness and School Improvement 5*(1): 2-24.

Louis, K., Kruse, S., & Raywid, A. (1996). Putting teachers at the center of reform: Learning schools and professional communities. *NASSP Bulletin 80*(580): 10-21.

Luke, A. (1998). Getting over method: literacy teaching as work in 'New Times'. *Language Arts 75*(4): 305-313.

Luke, A. & Freebody, P. (1997). The social practices of reading. In S. Muspratt, A. Luke & P. Freebody (eds.), *Constructing Critical Literacies: Teaching and Learning Textual Practice* (pp. 185-225). Creskill, NJ: Hampton Press.

Luke, A. & Kapitzke, C. (1999). Literacies and libraries – archives and cybraries. *Pedagogy Culture & Society 7*(3): 467-491.

Lunsford, K.J. & Bruce, B.C. (2001). Collaboratories: working together on the Web. *Journal of Adolescent & Adult Literacy 45*(1). Retrieved from http://www.readingonline.org/electronic/elec_index.asp?HREF=/electronic/jaal/9-01_Column/index.html

Maclean, M., Bryant, P. & Bradley, L. (1987). Rhymes, nursery rhymes, and reading in early childhood. *Merrill Palmer Quarterly 33*(3): 255-281.

Malhotra, Y. (1996). *Organizational Learning and Learning Organizations: An Overview.* Syracuse, NY: BRINT Institute. Retrieved 28/07/2004 from http://www.brint.com/papers/orglrng.htm

March, C. (1988). *Spotlight on School Improvement.* Sydney: Allen & Unwin.

Marsick, V. & Watkins, K. (1996). Adult educators and the learning organization. *Adult Learning 7*(4): 18-20.

Marton, F. (1994). Phenomenography. In *The International Encyclopedia of Education* (pp. 4424-4429). London: Pergamon.

Marton, F. & Booth, S. (1997). *Learning and Awareness.* Mahwah, NJ: Lawrence Erlbaum.

Marton, F. & Trigwell, K. (2000). Variatio est mater studiorum. *Higher Education Research & Development 19*(3): 381-395.

McGregor, J. H. & Streitenberger, D. C. (1998). Do scribes learn? Copying and information use. *School Library Media Research 1*: 1-17. Retrieved 28/07/2004 from http://www.ala.org/aasl/SLMQ/scribes.html

McKenzie, J. (1997). Making the Net work for schools: Online research modules. *From Now On 7*(1). Retrieved 28/07/2004 from http://www.fno.org/sept97/online.html

McKenzie, J. (1998). The information literate school community. *From Now On: The Educational Technology Journal 8*(1). Retrieved 28/07/2004 from http://fno.org/sept98/infolit.html.

McLuhan, M. & Quentin, F. (1967). *The Medium is the Massage.* New York: Bantam

Mesmir, H. A. (1999). Scaffolding a crucial transition using text with some decodability. *The Reading Teacher 53*(2): 130-142.

Mier, M. (1994). Comprehension monitoring in the elementary school. *The Reading Teacher 37*(8): 770-774.

Milam, P. (2002). *InfoQuest: A New Twist on Information Literacy.* Worthington, OH: Linworth.

Millennial Surveys (2000). Retrieved 15/03/2004 from: http://millennialsrising.com/survey.shtml

Mills, C. W. (1959). *The Sociological Imagination.* New York: Oxford University Press.

Mitchell, L., Cameron, M. & Wylie, C. (2002). *What's Needed to Support and Sustain Good Teaching.* Wellington: New Zealand Council for Educational Research.

Moore, P. (1995). Information literacy: past approaches and present challenges. *New Zealand Annual Review of Education 5*: 137-151.

Moore, P. (1998). *Teaching Information Problem Solving in Primary Schools.* Wellington: Ministry of Education.

Moore, P. (1999). Information literate school communities: beyond teacher librarians. In *The Information Literate School Community: Best Practice* (pp. 99-120). Wagga Wagga: Charles Sturt University.

Moore, P. (2000). *Towards Information Literacy: One School's Journey.* Wellington: New Zealand Council for Educational Research.

Moore, P. (2001). *Learning-inspired Connections.* Paper presented at 30th Conference of the International Association of School Librarianship, Auckland, New Zealand, July 9-12, 2001. Retrieved 28/07/2004 from http://www.iasl-slo.org/keynote-moore2001.html

Moore, P. (2002). *An Analysis of Information Education Worldwide: White Paper.* Presented at the UNESCO, the US National Commission on Libraries and Information Science, and the National Forum on Information Literacy for use at the Information Literacy Meeting of Experts, Prague, The Czech Republic, July.

Moore, P. & Page, N. (2002). Cognitive apprenticeships in education for information literacy. In *Continuing Professional Education in the Library and Information Science Professions.* (P. L. Ward, ed.). IFLA Publications, 100. Munich: K.G. Saur.

Moore, P. & Trebilcock, M. (2003a). *The School Library Team: How does it Influence Learning and Teaching.* Presented at the 32nd International Association of School Librarianship Conference, Durban, 7-11 July.

Moore, P. & Trebilcock, M. (2003b). *The School Library Team: What Does it do to Influence Teaching and Learning.* Unpublished research report, Auckland College of Education, Auckland.

Murphy, J. & Hallinger, P. (1993). *Restructuring Schooling: Learning from Ongoing Efforts.* Newbury Park, CA: Corwin.

Murphy, K. (2000). Ministry list ignores gays. *Xtra West 1*: 13.

Murphy P. K. & Alexander, P. A. (2002). What counts? The predictive powers of subject matter knowledge, strategic processing and interest in domain-specific performance. *Journal of Experimental Education 70*(3): 197-214.

National Center for Educational Statistics (2002). *The Nation's Report Card.* Retrieved 28/07/2004 from http://nces.ed.gov/nationsreportcard/reading/results2002.

National Clearinghouse for Comprehensive School Reform (2002). *The Catalog of School Reform Models*. Portland, OR: Northwest Regional Educational Laboratory.

National Commission on Teaching and America's Future (1996). *What Matters Most: Teaching for America's Future: Report of the National Commission on Teaching and America's Future*. Retrieved 28/07/2004 from http://www.nctaf.org/article/?c=4&sc=42

National Geographic Society (2003). *National Geographic Online*, 2 June 2003 Retrieved 02/06/2003, from http://www.nationalgeographic.com/.

National Reading Panel (2000). *Teaching Children to Read: An Evidence-Based Assessment for the Scientific Research Literature on Reading and Its Implications for Reading Instruction: Report of the Subgroup*. Washington, DC: National Institute of Child Health and Human Development.

Negroponte, N. (1995). *Being Digital*. New York: Vintage Books.

Neuman, S. & Celano, D. (2001). Access to print in low-income and middle-income communities. *Reading Research Quarterly 36*(1): 8-26.

Nevis, E. C., DiBella, A. J. & Gould, J. M. (1995). Understanding organizations as learning systems. *Sloan Management Review 36*(2): 73-85.

New London Group (1996). A pedagogy of multiliteracies: Designing social futures. *Harvard Educational Review 66*(1): 60-92.

New Zealand Department of Education (1988). *Tomorrow's Schools: The Reform of Educational Administration in New Zealand*. Wellington.

New Zealand Education Review Office (1997). *Literacy in New Zealand Schools: Reading*. Wellington.

New Zealand Ministry of Education (1993). *The New Zealand Curriculum Framework/ Te Anga Marautanga o Aotearoa*. Wellington.

New Zealand Ministry of Education (2002). *Digital Horizons: Learning Through ICT*. Wellington.

New Zealand Ministry of Education and National Library of New Zealand (2002). *The School Library and Learning in the Information Landscape: Guidelines for New Zealand Schools*. Wellington: Learning Media.

Nonaka, I. (1991). The knowledge creating company. *Harvard Business Review 69*(6): 96-104.

Nonaka, I. (1994). A dynamic theory of organizational knowledge creation. *Organization Science 5*(1): 14-37.

Nonaka, I. & Konno, N. (1998). The concept of 'ba': Building a foundation for knowledge creation. *California Management Review 40*(3): 40-55.

Nonaka, I. & Takeuchi, H. (1995). *The Knowledge-creating Company*. New York: Oxford University Press.

Nonaka, I., Toyama R. & Konno, N. (2001). SECI, ba and leadership: A unified model of dynamic knowledge creation. In *Managing industrial knowledge* (pp. 13-43). London: Sage.

NoodleTools. (2003). *The NoodleShop*. Retrieved 01/05/2003 from http://www.noodletools.com

Oberg, D. (1995). Principal support: What does it mean to teacher-librarians? In *Sustaining the Vision: A Selection of Conference Papers from the 24th Annual Conference of the International Association of School Librarianship, Worcester, UK* (17-25). Retrieved 28/07/2004 from http://www.slis.ualberta.ca/oberg_support.htm.

Oberg, D. (1997). The principal's role in empowering collaboration between teacher-librarians and teachers: Research findings. *Scan 16*(3): 6-8.

Oberg, D., Hay, L. & Henri, J. (1999). The role of the principal in an information literate school community: Findings from an international research project. In L. Lighthall & E. Howe (eds.), *Unleash the Power! Knowledge, Technology, Diversity: Papers Presented at the 3rd International Forum on Research in School Librarianship, Birmingham, USA* (pp. 163-168). Seattle, WA: IASL.

Oberg, D., Hay, L. & Henri, J. (2000). The role of the principal in an information literate school community: Findings from an international research project. *School Library Media Research 3*. Retrieved 28/07/2004 from http://www.ala.org/ala/aasl/aaslpubsand journals /slmrb/slmrcontents/volume32000/principal2.htm

O'Connell, J. & Henri, J. (1997). *Information literacy: Teachers' perspective of the information process*. Paper presented at the 1997 IASL Conference, Vancouver, BC.

Ollmann, H. E. (1993). Choosing literature wisely: Students speak out. *Journal of Reading 36*(8): 648-653.

Olson, D. R. (1994). *The World on Paper*. Cambridge: Cambridge University Press.

O'Reilly, B. (2000). Meet the future: It's your kids. *Fortune,* 24 July: 144-168.

Palinscar, A. S. & Brown, A. L. (1984). Reciprocal teaching of comprehension fostering and monitoring activities. *Cognition and Instruction 1*(2): 117-175.

Pellicer, L., Anderson, L., Keefe, J., Kelley, E. & McCleary, L. (1990). *High School Leaders and their Schools. Volume II: Profiles of Effectiveness*. Reston, VA: National Association of Secondary School Principals (ED 319 139).

Petrides, L. & Guiney, S. (2002). Knowledge management for school leaders: An ecological framework for thinking schools. *Teachers College Record 104*(8): 1702-1717.

Pinker, S. (1994). *The Language Instinct.* New York: Harper Collins.

Poskitt, J. (2001). Schools doing it for themselves: Successful professional development. *SET 1*: 4-7.

Pressley, M. (2000). What should comprehension instruction be the instruction of? In *Handbook of Reading Research 3.* Mahwah, NJ: Lawrence Erlbaum.

Pressley, M. (2002). Metacognition and self-regulated comprehension. In *What Research Has to Say About Reading Instruction.* Newark: International Reading Association.

Pressley, M., Johnson, C. J., Symons, S., McGodrick, J. A. & Kurita, J. A. (1989). Strategies that improve children's memory and comprehension of what is read. *Elementary School Journal 90*(1): 3-32.

Probert, E. (1999). Be in on the benefits of information literacy: Helping students THINK using information skills and information and communication technologies. *Computers in New Zealand Schools 11*(3): 11-14.

Purcell-Gates, V. (1997). Stories, coupons, and the TV guide: Relationships between home literacy experience and emergent literacy knowledge. *Reading Research Quarterly 31*(4): 406-428.

Redding, J. & Catalanello, F. (1992). The fourth iteration: The learning organization as a model of strategic change. *Thresholds in Education 18*: 47-53.

Reinking, D., McKenna, M. C., Labbo, L. D. & Kiefer, B. (1998). *Handbook of Literacy and Technology: Transformations in a Post-Typographic World.* Mahwah, NJ: Lawrence Erlbaum.

Rivkin, S. G., Hanushek, E. A. & Kain, J. F. (2000). *Teachers, Schools, and Academic Achievement.* Retrieved 28/07/2004 from http://www.utdallas.edu/research/tsp/pdfpapers/paper06.pdf.

Robbins, C. & Ehri, L. C. (1994). Reading story books to kindergartners helps them learn new vocabulary words. *Journal of Educational Psychology 86*(1): 54-64.

Rosenholtz, S. J. (1989). *Teachers' Workplace: The Social Organization of Schools.* White Plains, NY: Longman.

Rosenshine, B. & Meister, C. (1994). Reciprocal teaching; a review of the research. *Review of Educational Research 64*(4): 479-530.

Rossman, G., Corbett, D. & Firestone, W. (1988). *Change and Effectiveness in Schools: A Cultural Perspective.* Philadelphia, PA: Research for Better Schools.

Rudman, R. (1999). *Human Resource Management in New Zealand.* Auckland: Addison Wesley.

Rumelhart, D. (1980). Schemata: the building blocks of cognition. In R. J. Spiro, B. C. Bruce & W. F. Bruner (eds.), *Theoretical Issues in Reading Comprehension* (pp. 38-58). Hillsdale, NJ: Lawrence Erlbaum.

Ryan, S. (1995). Introduction: Beginner's mind. In S. Chawla and J. Renesch (eds.), *Learning organizations: Developing cultures for tomorrow's workplace* (pp. 279-292). Portland, OR: Productivity Press.

Samuels, J. (2002). Reading fluency: its development and assessment. In *What Research Has to Say About Reading Instruction*. Newark: International Reading Association.

Sarason, S. (1990). *The Predictable Failure of Educational Reform*. San Francisco: Jossey-Bass.

Scanlon, M. & Buckingham, D. (2002). Popular histories: 'education' and 'entertainment' in information books for children. *Curriculum Journal 13*(2): 141-161.

Scardamalia, M. & Bereiter, C. (1999). Schools as knowledge building organizations. In D. Keating & C. Hertzman (eds.), *Today's Children, Tomorrow's Society: The Developmental Health and Wealth of Nations* (pp. 274-289). New York: Guilford.

Schein, E. (1985). *Organizational Culture and Leadership*. San Francisco: Jossey-Bass.

Schön, D. (1983). *The Reflective Practitioner*. New York: Basic Books.

Schön, D. (1990). *Educating the Reflective Practitioner*. New York: Jossey-Bass.

School Library Association of South Australia (2003). *Role Statement for Teacher Librarians*. Retrieved 28/07/2004 from http://www.slasa.asn.au/rolestatement.html.

Schrader, A. M. (1995). *Fear for Words: Censorship and the Public Libraries of Canada*. Ottawa, ON: Canadian Library Association.

Schrock, K. (2003). *Kathy Schrock's Guide for Educators – Assessment & Rubric Information*. Retrieved 28/07/2004 from http://school.discovery.com/schrockguide/assess.html.

Selby, L. (1999). Information literacy: a blueprint for effective learning and teaching. *Computers in New Zealand Schools 11*(3): 3-4.

Selwyn, N. (2003). Schooling the mobile generation: the future for schools in the mobile-networked society. *British Journal of Sociology of Education 24*(2): 131-144.

Semali, L. M. & Pailliotet, A. W. (1999). *Intermediality: The Teachers' Handbook of Critical Media Literacy*. Boulder, CO: Westview Press.

Senge, P. M. (1990). *The Fifth Discipline: the Art and Practice of the Learning Organisation*. Sydney: Random House.

Senge, P. M. (1996). The ecology of leadership. *Leader to Leader 2*: 18-23. Retrieved 28/07/2004 from http://www.pfdf.org/leaderbooks/l2l/fall96/senge.html

Senge, P., Cambron-McCabe, N., Lucas, T., Smith, B., Dutton, J. & Kleiner, A. (2000). *Schools That Learn: A Fifth Discipline Fieldbook for Educators, Parents, and Everyone Who Cares About Education.* New York: Doubleday.

Senge, P., Roberts, C., Ross, R., Smith, B. & Kleiner, A. (1994). *The Fifth Discipline Fieldbook*. Toronto: Doubleday.

Sergiovanni, T. (1995). *The Principalship: A Reflective Practice Perspective*. Boston: Allyn & Bacon.

Shalla, V. & Schellenberg, G. (1998). *The Value of Words: Literacy and Economic Security in Canada.* Ottawa: Statistics Canada.

Sheppard, B. & Brown, J. (1996). One school district's experience in building a learning organization. *The Morning Watch 24*(1-2): 1-12.

Showers, J. & Joyce, B. (1996). The evolution of peer coaching. *Educational Leadership* 53(6): 12-16.

Silicon Literacies: Communication, Innovation and Education in the Electronic Age (2002). (Ed. I. Snyder). London: Routledge.

Sims, R., Dobbs, G. & Hand, T. (2002). Enhancing quality in online learning: Scaffolding planning and design through proactive evaluation. *Distance Education 23*(2): 135-48.

Slyfield, H. (1997). *New Zealand School Libraries in the Information Age.* Wellington: Research Unit National Library of New Zealand.

Slyfield, H. (2001). *Information Literacy in New Zealand Secondary and Primary Schools.* Wellington: Research Unit National Library of New Zealand.

Smith, E. G. (2001). *Texas School Libraries: Standards, Resources, Services, and Students' Performance. Texas State Library and Archives Commission.* Retrieved 28/07/2004 from http://www.tsl.state.tx.us/ld/pubs/schlibsurvey/index.html

South Australia Department of Education and Children's Services (DECS) (2001). *South Australian Curriculum Standards and Accountability (SACSA) Framework*. Retrieved 28/07/2004 from http://www.sacsa.sa.edu.au/index_fsrc.asp?t=Home

Sparks, D. (1996). A new form of staff development is essential to high school reform. *Educational Forum 60*(3): 260-266.

Spence, S. (2000a). *RBL Revisited*. Retrieved 28/07/2004 from http://www.adelaidehs.sa.edu.au/rblweb/index.htm

Spence, S. (2000b). *Webquests*. Retrieved 28/07/2004 from http://www.adelaidehs.sa.edu.au/rblweb/webquests.htm#integrating

Spence, S. (2002a). *Building an Intranet: Some Handy Hints*. Retrieved 14/04/2003 from http://rblonline.tripod.com/Quorn/INTRANEThints.doc

Spence, S. (2002b). *New Learning Tools 4 U*. Retrieved 14/04/2003 from http://www.adelaidehs.sa.edu.au/ahsintranet/Teachers/qtp/qtp.htm.

Spence, S. (2002c). Oh, where is a teacher librarian when you really need one? *AEU Journal, SA Branch,* June. Retrieved 28/07/2004 from http://www.teachers.ash.org.au/rblonline/Library/aeuarticle.pdf

Spence, S. (2002d). Survey highlights major problems with library staffing. *AEU Journal, SA Branch* December. Retrieved 17/04/2003 from http://www.teachers.ash.org.au/rblonline/Library/aeusurveyarticle.pdf

Spence, S. (2003). *RBL Online*. Retrieved 28/07/2004 from http://www.teachers.ash.org.au/rblonline/.

Spence, S. & Mitchell, P. (2002). *CoSLA Submission to the Senate Inquiry into the Role of Libraries in the Online Environment.*

Spender, D. & Stewart, F. (2002). *Embracing e-Learning in Australian Schools.* Commonwealth Bank. Retrieved 26/07/2004 from http://www.dollarsandsense.com.au/files/embracing_elearning

Stahl, S. A. & Murray, B. A. (1994). Defining Phonological Awareness and its Relationship to Early Reading. *Journal of Educational Psychology 86*(2): 221-234.

Stenmark, D. (2002). Information vs. knowledge: The role of intranets in knowledge management. *Proceedings of the 35thAnnual Hawaii International Conference on System Sciences*, Hawaii. Retrieved 25/03/2004 from http://csdl.computer.org/comp/proceedings/hicss/2002/1435/04/1435toc.htm

Sticht, T. G. & James, J. H. (1984). Listening and reading. In *Handbook of Reading Research.* New York: Longman.

Stoll, L. (2003). *It's about Learning: Leading the Learning School.* Paper presented at School Leadership in the Global Community, Convention of the International Confederation of Principals, Edinburgh, Scotland, July 13-16, 2003. Retrieved 28/07/2004 from http://www.aspa.asn.au/Confs/Icp2003/stoll.htm

Stoll, L & Fink, D. (1996). *Changing our Schools*. Philadelphia: Open University Press.

Street, B. (2003). What's 'new' in new literacy studies? Critical approaches to literacy theory and practice. *Current Issues in Comparative Education 5*(2). Retrieved 28/07/2004 from http://www.tc.columbia.edu/cice/articles/bs152.pdf

Strickland, D. S. & Taylor, D. (1989). Family storybook reading: implications for children, curriculum and families. In *Emerging Literacy: Young Children Learn to Read and Write.* Newark: International Reading Association.

Talisayon, S. D. (2001). *Knowledge Management Tools.* Retrieved 25/03/2004 from http://www.geocities.com/serafintalisayon/Tools.html

Tapscott, D. (1998). *Growing Up Digital: The Rise of the Net Generation*. New York: McGraw Hill.

Tharp, R. G. & Gallimore, R. (1988). *Rousing Minds to Life: Teaching, Learning, and Schooling in Social Context*. New York: Cambridge.

Thomas, J. C., Kellogg, W. A. & Erickson, T. (2001). The knowledge management puzzle: Human and social factors in knowledge management. *IBM Systems Journal 40*(4): 863-884. Retrieved 28/07/2004 from http://researchweb.watson.ibm.com/journal/sj/404/thomas.html

Tichy, N. M. & Cardwell, N. (2002). *The Cycle of Leadership*. New York: Harper Collins.

Tierney, G. & Whitney, M. (1993). Writing a school library resource centre policy. *Access 7*(2): 12-14.

Tierney, G. & Whitney, M. (1998). Policy writing framework review. *Access 12*(3): 16-17.

Todd, R. (1999). Information, technology and learning: collaboration critical. *Computers in New Zealand Schools 11*(3): 5-10.

Todd, R. (2000). Information literacy in electronic environments: Fantasies, facts and futures. In *Virtual Libraries: Virtual Communities: 2000 IATUL Conference*. Abstract retrieved 28/07/2004 from http://dois.mimas.ac.uk/DoIS/data/Articles/juliatulpy:2000:v:10:p:4860.html

Todd, R. (2001a). Knowledge management: The human dimension of collection management. In J. McGregor, K. Dillon & J. Henri (eds.), *Collection management for school libraries* (pp. 71-88). Lanham, MD: Scarecrow Press.

Todd, R. (2001b). Transition for preferred futures of school libraries: Keynote Address. *International Association of School Librarianship Conference & International Research Forum on Research in School Librarianship*, 9-12 July, Auckland. Retrieved 28/07/2004 from http://www.iasl-slo.org/virtualconf2001.html.

Todd, R. (2005). Adolescent information behaviours. In *Reality bytes: Information literacy for independent learning* (pp. 3-17). Carlton, Vic.: School Library Association of Victoria.

Torgesen, J. K., Wagner, R. K. & Rashotte, C. A. (1994). Longitudinal studies of phonological processing and reading. *Journal of Learning Disabilities 27*: 276-286.

Toronto Board of Education (1996). *The Role of the Teacher Librarian in the Toronto Board of Education*. Toronto.

Turner, P. M. (1980). The relationship between the principal's attitude and the amount and type of instructional development performed by the media professional. *International Journal of Instructional Media 7*(2): 127-138.

UNICEF (1995). *The Convention on the Right of the Child.* London: UK Committee for UNICEF.

United Nations (1948). *Universal Declaration of Human Rights.* Office of the High Commissioner for Human Rights. Retrieved 28/07/2004 from http://www.unhchr.ch/udhr/

University of Michigan (2003). *The Internet Public Library-Pathfinders.* Retrieved 28/07/2004 from http://www.ipl.org/div/pf/

Vail, K. (1996). Data-driven decisions. *The Executive Educator 18*(4): 28-30.

Van Merrienboer, J., Kirschner, P. & Kester, L. (2003). Taking the load off a learner's mind: Instructional design for complex learning *Educational Psychologist 38*(1): 5-13.

Vine, R. (2003). *How Does the Infolink: Information Literacy Skill Course Impact on Teaching Practice.* Auckland College of Education, Auckland.

Walsh, K. (2003). Basal readers: the lost opportunity to build knowledge that propels comprehension. *American Educator 27*(1): 24-27.

Watkins, K. E. & Marsick, V. J. (1993). *Sculpting the Learning Organization: Lessons in the Art and Science of Systematic Change.* San Francisco: Jossey-Bass.

Weick, K. E. (1976). Educational organizations as loosely coupled systems. *Administrative Science Quarterly 21*(1): 1-19.

Wells, G. (1986). *The Meaning Makers: Children Learning Language and Using Language to Learn.* Portsmouth: Heinemann.

Wenger, E. C. & Snyder, W. M. (2000). Communities of practice: The organizational frontier. *Harvard Business Review 78*(1): 139-145.

West, J., Denton, K. & Germino-Hausken, E. (2000). *Early Childhood Longitudinal Study: Kindergarten Class of 1998-99.* Washington, DC: National Center for Educational Statistics.

Western Australia Department of Education (2001). *CMIS Selection Policy.* Retrieved 28/07/2004 from http://www.eddept.wa.edu.au/cmis/eval/library/selection/sel22.htm

Western Australia Department of Education and Training (2003). *Pathfinders Online.* Retrieved 28/07/2004 from http://www.eddept.wa.edu.au/cmis/eval/curriculum/pathfinders/index.htm

Whelan, D. L. (2003). Why isn't information literacy catching on? *School Library Journal 49*(9). Retrieved 28/07/2004 from http://www.schoollibraryjournal.com/index.asp?layout=article&articleid=CA318993.

Wicks, J. (1995). Patterns of reading among teenage boys: the reading habits and book preferences of 13-15 year-old boys. *New Library World 96*: 10-16.

Wiegand, W. A. (2000). *Irrespressible Reformer: A Biography of Melvil Dewey.* Chicago: American Library Association.

Williams, C. L. & Dillon, K. (1993). *Brought to Book.* Melbourne, Vic.: D.W.Thorpe/ALIA Press.

Williams, P. (1998). Censorship, the law and school libraries. *Access 12*(1): 18-20.

Wilson, P. (1983). *Second-hand Knowledge: An Enquiry into Cognitive Authority.* Westport, CT: Greenwood Press.

Wilson, P. J. Blake, M. & Lyders, J. A. (1993). Principals and teacher-librarians: A study and a plan for partnership. *Emergency Librarian 21*(1): 18-24.

Wisner, W. H. (2000). *Whither the Postmodern Library? Libraries, Technology, and Education in the Information Age.* Jefferson, NC: McFarland.

Wittgenstein, L. (1997). *Philosophical Investigations*, 2nd ed. Cambridge, MA: Blackwell.

Wolf, M. & Katzir-Cohen, T. (2001). Reading fluency and its intervention. *Scientific Studies of Reading 5*: 211-238.

Wood, W. & Wood, H. (1996). Vygotsky, tutoring and learning. *Oxford Review of Education 22*(1): 5-17.

Worthy, T. & Broaddus, K. (2002). Fluency beyond the primary grades: from group performance to silent, independent reading. *The Reading Teacher 55*: 334-343.

Wylie, C. (1997). *Self-Managing Schools Seven Years On: What Have We Learnt?* Wellington: NZCER.

Yetter, C. L. (1994). Resource-based Learning in the Information Age School: The Intersection of Roles and Relationships of the School Library Media Specialist, Teachers, and Principals. Unpublished doctoral dissertation, Seattle University. In *Dissertations Abstracts International* (1130A, p. 55).

Yopp, R. H. & Yopp, H. K. (1992). *Literature-based Reading Activities.* Boston: Allyn & Bacon.

Yopp, R. H. & Yopp, H. K. (2000). Sharing informational text with young children. *The Reading Teacher 5*: 410-413.

Young, J. P. & Brozo, W. G. (2001). Boys will be boys, or will they? Literacy and masculinities. *Reading Research Quarterly 36*: 316-325.

About the Editors and Contributors

MARLENE ASSELIN is an Associate Professor, Department of Language and Literacy Education, University of British Columbia (UBC), Canada and the Coordinator of the UBC diploma and masters programs in teacher-librarianship. Her research interests include: school libraries, information literacy, elementary literacy development and instruction, teacher education, and teacher knowledge. Dr Asselin is a member of the editorial and advisory boards for: *School Libraries Worldwide*, *Studies in Media and Information Literacy Education* (SIMILE), and *Reading Teacher*. Recent publications include:

> Asselin, M. & Doiron, R. (2003) An analysis of the inclusion of school library programs and services in the preparation of preservice teachers in Canadian universities. *Behavioral and Social Sciences Librarian 22*(1): 19-32.
>
> Asselin, M., Branch, J. & Oberg, D. (eds.) (2003) *Achieving information literacy: Standards for school library programs in Canada*. Ottawa: Canadian Association of School Librarians and the Association of Teacher-librarians in Canada.
>
> Asselin, M. & Lee, E. (2002) I wish someone had taught me: Information literacy in a teacher education program. *Teacher Librarian 30* (2): 10-17.

Contact at: marlene.asselin@ubc.ca

JEDD BARTLETT is an independent professional development provider in the areas of information literacy, ICT and curriculum integration to schools in the Wairarapa and Hutt Valley region of New Zealand. Jedd has a particular interest in developing student-centred learning programs at the secondary school level, and is currently researching teaching and learning in constructivist-based learning environments. Jedd is supervising an action research project involving teachers in an online integrated studies program for secondary students at the New Zealand Correspondence School during 2004.
Contact at: jedd@ihug.co.nz

JEAN BROWN is currently Professor in the field of Educational Leadership at Memorial University, Newfoundland, Canada and Director of the Centre for e-Learning. Her research interests relate to implementation of computers across the curriculum, with a focus on educational leadership, educational change, and teacher leadership. Jean was the principal investigator in the Newfoundland study for the Canadian Education Association Exemplary Schools Project. Additionally, she has been active in the field of learning resources. She chaired the committee for the development of the Learning to Learn document, the first policy statement on school libraries and resource-based learning in the province of Newfoundland and Labrador. She prefers working with action research teams at the school and district level, and is interested in schools as community learning centres. She supervises graduate students interested in educational leadership, teacher-librarianship, and as Director of the Centre for e-Learning is currently actively involved with facilitating research in the areas of distance learning.
Contact at: jbrown@mun.ca

L. ANNE CLYDE is Professor and Chair of the Library and Information Science Department at the University of Iceland where she teaches and carries out research in the areas of online information services and the Internet. Dr. Clyde's recent publications include: *Managing InfoTech in School Library Media Centers* (1999), *School Libraries and the Electronic Community: The Internet Connection* (1997), and a new book entitled *Weblogs and Libraries* (2003).
Contact at: anne@hi.is

LESLEY FARMER is Professor at California State University Long Beach, and coordinates the Library Media Teacher program. Her research interests include information literacy, collaboration, and educational technology. Dr. Farmer's most recent publications include *Student Success and Library Media Programs: A Systems Approach to Research and Best Practice* (Libraries Unlimited 2003), *How to Conduct Action Research: A Guide for Library Media Specialists* (AASL 2003), and *Teaming with Opportunity: Media Programs, Community Constituencies and Technology* (Libraries Unlimited 2001).
Contact at: lfarmer@csulb.edu

KEN HAYCOCK is Professor in the School of Library, Archival and Information Studies at the University of British Columbia in Vancouver, Canada and executive editor of *Teacher-Librarian: The Journal for School Library Professionals*. Recent publications include *Foundations for Effective School Library Media Programs* (Libraries Unlimited 1999), *The Neal-Schuman Authoritative Guide to Kids' Search Engines, Subject Directories and Portals* (Neal-Schuman 2003), and *The Crisis in Canada's School Libraries: The Case for Reform and Re-investment* (Association of Canadian Publishers 2003).
Contact at: haycock@interchange.ubc.ca

JAMES HENRI is an Associate Professor and the Deputy Director of the Centre for IT in Education, in the Faculty of Education, at the University of Hong Kong. His current research interests include: principal influence, role of teacher librarian, pedagogical practice online, the information literate school community, and information policy. Recent publications include:

> Dillon, K., McGregor, J. & Henri, J. (eds.) (2003) *Collection Management for School Libraries.* Lanham, MD: Scarecrow Press.
> Eustace, K., Meloche, J. & Henri, J. (2003) Developments in tele-learning professional practice in higher education: less teaching, more learning. e-*JIST: the e-Journal of Instructional Science and Technology* 6(2). Retrieved from http://www.usq.edu.au/electpub/e-jist/index.htm
> Henri, J. (2002) Assessing learning: Points for consideration. In S. Capra & J. Ryan (eds.) *Problems are the Solution: Keys to Lifelong Learning* (pp. 27-52). Brisbane, Q: Capra Ryan & Associates.
> Henri, J. & Boyd, S. (2003) Teacher librarian influence: Principal and teacher librarian perspective. *School Libraries Worldwide* 8(2): 1-18.

Contact at: james@cite.hku.hk

CUSHLA KAPITZKE is a Senior Lecturer in the School of Education at the University of Queensland, Australia. Her research interests focus on the political economy of information access and its pedagogical implications. She is currently completing an ARC Discovery project examining multiliteracies in school libraries and cybraries. Selected publications include *Literacy and Religion* (John Benjamins 1995) and an edited volume, *Difference and Dispersion: Educational Research in a Postmodern Context* (Post Pressed 2000). *Contact at: c.kapitzke@uq.edu.au*

ELIZABETH A. LEE is an Assistant Professor in Language and Literacy, Faculty of Education, Queen's University, Canada. Her research interests include instruction in reading, information literacy and adolescent literacy. Recent publications include:

> Lee, E.A. (2002) Adolescent literacy: Current status. *English Quarterly 34*(3/4): 63-67.
> Asselin, M. & Lee, E. (2002) I wish someone had taught me: Information literacy in a teacher education program. *Teacher Librarian 30*(2): 10-17.
> Lee, E. A., Torrance, N. & Olson, D. R. (2001) Young children and the say/mean distinction: Verbatim and paraphrase recognition in narrative and nursery rhyme contexts. *Journal of Child Language 28*: 531-534.

Contact at: leee@educ.queensu.ca

SANDRA LEE is a College Lecturer in the Faculty of Education at the University of Hong Kong. Her research interests include knowledge management, information retrieval, LIS education, information policy and reading research. She is currently involved in several research projects including a collaborative project about self-directed learning behaviour in adult part-time students and recently published:

> Henri J. & Lee S. (2003). Building the self-directed learner: Improving teaching practice in education for teacher librarianship in Hong Kong. *Impact 12*(3): 28-31.

Contact at: sandra@cite.hku.hk

LOUISE LIMBERG is Senior Lecturer at the Swedish School of Library and Information Science, University College of Borås and Göteborg University, Sweden. Her research interests concern the interaction between information seeking and use and learning. She is currently concluding a research project on teachers' and librarians' views of information literacy education. She is also the coordinator of a recently initiated three year research project on libraries, ICT and learning, funded by the national Swedish LearnIT program. She is a member of the permanent committee of the international research community, Information Seeking in Context (ISIC). She has published internationally as well as in Sweden. Recent international publications include:

> Limberg, L. & Alexandersson, M. (2003) The School Library as a Space for Learning. *School Libraries Worldwide 9*(1): 1-15.
> Alexandersson, M. & Limberg, L. (2003) Constructing meaning through information artefacts. *The New Review of Information Behaviour Research 4*(1): 17-30.
> Hultgren, F. & Limberg, L. (2003) A study of research on children's information behaviour in a school context. *The New Review of Information Behaviour Research 3*: 1-16.

Contact at: Louise.Limberg@hb.se

DIANNE OBERG is Professor and Chair, Department of Elementary Education, University of Alberta, Canada. Her research interests include: school library program implementation and evaluation, resource-based learning, inquiry-based learning. Dr Oberg is the editor of *School Libraries Worldwide*, journal of the International Association of School Librarianship. Recent publications include:

> Henri, J., Hay, L. & Oberg, D. (2002) *The School Library-Principal Relationship: Guidelines for Research and Practice* (IFLA Professional Report, No. 78). The Hague: IFLA.
>
> Oberg, D. (2002) The affective dimension of information literacy. In S. Capra & J. Ryan (eds.) *Problems are the Solution: Keys to Lifelong Learning* (pp. 37-56). Brisbane, Q.: Capra Ryan & Associates.
>
> Donham, J., Kuhlthau, C. C., Oberg, D. & Bishop, K. (2001) *Inquiry-based learning: Lessons from Library Power*. Worthington, OH: Linworth Press.

Contact at: doberg@ualberta.ca

LINDA SELBY is the Director, Centre for Professional Studies, Faculty of Postgraduate Studies and Research, Auckland College of Education, New Zealand. Her research interests include information literacy, teacher professional development, the use of ICT in educational settings, teaching and learning with the internet, equity issues and computing, ICT and special education. She is the author of several book chapters and is editor of *Computers in New Zealand Schools*.

Contact at: l.selby@ace.ac.nz

BRUCE SHEPPARD is currently Director of Education and Chief Executive Officer for Avalon West School Board and adjunct professor, Faculty of Education, Memorial University of Newfoundland. Prior to his current appointment, Dr Sheppard has served as Associate Dean of Graduate Programmes and Research in the Faculty of Education at Memorial University, assistant superintendent in a school district in western Newfoundland and principal of Ascension Collegiate in Bay Roberts, Newfoundland. As well as having extensive experience in the K-12 school system, Bruce has taught both graduate and undergraduate courses at Memorial University of Newfoundland. He has also taught graduate courses in educational administration at the University of Ottawa, Ontario and St. Francis Xavier University, Nova Scotia, Canada. His research interests include educational leadership, educational change, school improvement, organizational learning in educational settings, program implementation, and effective schooling in telelearning environments. Bruce is a member of the Editorial Advisory Board for the *International Electronic Journal for Leadership in Learning*. He has presented papers at various national and international conferences and has published widely in academic and professional journals. Among his recent accomplishments, Dr. Sheppard was awarded the 2002 CEA-Whitworth Award for research and scholarship in Canada.

Contact at: sheppardb@awsb.ca

SUE SPENCE is Teacher Librarian at Adelaide High School. She is the creator of an effective Virtual Library for her school and professional development materials available at: rblonline.tripod.com. Recent publications include:

Spence, S. (2002) Oh, where is a teacher librarian when you really need one? *AEU Journal,* SA branch, June.

Spence, S. (2002) Survey highlights major problems with library staffing. *AEU Journal*, SA branch, December.

Spence, S. & Mitchell, P. (2002) CoSLA submission to the Senate Inquiry into the Role of Libraries in the Online Environment, August 2002. http://www.aph.gov.au/Senate/committee/ecita_ctte/online_libraries/submissions/sub70.rtf

Contact at: sspence@adelaidehs.sa.edu.au

MAUREEN TREBILCOCK is Teacher Librarian at the Western Academy of Beijing and formerly Senior Lecturer at the Auckland College of Education where she managed professional development programs for teachers in the area of teacher librarianship and ICT. Her research interests include teacher professional development, teacher librarianship, information literacy and online learning.

Contact at: mtrebilcock@westernacademy.com

Index